NF

HOME-BASED EMPLOYMENT AND FAMILY LIFE

HOME-BASED EMPLOYMENT AND FAMILY LIFE

Edited by
Ramona K. Z. Heck,
Alma J. Owen,
and Barbara R. Rowe

Foreword by
Paul Edwards and Sarah Edwards

AUBURN HOUSE
Westport, Connecticut • London

Library of Congress Cataloging-in-Publication Data

Home-based employment and family life / edited by Ramona K. Z. Heck,
Alma J. Owen, and Barbara R. Rowe ; foreword by Paul Edwards and
Sarah Edwards.
    p.   cm.
    Includes bibliographical references and index.
    ISBN 0–86569–214–9 (alk. paper)
    1. Home-based businesses—United States. 2. Home labor—United
States. 3. Self-employed—United States. 4. Work and family—
United States. I. Heck, Ramona K. Z. II. Owen, Alma J.
III. Rowe, Barbara R.
HD2336.U5H657 1995
306.3′6—dc20   94–39484

British Library Cataloguing in Publication Data is available.

Library of Congress Catalog Card Number: 94–39484
ISBN: 0–86569–214–9

First published in 1995

Auburn House, 88 Post Road West, Westport, CT 06881
An imprint of Greenwood Publishing Group, Inc.

Printed in the United States of America

The paper used in this book complies with the
Permanent Paper Standard issued by the National
Information Standards Organization (Z39.48–1984).

10 9 8 7 6 5 4 3 2 1

This book is dedicated to Dr. Sarah Lydia Manning, Professor Emerita, Buffalo State College, for her insightful simplicity, undaunted perseverance, and resourceful creativity. With her support, this research became.

Two Kenneths, Raymond, Bernita, Ginger, Amanda, and Neil imbued the words of this book.

The group, composed of the researchers, writing here has shown that the whole is truly more than the sum of its parts.

Contents

Illustrations

NA

BR Title:

Foreword

Paul Edwards and Sarah Edwards

"I can't die. Not now. My son is too young." Even though I had a deliriously high fever, I still remember saying these words to the nurse. A few days later I learned I had almost died that night from a sudden stress-related illness, and the doctor warned when he released me from the hospital that if I didn't change my lifestyle, I might not be so lucky next time.

Our son was only two years old when Sarah discovered that our two-career-couple life was not working as well as we thought. We should have realized it before. We were up early every morning, often racing to the airport to catch separate planes. We'd come home late and go into our son's darkened bedroom to wake him up for a little quality time. Our only real time together as a family was on weekends, but they too were filled with the rush and pressure of completing the many errands, household tasks, and other responsibilities of a family.

What options did we have? We both wanted to pursue our careers. We both wanted a lifestyle only a two-career income could produce. It wasn't until Sarah attended a meeting at the office of an outside consultant that we discovered there was another choice. Rare as it was at the time, this consultant's office was in his home.

We liked the idea immediately. Sarah would quit her job and open a private psychotherapy practice in our home—the one we had to buy so she could have a separate office. Paul would run his consulting firm from his downtown office. That plan lasted only a few months. Why should Paul pay all that extra rent and overhead when he too could work from our new home? When he started working from home, however, the neighbors thought he was unemployed! Why else would an able-bodied man be at home during the day?

Our solution was peculiar at the time, but today it is commonplace and becoming more so. We have dedicated the last 14 years of our lives to providing people with the information they need to decide how working from home could be an option for them and their families. As wonderful as it has been for us and so many families and can be for still others, working and living under the same roof presents its own challenges, primarily because most of us are completely unprepared to do it. In fact, many people would like to work from home but can't imagine how they could make it work.

For several generations and many decades, families have been taught that home is home and work is work and never the two shall meet. But times have changed so dramatically over the past 20 years, and with them our lives, that every day it becomes increasingly difficult to keep our family lives and our work lives neatly segmented between 9 and 5. The struggle to earn a living while simultaneously managing a family has reached near crisis proportions in many households. For some, it's a matter of juggling shifts so that one parent can be home while the other is at work. For others it means lugging kids to day care before sunrise, picking them up after sunset, and spending several hours in round-trip commuting. For some it means placing aging parents in nursing homes when they would rather have them at home with the family. For others it means going on welfare or cutting back living expenses to near survival levels so that one parent can stay home while the other works. Frequently these solutions give only the illusion of working out. As was true for us, they too often leave family members feeling as desperate, exhausted, and isolated from one another as we did before a near tragedy alerted us to the need to find another way.

Fortunately, now a growing number of books, magazine columns, and seminars, even radio and television shows, including ours, provide families with a wealth of information about how to work from home successfully if they so choose. But it was only slightly over 10 years ago that we didn't know how many people were working from home and even more recently that we have had any idea how many of them involved families, let alone the nature of these families and how they actually manage both work and family.

Although our own research is almost exclusively qualitative—in the parlance of the research world—we eagerly consume the quantitative research that has been done by others on home-based work. A review of the findings of government agencies and private research firms provides disparate views of how many people work at home, who they are, and why they do so.

That is why publishing books of this kind is so important. It is the first publication of a serious longitudinal academic study from nine states that examines the phenomenon of working from home, who is doing it, what they are doing, how they are doing it, and, most important, how it affects family life and our communities. The book provides a historical context of how and why so many people are choosing this option. It points to the significantly positive impact at-home workers are having not only on their own families' lives, but also on their neighborhoods, their communities, and their regions.

This book also provides insights into how families are coping with combining work and family under one roof and points to the other questions we must ask and answer if we are to give better help to people who are making the choice to work from home as well as those who would like to but still can't imagine how they could. We hope that this book will lead to many further studies that will give us an ever clearer picture of this phenomenon and enable us to answer many remaining questions that are waiting to be addressed.

Most important, it is an acknowledgment of the future that is unfolding before our eyes, and it will help us shape that future so that families can better support one another through all stages of life financially, socially, and emotionally. Perhaps it can help us to blend the best from times long past, when families shared most aspects of their daily lives together, with the best of this modern era, when most of us not only live above the poverty level but can truly enjoy both personal and financial satisfaction.

Acknowledgments

Ramona K. Z. Heck would like to credit Justine Lynge for secretarial assistance and her willingness to read the word-processing manuals as well as her calmness in the "eye" of this book's production. I want to thank Frank Chiang and You-Hyun Cho for earlier computer assistance for the nine-state study and, currently, I am greatly indebted to Likwang Chen for her dedicated and untiring efforts on the computer. Dandan Pan and Lisa Wilson offered much help with checking the references for this book.

Suzanne Loker and Elizabeth Scannell would like to credit Diantha Howard for her early statistical support for the project, particularly her advice related to sampling rare populations. We would also like to thank Sue Lang for the computer analyses that helped shape the macro comparisons using the census data.

Diane Masuo would like to credit Johnny M. H. On, Department of Electrical Engineering, and Ronnie S. Natawidjaja, Department of Agricultural and Resource Economics, both at University of Hawaii at Manoa, for their capable computer assistance.

Alma J. Owen graciously thanks Vena Oliver for always being there, following through, and organizing my professional energies, activities, and efforts that have been realized, in part, by the culmination of this book. I will miss you. Thank you, Vena, for so much.

Barbara Rowe would like to thank for their able assistance Lien-Ti Bei and Shuling Liao, who are currently Ph.D. students in the Department of Consumer Sciences and Retailing, Purdue University, West Lafayette, Indiana, and Meng-Kuang Lai, now teaching at the Graduate School of Business Administration,

National Cheng Kung University, Tainan, Taiwan. Both were instrumental in my completing analyses.

Kathryn Stafford would like to express appreciation to Xiao Jing Jessie Fan, Assistant Professor in the Department of Family and Consumer Studies at the University of Utah at Salt Lake City. During her graduate studies at Ohio State, she spent hours on the computer helping to complete my work on the nine-state study. I would also like to thank two current graduate students in the Department of Consumer and Textile Sciences at Ohio State University at Columbus, Patricia D. Olson and Virginia S. Zuiker, for diligent, continuous, and global computer work.

Rosemary Walker would like to thank Ishien Li for her expertise and endless patience in running more and more analyses as the research presented in this book evolved.

Mary Winter would like to credit Hyochung Kim and Herien Puspatawati for their constant attention to the details of computer analyses and printouts.

Chapter 1

Harmonizing Family and Work

Alma J. Owen, Ramona K. Z. Heck, and Barbara R. Rowe

INTRODUCTION

This book is about home and work. More specifically, it is about families who try to combine home life and income-producing work under the same roof.

One of the hottest media topics in the 1980s was home-based work: Who did it? Why did they do it? Was it profitable? Should it be prohibited, regulated, unionized, or ignored? This interest was occasioned by the rapid increase in the numbers of people working at home and by the easing of federal regulations prohibiting work at home in several textile craft industries.

Families were looking at home-based work as one solution to the work-family crunch. The term "work and family" is a succinct way of portraying the conflict faced by many American couples. It refers to the challenges people confront when trying to find a way to balance the needs and demands of raising children or caring for an elderly parent with the restrictions on time and energy that employment imposes.

Work and family terminology is often combined with phrases like balancing act, resolving conflict, fitting the pieces, or meeting the challenge—all implying that the work-family snarl is a personal conflict that individuals have to fix within set bounds. These boundaries include the need to work 40 hours or more each week, usually from 8 to 5; responsibility for arranging care for dependent family members; an employer's control of the work locale and atmosphere; and employment insecurity.

Small wonder that in the 1980s many individuals began looking for ways other than the standard on-site 8-to-5 employment to garner an income while fulfilling family responsibilities and enjoying some personal freedom. In particular, the movement of married women with children into the labor force created a need for more flexibility. Whether working for others or for themselves, home-based workers have more control over income production, work schedules, household responsibilities, and care of dependents than their fellow workers located at centralized work sites. Further economic, technological, demographic, social, and political forces have contributed to an increasing number of individuals working at home for pay.

NATIONAL TRENDS THAT STIMULATE HOMEWORKING

Both the popular press and research literature emphasize the personal, family, and social benefits derived from the flexibility afforded to home-based workers as the reason for the reemergence of homeworking.[1] The mother enjoying a view of snow-capped mountains while knitting personally designed sweaters, occasionally looking in on her sleeping baby while the stew simmers and bread bakes, is the idyllic picture. Another perspective is the harried medical claims processor, 2 days behind on work to teleport into the office. He is at a poorly lit computer screen while a 2-year-old pesters him to come and play. Outside, the leaves are unraked and downstairs, the laundry is threatening to expand to upper floors of the house if he doesn't get it done soon.

Articles about home-based work in the last decade have used both pictures, in part because both public policy and a changing economy are factors in the revival. In 1981, the Reagan administration attempted to lessen workplace controls by withdrawing the ban on home knitting that had stood since 1938. Regulation of homework, particularly in the needle trades, had begun in the 1800s both as a way to protect consumers against possibly contaminated tenement-made goods and as a crusade to end exploitation of homeworkers. The difficulty of regulating homework led to an outright prohibition of home-based work in seven industries: women's apparel, jewelry, gloves and mittens, buttons and buckles, handkerchiefs, embroideries, and knitted outerwear. Labor codes prohibiting homework, the growth of out-of-home employment opportunities for women, and policies that encouraged married women to devote themselves exclusively to child care and housekeeping led to a downward trend in homework in the United States that lasted almost 30 years (Boris, 1985). The resurgence of homework over the last 10 to 15 years was brought to public attention by a group of Vermont home knitters. Following a test relaxation of the ban on home-based labor in the knitted outerwear industry, the International Ladies Garment Workers Union brought suit against the U.S. Department of Labor (DOL) for wage and hour violations; this suit led to the eventual elimination of most outright prohibitions coupled with a more rigorous manner in which to track compliance and assure protection of the workers from exploitation (Boris, 1987).

Three reasons are generally cited to explain increases in the numbers of people who work at home. In the mid-1980s, as the baby boom generation aged, women with careers were having children and wanting to continue working while having more family time. At the same time, readjustments of the U.S. economy from a manufacturing base to a service/information base left many workers torn between joblessness or leaving their homes and communities in search of work. In addition, technological advances in computers and telecommunications equipment were providing small, powerful, and affordable tools that gave home-based business people the same capability as big businesses to perform information-age work (Pratt, 1993). Although the factors leading people to work at home have produced diverse concerns, efforts are being made to find common interests and issues about the home-based work force. A major distinction remains between home-based workers who are self-employed and those who are wage workers.

Self-Employment and Home-Based Work

Without independent wealth, there is little chance to ensure income security in the U.S. economy except through exchanging one's labor for salaries and wages. In 1993, about 10.3 million Americans were taking control of their work schedules and work atmosphere through self-employment (U.S. Bureau of Labor Statistics [BLS], 1994). This was a significant increase over the number of Americans working for themselves in 1976 (Steinmetz & Wright, 1989). Self-employment has historically provided a mechanism for individual workers to exchange their labor and expertise for monetary rewards. But only recently have scholars begun to understand how self-employment assists individuals and families in meeting their simultaneous need for income and desire for a satisfying personal life.

Although men continue to outnumber women in these ranks, women are the fastest-growing segment of self-employed people (Hagan, Rivchun, & Sexton, 1989; U.S. Small Business Administration [SBA], 1992). This attests to the unique objects or rewards that women seek through employment patterns. Women have traditionally had more responsibility and expectations than men for maintaining family standards and meeting the needs of children and other family members who require care.

Adding to the family's income stream is a particularly time-consuming responsibility for many American women, especially those in their child-bearing years. Mothers usually perform the majority of household tasks and do most of the parenting before and after 8 hours on the job (Hochschild, 1989).

Some women with family responsibilities remain in the paid labor force because of their professional preparation and desire to maintain job skills and earnings potential for midlife careers. Other women take what they intend to be temporary employment during times the family needs more income (e.g., to buy a home, when a child enters college, or while a spouse is laid off). Lifestyle adjustments or shrinking purchasing power makes these jobs permanent. Successful self-employment can provide an income stream as well as allowing for some flexibility in work obligations.

Employed Home-Based Wage Workers

Self-employment is not the only solution for addressing the simultaneous demands of work and family life. Many people lack the start-up capital or the expertise to run their own company, or self-employment may be unrealistic within the isolated local economy in which they live. These people look for ways to work for others while still garnering an income and attending to home responsibilities. Home-based knitters (Loker, 1985), midwestern auto parts assemblers (Gringeri, 1990), and telecommuters (Christensen, 1985; Pratt, 1987) are significant homeworking employee populations that have been studied in recent years. Along with the family benefits observed by some researchers, exploitation by employers through lower salaries, the absence of fringe benefits, and lack of protections such as workers' compensation, Social Security, unemployment insurance, and health and safety regulations are commonly reported disadvantages for these workers. In addition, homeworkers routinely pay the cost of utilities, of transportation to pick up materials and return finished products, and of the rent or purchase of tools and machinery to do the work (Dangler, 1986; Silver, 1989).

Some homeworkers, especially illegal immigrants, labor under deplorable working conditions: subminimum wages, lack of legal protections, seasonal ebbs and flows in production, and exposure to hazardous substances. Paid by the piece or job lot, they tend to work excessively long hours at a continually stepped-up pace. Even white-collar telecommuters may have job-related stress from the simultaneous pressures of paid work and family responsibilities. Not only can unmade beds and dirty dishes be seen as rebukes, but the dark computer screen, idle knitting machine, or unused lathe is a reminder of work that could or should be done and of income forgone (Carsky, Dolan, & McCabe, 1988).

Self-exploitation may exist because workers tend to underestimate the absorptiveness of the work contracted. Absorptiveness refers both to the imposition of the occupation on family life and the extent to which the work requires the full, uninterrupted attention of the worker. Most of the occupations typifying home-based work today cannot take place with repeated intrusions into concentration.

Income Disruption in Rural America

Rural areas of the United States were among the hardest hit during the recession and economic restructuring of the 1980s. A strong U.S. dollar, coupled with a decline in commodity prices and cheaper competing imports, brought extreme shifts in income to farmers and other rural families. Factories in small towns closed in favor of lower-wage labor overseas. The boom that rural economies experienced in the 1970s gave way to economic depression in the 1980s (Flora & Christenson, 1991; U.S. Bureau of the Census [BOC], 1990c).

Rural families also have less access to health care services, social services, and vocational training opportunities than urban residents (Bokemeier & Garkovich, 1991). Child or elder day care and after-school programs are sparse or nonexistent so that caregivers have no respite from family responsibilities. Retail and service markets in rural communities generally adhere to 5-day, 9-to-5 schedules, making otherwise routine chores—shopping, appliance repair, or medical appointments—major life events.

In spite of these obstacles, rural families lead satisfying, stable lifestyles. They live in communities where they raise their children in relative safety and rely on friends and neighbors for camaraderie and support. Farm ownership often represents generations of effort and accomplishment for these families. They are reluctant to relinquish these tangible and intangible rewards of rural life when traditional sites of off-farm employment either close or move away.

Although often seen in midwestern communities, families with similar lifestyles and concerns exist throughout rural America. Pennsylvania, which has the largest rural population in the United States, has many; Vermont has more than its share of farmsteads held by one family for a century or more. In the West, states such as Utah have experienced in-migration from populations intent on moving away from urban influences. The original impetus for this study was these rural families, some in economic hardship, some living in intentional simplicity. However, the study and this book go beyond rural homeworking families to explore, examine, and compare a range of populations who work at home for income.

THE NINE-STATE RESEARCH STUDY ON HOME-BASED WORK

This book reports the major findings of a nine-state research study that examined the issues involved in home-based work.[2] The study, entitled "At-Home Income Generation: Impact on Management, Productivity, and Stability in Rural/Urban Families," grew from two vantage points. For some researchers involved, concerns about the individual welfare and implications for families and communities of the agricultural economic depression in their states were motivating factors. Thus special emphasis was placed on securing a representative sample of rural households. In addition, researchers and educators in the northeastern portion of the United States were being drawn into the public policy debate concerning the legality of home-based employment in the knitted outerwear industry, a case largely centered in Vermont but affecting contiguous states. For them, this research was part of an endeavor to understand the advantages and disadvantages of home-based wage working, including the potential for exploitation as well as the benefits to family life.

Objectives of the Research Study

The specific purposes of the nine-state research project were (a) to determine a profile of characteristics for households that generate income at home and the communities in which they live, (b) to analyze and assess the effectiveness of managerial strategies and behaviors used in these households, and (c) to examine the relationship among work activities, work environments, and family functioning within homeworking families. Thus the research objectives encompassed not only an understanding of the work and the worker but an examination of the interface between work activities and family activities, both taking place in the same or contiguous space.

Conceptual Perspective for the Nine-State Study

Home-based workers and the work they do are the heart of this study. Close to them are the families in which they live and work because most people work not for work's sake but for the goods, services, and satisfactions that income affords. Few people purchase for themselves alone: the needs and desires of family members as well as other associates shape their spending patterns.

Researchers involved in this nine-state study followed a holistic model in which individuals, social structures, and material infrastructures form an embedded whole. Although the first objective of the study did not necessitate an integrated conceptualization, the objectives on management and family functioning did. These latter two concepts are both based on systems models—Deacon and Firebaugh's (1988) family resource management system and Kantor and Lehr's (1975) family systems as organized and elaborated by Constantine (1986). These models were combined into a single sytems model conceptualized specifically for this nine-state research study (Owen, Carsky, & Dolan, 1992).

Use of a systems model allowed the researchers to go beyond simple descriptive statistics of the families in which home-based work occurs. The model guided collection of the data, which yielded a large, useful data set within austere resource constraints. The model was used to combine data across various spheres—family life, household management, and work execution— for multivariate analyses. Finally, implications that were derived from the analyses were guided by the same systems model.

The Home-Based Work Survey

The respondents in this nine-state study represented households in which at least one individual generated income by working *at* or *from* home for at least

312 hours during the 12 months before the telephone survey conducted in the spring of 1989. The definition of home-based employment or at-home income generation for the study included self-employment, traditional marketplace jobs relocated in the home, artistic and craft work, home sales, and nontraditional farming.

During the spring of 1989, 30-minute telephone interviews were conducted with the household manager (defined as the person who took care of most of the household meal preparation, laundry, cleaning, scheduling of family activities, and overseeing any child care) in 899 households in which there was home-based employment, according to the study's criteria. Because many respondent households had more than one home-based worker and more than one income-generating activity, a decision had to be made about which work or worker would be the focus of the interview. If more than one worker in the household was engaged in home-based work, or if one individual did more than one activity that qualified as home-based work, the primary worker was designated as the household member who spent the most hours in home-based work. An exception to this rule was when the household manager met the criterion for minimum number of hours but did not spend the most time in home-based work. In those cases, the household manager was considered the primary home-based worker. When the home-based worker had more than one home-based job, questions about the work referred to the one that was the most time-consuming.

The study was designed to oversample rural populations. Each of the nine participating states was divided into rural and urban strata by designating counties containing at least one city with a population of 25,000 or more as urban and the remaining counties as rural. Nine counties consisting of major metropolitan areas were excluded from the study.[3] The stratified random sample was then selected from household telephone listings. In the analyses reported in this book, the data have been weighted to represent the total number of households in each stratum using the numbers of rural-urban households in 1985 as estimated by the U.S. Bureau of the Census. Detailed information about the sampling procedure is presented in Appendix A.

The data included detailed information about individual and household demographic characteristics; home-based work characteristics and circumstances, including self-employment or wage work; management strategies used in family life as well as in the home-based employment; and community information and circumstances.

Community Characteristics and Longitudinal Analyses

In addition to the telephone interview, community-level data were gathered on each case. Each household was identified by county of residence. Secondary data from various state and federal sources were used to examine how homeworking households in this study were similar or dissimilar to their geographic and economic neighbors. The 899 households in the sample were recontacted in 1992 to ascertain if they were still working at home and how their work and family life had changed or remained the same in the 3-year interval.

Uniqueness of the Study and Its Data

This study, its data set, and its analyses are unique for three reasons. First, households in rural counties were oversampled so that the numbers were great enough to examine in detail the nature of home-based work in rural communities. Questions were asked so that the relationship between the household engaged in home-based work and its community could be explored to some extent. Second, the phenomenon of home-based work is essentially a rare event from a statistical standpoint. Although this form of employment is growing and is seen as a strategy for families to cope with a changing economic climate, few have studied its impact on the family. Third, data from this project permit researchers to examine the household's management and decision-making practices and the household's economic welfare.

Like all large data sets, the research results are strongest for the entire sample. This book presents overall major research findings. Many of the book's contributors have written other publications that highlight the unique aspects of their state samples. In other publications, the homeworking sample is segmented along demographic or issue lines. For those wanting more information in addition to the results presented here, over 50 publications have been produced from this nine-state study. The major pieces are shared in an annotated bibliography in Appendix B.

Limitations of the Nine-State Study

Although the nine-state study has added significantly to the empirical literature on work and family life, its exclusion of family businesses located away from the household limits the applicability of its findings to the larger universe of family firms. In addition, the nine-state sample excluded traditional farming operations and three major metropolitan areas.

The qualification of having the work take place at or from home probably resulted in loss of those businesses that started at home and subsequently outgrew or left those environs. It is not known whether size of the business, intrusiveness, or other factors lead to relocation away from the family dwelling. Finally, special populations were not the focus of the nine-state study. Although the sample allowed for the analysis of males versus females, questions about race and ethnicity were not asked.

A primary focus of the nine-state study was to examine specific interactions of work and family. The research sample deliberately excluded those who had been involved in home-based work for less than a year or who had just started. Hence only those households that were established in a homeworking situation were included in the nine-state study. Members of households working at least a year before the survey were thought to have more stable family and work patterns, a major focus of the research. New home-based workers were excluded because the entrance and exit rates of such start-ups were unknown at the time of the nine-state study; thus the average longevity rate of the home-based workers surveyed was deliberately skewed toward longer periods. Given the difficulty and cost of sampling start-ups and the lack of focus on such new employment endeavors, the benefit of having a reasonably sized and representative sample of ongoing or continuing home-based workers was preferred over any forgone benefits of including start-ups in the sample.

A telephone interview with a single respondent from each household cannot capture the fullness of family life or the intermingling of family and work spheres. Success in either of these domains is elusive and subtle to measure; they often involve an interplay of various factors that cannot be measured by any outsider, even if household members are observed directly. However, such interviews can offer insight into the salient questions necessary to highlight issues to be addressed in more qualitative research and, along with a mix of measures, can pinpoint areas in need of further study.

Consistent with the framework of statistical inference, few assumptions reported in this book go beyond the states that funded and participated in this research. However, having a large sample gathered specifically to explore the work and family lives of home-based workers strengthens understanding wherever home-based work is taking place.

OVERVIEW OF MAJOR RESEARCH FINDINGS

Several themes emerged as the findings from the nine-state study were analyzed. First, the workers were better educated, lived in larger households, and were more attached to their place of residence than the average reported in the U.S. census. Second, business owners and wage earners operated in fairly distinct work worlds, and the gender factor was pronounced within each group of workers. Third, although households in the sample were not screened to yield families as opposed to single residents, overwhelmingly, people in the sample lived in households of more than one member. A spouse or identified life partner was usually present; a surprising number of households contained relatives beyond the nuclear family and children over the age of 18. Fourth, the economic contributions of home-based work to the family, the local community, and the larger macro economy were significant. Extrapolating from the data in this study, researchers estimated that the net income of home-based business owners equaled over one-half of the net income of all nonfarm proprietorships in the country. Finally, the continuation of home-based work was related more to the worker's satisfaction with the work than to the income earned or expected.

Specific major research findings showed that home-based employment was a vital economic link to the survival of some households and communities. The prevalence rate resulting from this study showed that an average of 9.6% of all households in the nine states participated in some type and level of home-based employment. The highest rates of participation consistently occurred in small towns and rural communities. Using the study's criteria for home-based work reduced the average prevalence rate to 6.4% of all households in the nine states.

Selected major findings of the nine-state study include the following:

1. The typical home-based worker was a 44-year-old (43.6 years) male who was married and had children, had 13.9 years of education, and was a homeowner who had lived in a town with greater than 2,500 population for an average of 19.8 years.

2. The frequencies for the occupational categories were as follows:

marketing and sales	24.3%
contracting	14.9%
mechanical and transportation	13.2%
services	12.1%
professional and technical	11.9%
crafts and artisans	11.6%
clerical and administrative support	5.8%
managers	3.5%
agricultural products and sales	2.7%

3. Income figures for home-based workers were as follows in 1988 dollars:

mean annual gross business income	$53,164
mean annual net business income	$15,628
mean annual net wage income	$24,300
mean annual household income from all sources, including home-based work	$42,263

The mean net income from both kinds of home-based work was $17,835, and on average the proportion of household income derived from home-based work was 39.7%.

4. Although 89.3% of the home-based workers in the sample had some health insurance coverage, the most common source of payment for the coverage was from another employment not related to the home-

based work. Either another job held by the home-based worker or the employment of another family member accounted for 44.0% of the medical insurance coverage of the worker sample.

5. Families that contain someone who earned income by working at or from the dwelling included a high proportion (60.9%) of married-couple-with-children families and a comparatively small proportion (24.5%) of adult-only families or families with only adult children at home. The number of single-parent families fell far below the national average.

6. For all home-based workers, the presence of children under the age of 18 in the household reduced the number of hours involved in home-based work by approximately 8 hours per week during the year or 1 workday per week; having a child under the age of 6 in the household reduced the number of work hours by approximately an additional 6 hours per week during the year, or about three-quarters of a workday per week.

7. Compared to wage workers, paid child care was less likely for all home-based business owners. However, business owners who had hired employees (i.e., who were presumed to have larger firms) were more likely to have paid child care.

8. In comparison to census data, the sample respondents had high levels of homeownership (87.3%) and were more likely to live in rural areas, defined as in open country or in communities of under 2,500 people.

9. Nearly two-thirds (63.3%) have lived in their community more than 10 years, and the worker has been engaged in the home-based work for an average of 9.1 years.

10. Over one-half (58.8%) of the home-based workers had places in their homes devoted exclusively to work, and slightly over one-third (37.3%) had their first work site in an office/workroom/study, or attached cottage, business, shop, or studio office.

11. Seventy-five (74.6%) percent of the sample were home-based businesses; the remaining 25.4% were wage earners.

12. As compared to wage workers, owners of home-based businesses were older, had less education, lived in larger households, had lower incomes from home-based work, tallied fewer home-based work hours, had been engaged in home-based work longer, were more likely to be involved in seasonal work, and were more likely to have other employment.

13. The effects of gender were identified in a variety of analyses, and the following have been shown to be related to the gender of the home-

based worker: (a) income, (b) occupational type, (c) health insurance coverage, (d) restructuring of work time, (e) time management strategies used when the home-based work was especially demanding, and (f) effects of children on the number of hours worked.

14. Household managers who also work at home for pay engaged in different managerial practices for their paid work than for their family work.

15. Workers were more likely to reallocate personal time than to obtain additional help for either the home-based work or household production.

16. As measured by mean scores, the majority of the households were satisfied with their quality of life and control over life but somewhat less satisfied with the adequacy of their incomes.

17. General community services provided to households such as food stores, routine medical care, and postal services were usually more readily accessible to the sample of home-based workers than were needed business services. Home-based workers used banking and supply services provided by their local communities in higher proportions than they used accounting, legal, and copying services. Such services were considered necessary for nearly all businesses and most wage earners, although usage of individual types of services varied slightly by residential location.

18. For the nine-state sample, the total net (i.e., after taxes and, in the case of a home business, after all other expenses) income generated from home-based work, based on the prevalence rate and the mean home-based income, was in excess of $18 billion. Using these figures and extrapolating to the U.S. population, researchers estimated that the 1988 net income from home-based work was nearly $108.4 billion after taxes and any other business expenses, if applicable. This accounted for nearly 3.4% of the total personal income (i.e., income available to families and individuals to spend for their everyday needs and wants) in the United States.

19. Compared to the populations of the counties where the survey sample resided and the total U.S. population, the sample households had fewer females in the labor force, had lower median ages for household members, had higher levels of education, had larger-sized families, and were much less likely to contain either male or female single parents. The sample had higher median family and household incomes but lower mean per capita incomes.

20. After 3 years, factors associated with the continuation of the home-based work included higher levels of education for the home-based

worker, smaller household sizes, higher home-based work incomes, more years in home-based work, positive feelings about the work, and expectations of changing attitudes about the work. Neither income nor attitudes about income from the home-based work were significant predictors of the worker performing the same work three years later.

Research findings from the nine-state study expand the knowledge base for making community infrastructure and policy decisions and for designing educational programs to inform families about decisions regarding home-based work as an employment alternative. In addition, other groups of consumers and families who are not currently involved in home-based employment may greatly benefit from enhancing their chances of being able to engage in such employment situations. Furthermore, this research documents the effects of home-based employment on small towns and rural communities. In these ways information generated from this research can assist people who seek to fulfill the dual roles of society—to be financially independent and to nurture strong and healthy children for the next generation.

ISSUES EXPLORED IN THIS BOOK

Chapter 1 gives an overview of the nine-state study offering motivations for such a study, the approach and sampling design of the study, and an overview of the major findings. Chapter 2 discusses salient current issues surrounding home-based work along with a historical overview of such work, the current labor force trends leading to home-based work, and a discussion of public policies and private employer policies that shape the work force and the choice of home-based work.

Chapter 3 presents details about the characteristics of the worker and the work, including special topics of health insurance coverage, work space usage and intrusiveness, management, and perceptual outcomes of home-based work. Chapter 4 shares the known details of home businesses in comparison to the wage workers in the nine-state study. A multivariate research model of ownership is discussed. Additionally, gender comparisons are made between owners and earners for income, hours, occupation, and other general work characteristics. Home-based businesses are examined via their financial and marketing practices. Finally, special topics are explored, such as the differences between males and females in net income and hours worked, the use of employees and helpers in the home business, and subjective outcomes of the home business.

Chapter 5 explores in detail the family side of home-based work by examining the structure and composition of homeworking families, the effects of children on home-based work, and the use of child care services. Family functioning, management, and adjustment strategies are studied in detail using established theory or conceptualizations in each case.

Chapter 6 discusses the characteristics of the family and community interface. The economic effects of home-based work on the family and its contribution to local communities and the national economy are documented. The character of the counties within which the home-based workers resided is explored along with comparisons to the population in these counties and the nation.

Chapter 7 examines the households with home-based workers 3 years after the main study in 1989. Retention rates of the home-based work done in 1989 are calculated to be between 71.2% and 75.5%, reasons for exiting are explored, and comparisons are made between those who continued their home-based work and those who did not. A model for predicting the continuation of both home-based work in general and business ownership is presented.

Finally, Chapter 8 delineates the major research findings and their implications for home-based workers, their families, their communities, and an array of professionals who come in contact with these workers, including researchers, educators, practitioners, and policy makers at all levels of government. Suggestions for future research, education, practice, and policy are also offered, as well as suggestions for current and potential homeworking households and workers.

NOTES

1. Throughout this book, the following terms will be used interchangeably: home-based work, homeworking, homework, and at-home income generation.

2. The following Agricultural Experiment Stations, associated with state land-grant universities, cooperated in funding this research: University of Hawaii, Iowa State University, Michigan State University, Lincoln University (Missouri), Cornell University (New York), Ohio State University, Pennsylvania State University, Utah State University, and University of Vermont.

3. The five counties that make up New York City; Philadelphia County, Pennsylvania; and three counties in metropolitan Detroit were excluded from the nine-state study.

Chapter 2

The Changing Environment of Work

Alma J. Owen, Barbara R. Rowe, and Nancy C. Saltford
with the assistance of Ramona K. Z. Heck and
Diane M. Masuo

INTRODUCTION

The research reported in this book is, in part, a direct result of the political attention paid to legal disputes arising from the need of home-bound women to supplement family income in an especially troublesome labor market. Researchers at the University of Vermont sought to assist that state's citizens in arguing their case for the need for paid home-based labor. Coupled with Vermont's rugged terrain and harsh winters is the unusual geographic dispersion of its population, which seems to have followed jobs to just one centralized area. Steady, full-time employment is available in few towns outside metropolitan Burlington. Hence the state is a fertile milieu conducive to the pursuit of home-based employment. Understanding the plight of these citizens, mostly women, illuminates the manner in which the entities of family, workplace, community, and political bodies interact to influence the way families can make a livelihood while having the life they desire.

One body of literature has concentrated on the infringement of work on family life (Kanter, 1977), the increasing amount of time spent on the job by Americans (Schor, 1991), and the loss of meaning that results when employment takes control of family lives and schedules (Illich, 1981; Lasch, 1977). Some of the labor force issues that have influenced scholarly interest in home-based work include the participation of married women with children, the compatibility of employee benefits with employees' needs, and working conditions, especially scheduling, that restrict or promote income maintenance and family care duties done by the same person(s).

This chapter outlines the labor force issues that have led to a resurgence of interest in home-based work. The first section discusses the current political attention and policy issues surrounding work at home. The second section encapsulates the history of home-based work in the United States. Next, overall labor force participation, especially changes in the nature of women's work, is reviewed. Of special interest in the overall labor market is the extent to which laws and regulations affect the workplace needs of working families and constrict personal control over the timing and location of employment; hence both public policies and employers' responses to working families are reviewed. Finally, in light of all these forces, the role of home-based work is explored.

POLITICAL AND PUBLIC ATTENTION TO HOME-BASED WORK

Background

As discussed in Chapter 1, in 1942 the U.S. Department of Labor (DOL) imposed restrictions on seven industries in which homework prevailed, generally under sweatshop conditions. The DOL Wage and Hour Administration outlawed homework in knitted outerwear, women's apparel, buttons and buckles, handkerchiefs, embroidery, gloves and mittens, and jewelry (Boris, 1985) because the Fair Labor Standards Act (FLSA), which prescribes minimum wages, maximum hours, and other labor standards, could not be adequately enforced in these industries. Industrial homework in these seven industries could not be regulated because employers used the system to reduce wages, avoid paying benefits, and eliminate overhead costs (Mazur, 1987). Enforcement officials repeatedly found long hours and below–minimum wage pay, child labor, and unfair competition with legitimate employers and factory workers. The ban on homework applied only to women's apparel and infants' and children's wear. Other types of homework were never subject to such restrictions (Staff, 1986).

Early in the Reagan administration, attempts were made to relax these bans as a part of overall efforts to deregulate the workplace. The ban on knitted outerwear was tested in the 1981 federal DOL suit against CB Sports, Inc., which had hired New Englanders to knit ski wear in their homes. The company was charged with violating regulations banning work in the home in certain industries and not paying its homeworkers the minimum wage. For years CB Sports had paid 50 Vermont women about $1.25 a cap for ski hats they knitted at home. The women insisted that almost all of them earned the minimum wage—$3.35 per hour at that time—and that the fastest earned considerably more. They did not feel exploited. Some preferred working in their rural homes to commuting to a factory. Others were young mothers who wanted to stay home with their children. By 1984, this was resolved by the federal DOL substituting a certification system for the ban on homework in the knitted outerwear industry (Hukill, 1990; Rauch, 1981). Under this system, an employer could hire homeworkers only if each worker acquired a certificate from the DOL.

The International Ladies Garment Workers Union (ILGWU) argued that homework was often an excuse for businesses to abuse workers (Staff, 1984) and brought suit against the commissioner of the federal DOL, challenging these new regulations. The struggle between the Reagan administration's desire to deregulate the industry and the ILGWU's desire to control the work force continued when the union pressed a case concerning a group of Iowa farm women who did embroidery piecework. By 1986, the Iowa company had sales of $3.5 million. The work force varied from 100 to 150 women who sewed at home using their own machines and the company's materials. They were paid about $2.25 per piece, or $1.12 if the work did not pass inspection. Although some of the workers were very happy with the arrangement and calculated that they earned $4.00 to $9.00 per hour, others felt "oppressed." One woman estimated that she made $1.85 per hour at the most. She and other seamstresses complained to the union about lack of overtime pay and benefits. The company claimed that it did not need to provide such extras because its workers were "independent contractors."

Despite the opposition from organized labor, in January 1990, 4 years after the DOL issued the first certificate for homeworkers in knitted outerwear, the department lifted the restrictions in five of the six remaining industries (gloves and mittens, buttons and buckles, embroidery, handkerchiefs, and jewelry that does not involve hazardous materials). The ban on homework remains in effect for women's apparel and for hazardous jobs in jewelry (Hukill, 1990).

Current Issues in Home-Based Work

Home office deduction. In 1993, a U.S. Supreme Court decision limited the number of home business owners who can deduct expenses for a home office. The case in question involved an anesthesiologist who saw patients at three area hospitals for 30 to 35 hours a week but had no office at any of them. He kept patient records and telephoned patients and colleagues from a spare bedroom in his home 10 or 15 hours a week. The high court said it was not enough that work done in his office (i.e., the spare bedroom) was essential to the doctor's business. Rather, the central question in judging whether home office expenses are deductible is a comparative one: whether the home office is where the taxpayer's most important professional activities are performed, based on the relative importance of the activities and the time devoted to them. Business expenses for rental office space, however, are fully deductible. Thus this decision speaks to the nature of the home-based business, not to the valuation of business expenditures.

In writing the majority opinion, Justice Anthony Kennedy (*Commissioner v. Soliman*, 1993) said that because "the essence of the professional service" (p. 646) provided by an anesthesiologist is putting people to sleep, not maintaining patient records, the doctor's home office "must be regarded as less important" (p. 646) than the hospital operating rooms in which he worked. The long-standing confusion over home office deductions stems from an effort by Congress[1] to tighten the rules by limiting deductions to home offices that were the "principal place of business" but not defining "principal place" (Asinof, 1993; Greenhouse, 1993).

Employee or independent contractor status. Since the DOL bans on homework were lifted, home-based workers who are not clearly self-employed have had to establish their status as either independent contractors or employees. Many employers prefer to classify their workers as independent contractors to avoid paying Social Security taxes and unemployment compensation for them. These designations are determined for the purposes of state labor laws and federal and state tax codes. The federal government, however, can audit both public and private employers to determine that their work force is made up of employees so as to maximize tax revenues.

The U.S. District Court of Northern Iowa rendered a decision that no one factor is controlling and that the entire circumstances must be viewed in determining if a person is an employee. The single most important factor is the degree of control exercised by the worker. This opinion echoes the issues of control of work time and place as a determining reason for and factor in the decision to engage in home-based work. Beach's (1989) study of Maine shoe workers was seminal in ascertaining the factors to observe in determining the issue of control. Generally a worker is an employee if the business can say when and how the work is to be done.[2] For example, a homeworker who comes to a central point on Monday morning to pick up materials to be worked on during the week and is instructed on the quantity to be completed and when the items must be returned would probably not qualify as an independent contractor.

Recent economic cycles have led to the downsizing of major corporations (Crouter, 1994). As people lose or cannot find jobs, they may turn to other employment alternatives and, in turn, there has been an increase in the incidence of part-time workers, freelancers, temps, and independent contractors. Workers in these categories are becoming known as the "contingent" work force; they have an array of special concerns, including financial instability and insecurity, lack of health insurance coverage, and lack of access to career ladders (Castro, 1993; Employee Benefit Research Institute, 1994; Lozano, 1989). These workers may increasingly turn to home-based work on a permanent basis out of necessity.

Local zoning ordinances. Although some federal laws and regulations have been removed, state, city, and local legal restrictions remain or are changing slowly. In Chicago, for example, it is illegal to do work at home that requires electrically driven machinery (Edwards & Edwards, 1994a). This is a far cry from the support rural electric cooperatives provide to encourage home-based work as a means to maintain a load sufficient to justify the continued structure of electrical service to remote areas.

These two extremes reflect both the failure of laws to keep up with changing times and the differences in the mutual support that businesses and family provide as they interact within the infrastructure of community. The Chicago law may have been spurred by noise pollution, unsafe work conditions, or simply power lines that were inadequate to deliver the amount of electricity needed to run wood lathes and spinning jennies. These reasons are irrelevant in an age where electricity is delivered to residential communities in massive amounts to run air conditioners, color televisions, and home-use carpenter's tools and when the electricity used for home-based work is more likely to power a sewing machine, computer, or typewriter.

Community needs also vary more than are adequately reflected in legal constraints. This issue will be treated in detail in Chapter 6. However, it is clear that smaller communities lack the resources to research and design zoning regulations that are uniquely suited to the social, geographical, and economic needs and assets of all their businesses, citizens, and institutions. Community governance boards often look to laws made by other entities to pattern their own restrictions, usually to a community they seek to emulate, which may or may not contain the same mix of needs and assets.

Many zoning issues related to home-based work reflect the codification of antiquated concerns from an industrial or preindustrial era. They are designed to protect the health, property values, and safety of the places where we relax from work, raise our children, and enjoy recreation. However, this separation of work and family life is not an inherent characteristic of the work-family dynamic. The next section details the history of human labor that has culminated in this separation.

HISTORY OF EMPLOYMENT IN THE UNITED STATES

Work has consumed a major portion of life throughout human history. For prehistoric tribes, it was immediately tied to survival. More recently the definition of work has been related to labor force participation. Today, the enhancements of material life that have resulted from industrialized work and labor specialization form the foundations of economic life in both production and consumption activities of individuals and families.

Work in the American Colonies

At the time of its colonization, the resource base, settlement patterns, and independent character of its citizens made the United States a prime location for home-based work. Most settlers had come from Europe, where cultures thrived on personal initiative as the mainstay of survival. In the new nation, there were few persons within trading distance of each other, so families had to produce everything they needed for survival. The abundance of the land allowed for a rugged but substantial life.

The family was the center of production in the colonial economic system. All members, including adults and children as soon as they were capable, contributed. Families, sometimes assisted by neighbors, erected their own houses, produced and preserved their own food, made household furniture, and created their own garments from homespun and woven cloth (Cowan, 1987; Mintz & Kellogg, 1988). Household space was not distinct from work space; most work was performed within or near the living structure (Clark, 1986; Googins, 1991). Craftsmen manufactured some items that required a high level of skill or special tools that were seldom available on the homestead. Saddlery, ironwork, and grain milling are examples of common early trades that were done at or near the home of the laborer. When people worked for others, barter goods were usually exchanged in lieu of money. The person having flour ground left some grain for the miller. The horseman left leather for the saddler to make items for other customers.

In this preindustrial agrarian society, work was frequently allocated on the basis of gender, although all work was home-bound and family-defined. Jobs that were outside the household or that required long and uninterrupted commitments of time were performed by men; women's work permitted flexible time arrangements and was centered near the home (Anderson, 1988; Scott & Tilly, 1980). Despite their different responsibilities, men were not necessarily the main providers for the family and women were not necessarily dependents. Both spouses were responsible for economic maintenance and child rearing (Kahn-Hut, Daniels, & Colvard, 1982).

Family ties not only marked the beginning but also the end of many communities. Although it was rare for more than two generations to share a household, relatives lived close to each other. Establishment of households of married children and settlement of immigrant relatives built on this family network. These networks provided assistance and support to social, economic, and political community life (Googins, 1991; Hareven, 1991).

From Homework to Wage Work

The shift from an economy centered on household work to one based on market work took place over the nineteenth century (Kahn-Hut et al., 1982). Self-sufficiency in household goods declined as trade accelerated. Increased use of currency, the potential for expanding wealth beyond that of one's neighbors, and the increased availability of manufactured goods combined to relieve family members from being Jacks and Jills of all trades in order to have the necessities of life. Although farming continued to be the primary industry, it as well as other occupations came to be carried on in environments dedicated to commerce (Googins, 1991). Even tradespeople moved their shops away from the homestead and began the daily trip to town to work (Kahn-Hut et al., 1982).

For home-based workers, expansion of a market-oriented economy changed the conditions of labor. Rather than producing for themselves or persons they knew, home-based workers were now part of a putting-out system where employers arranged for segments of a larger manufacturing process to be "put" into homes on a pickup and delivery basis. Merchants would supply individual households with the raw materials needed to make cloth, beer, thread, or shoes. The family would then earn piecework wages by spinning yarn, sewing dresses, or setting up a tavern or inn in their home (Kahn-Hut et al., 1982; Mintz & Kellogg, 1988). Consequently, households no longer controlled what they produced. Yet they did control the pace and organization of work and so were able to integrate wage work with domestic work, including child care.

Industrialization

Industrialization changed this remnant of an earlier, more integrated work and family interaction. In the second half of the nineteenth century, institutions, values, and customs associated with work were transformed and reshaped. In the early phases of industrialization, many manufacturers hired whole families in their mills or set up special dormitories and boardinghouses to provide single employees with surrogate families (Kessler-Harris, 1982). Factory owners also permitted employees to select their older children as assistants or apprentices, thus allowing parents to work alongside their children so that work did not constitute a major break with families or family values (Hareven, 1987).

When companies began to introduce elements of scientific management into the workplace—centralized hiring, promotions, and firing; adopting the time clock; and other methods to gain tighter control over the work process—extended kinship groups diminished in power (Gutman, 1976; Hareven, 1987). Employers' increased control was accompanied by the development of assembly lines and the breakdown of production into monotonous, repetitive tasks. Whereas previously work and family life had been almost synonymous, the process of industrialization made the centralized workplace predominant. As a result, family life was adapted to better meet the demands of centralized wage work (Googins, 1991). The interaction between work and family seemed one-sided, with the tilt toward employment.

The Roots of Women's Paid Labor

By the late 1800s, mills and factories had been established in most northeastern towns. Laborers came from the surrounding farms although the seasonality of farming left mills vulnerable to inconvenient and costly down times during planting and harvesting (Kessler-Harris, 1982). To overcome this problem, factories turned to a relatively cheap and more reliable wage labor force made up of unmarried women and children.

Except for this segment of the work force, industrialization did not, at first, radically change women's work or the amount of time they devoted to production for the market versus for household use. Most women continued to work at home, or if employed, they worked as domestic servants, farm family workers, or garment workers doing piecework (Epstein, 1982; Tilly & Scott, 1987).

As the cost of manufactured goods declined and their quality improved, fewer and fewer families made their own clothing, soap, or shoes. The appearance of more and better products on the market meant that more factories and offices were being built, creating a demand for people who were willing to trade their labor for cash. Consequently households needed more cash with which to buy the newly available items (Cowan, 1987).

Changes in the structure of work and its locations worked to exclude married women from the labor market. On-site employment established a more rigid separation of labor and location than had previously existed between production for the household and production for the market (Coontz, 1992; Cowan, 1987; Googins, 1991). Thus began a period of more than 50 years when men's work was marked by wages and a clearly defined working day. Women's work was unpaid, task oriented, and at home (Anderson, 1988; Tilly & Scott, 1987).

Industrialization and immigration. Centralized factory work both allowed for and promoted increasing population density. As towns grew into cities they absorbed a huge number of immigrants who came to the United States. Some planned to work in their new country temporarily and then return to Europe; others, fleeing economic and political oppression, came intending to settle permanently. This abundance of immigrant labor fueled the process of industrialization. Without it, more native-born men and women would have been pulled into industrial work (Blau, 1978; Epstein, 1982).

Immigrant and working-class families moved frequently, seeking jobs and subsistence wherever they could be found. When they were working, wages kept most of these families only a shade above poverty. Nearly 60% of American families had incomes that were at or below a basic subsistence level (Googins, 1991; Mintz & Kellogg, 1988).

Persistence of the putting-out system. Many married women added to their family's collective economy by running boardinghouses, taking in laundry and sewing, and doing piecework in the home (Anderson, 1988; Mintz & Kellogg, 1988). Piecework rates were so low that workers had to put in long hours to make any money, but this was the most common form of employment for immigrant women in the nation's largest cities (Kessler-Harris, 1982). Compared to the very small number of married women who went out to work, the number who took in work was large. Most married women still spent the majority of their time caring for their large households, preparing food for their families, and organizing the activities of their children (Kessler-Harris, 1982).

Technology had made certain household tasks obsolete, but the time demands on homemakers did not lessen, because other domestic duties were expanded. Labor-saving devices such as vacuum cleaners and clothes-washing equipment decreased the time spent on each task, but these devices encouraged higher living standards: clothes were washed more often and houses were kept spick-and-span with less servant help (Cowan, 1987; Oakley, 1974). Most food was still bought unprocessed, and much of it was grown and preserved at home (Anderson, 1988; Blau, 1978; Cowan, 1987; Mintz & Kellogg, 1988).

As the economic development accompanying industrialization proceeded, the range of jobs available to women expanded. Employers began hiring women for teaching, clerical work, and retail sales. However, they were viewed as a temporary labor force, expected to return to the home as soon as they married (Anderson, 1988; Cowan, 1987). Outright prohibitions against hiring married women and the firing of single women as soon as they married reinforced social mores about women's rightful place being in the home. Male trade-union members argued against women's employment in manufacturing because they would work for less pay at a time when men were arguing for a "family wage"—income enough to support a wife at home and children (Kessler-Harris, 1982; Rose, 1987; Schor, 1991).

Domestic service work. In the early nineteenth century, the domestic and agricultural sectors of the economy provided much of the work available to African American and Latino women, reflecting the overall racial prejudice of the country toward women of color. Even in the northern states, these women were relegated to jobs as domestic servants, laundresses, and cooks (Anderson, 1988; Blau, 1978; Kessler-Harris, 1982). If household help from these classes was unavailable, immigrant women filled the gaps in the labor pool for these jobs.

If paid help was not available or a household could not afford it, all the onerous tasks of the household fell to the wife and older children. Oakley (1974) traces the belittling of domestic labor, in part, to this transformation of household work from an act of necessary subsistence to one of servant labor.

The 20th Century

After the Civil War, the nation's farm families began to sell an increasing share of their crops in commercial markets and to work land that was not their own. Urban dwellers had little or no control over resources that they could use to secure their livelihood. They were dependent on employers for income. Mill and mine workers were especially dependent on their jobs because their dwellings were usually owned by the company for which they worked.

The Great Depression. In an era when workers were increasingly forfeiting control of their means to maintain their lives and livelihood, the Depression of 1929 was devastating. It marked a dramatic change in patterns of employment. By 1932, 28% of the nation's households did not have any employed wage earner. Worse, few of the jobless found new work quickly. Those fortunate enough to hold jobs suffered drastic pay cuts and reductions in hours. By mid-1932, three-quarters of the nation's workers were on part-time schedules (Mintz & Kellogg, 1988).

Few images have been etched deeper on the nation's collective memory than the picture of midwestern and southern farm families piling all their possessions into an old jalopy and heading to California. Nearly eight million sharecroppers and tenant farmers took to the nation's highways and railroads in the 1930s, increasing the number of unemployed persons living in urban areas (Mintz & Kellogg, 1988).

Falling back on their own resources, families tried to return to an earlier state of self-sufficiency. Unemployed textile workers set up looms in their living rooms. Wives and mothers took in sewing and laundry (Mintz & Kellogg, 1988). Ideology and structures that had once been used to keep married women in the home and out of paying jobs were called into question when sometimes only women could get work (Anderson, 1988; Kessler-Harris, 1982).

World War II. If the Depression kept male workers in bread lines, New Deal programs (i.e., a broad set of social programs initiated during the presidency of Franklin D. Roosevelt to address the severe economic problems of the day), combined with the expansion of the economy during World War II, created a labor shortage. The war not only brought large numbers of women into the work force, it induced a new group of women to work outside the home. Before 1940, most employed women were young and unmarried. Now, for the first time, more than half of America's women workers were older, married women entering or reentering the labor force (Shank, 1988). Between 1940 and 1945, the number of working mothers of small children jumped by 76% (Anderson, 1988; Blau, 1978; Mintz & Kellogg, 1988). The government provided a large shift in attitudes toward the employment of married women by financing child care centers for mothers working in defense industries (Coontz, 1992).

When war production ended and men came back to their homes and factories, women were urged to leave their jobs to make room for returning veterans. Those who did not quit voluntarily were discharged. For a short period, the general pattern of employment returned to prewar status (Kessler-Harris, 1982). But most women did not lose their jobs permanently; by the end of 1947, the rate of female employment began to climb again (Coontz, 1992).

Family life and employment patterns from the 1950s forward. The image of family life was transformed in the postwar era. It differed from the structure of family life both earlier in the nation's history and since (Coontz, 1992). Young people of the 1950s reacted to the double hardships of depression and war by marrying unusually early (Mintz & Kellogg, 1988). Women were discouraged from higher education and careers outside the home. They were told—by advertising, television, and peer pressure—that they should find fulfillment only through their roles as wives, mothers, and homemakers.

The suburban family was the symbol of an appropriate lifestyle in the postwar period. This image, reinforced by television series such as "Leave It to Beaver" and "The Donna Reed Show," was attainable only because of the sustained economic growth afforded by capital expansion of the war economy, the increasing flow of cheap energy sources, and their use. Real income rose nearly 20% (U.S. Bureau of the Census [BOC], 1981). Housing construction boomed under veterans and federal home mortgage assistance. Transportation was cheap. Many families could own homes in the suburbs and support their lifestyle on the earnings of just one worker, invariably male (Googins, 1991; Mintz & Kellogg, 1988).

THE MAKING OF AMERICA'S CONTEMPORARY WORK FORCE

Over the centuries, America's work patterns have changed dramatically. The process of industrialization shifted the primary locus of employment from the household to the marketplace and separated the productive activities of women and men. For years, discrimination and social mores discouraged women from paid employment, reinforcing the division and specialization of labor by gender. Long-term changes in the composition of the labor force did not begin until after World War II with the sequential entry of two new groups of workers into the labor force—older married women followed by women with preschool children—and the slow decline of men's work force participation. These changes incorporated both new developments and a return to old patterns. The influx of mothers into the paid labor force constituted an important change in the roles available to women. Women's market involvement also represents a reinstitution, though in a new form, of the contribution women have always made to family production.

Women's Employment and Other Labor Force Issues

Although some commentators view feminization of the labor market as liberating women, critics warn of a threat to traditional values and the decline of a system that provided a warm and comfortable home life. These two factions disagree on whether employing women increases the productive capacity of the nation or simply floods a labor market unable to provide enough jobs (Bergmann, 1986; Smith, 1979). This controversy provides fuel for debate about family values and the social consequences of mothers working. Set against this background, the changing environment of work continues to touch the lives of families and to provide policy implications for employers and governments.

Long-term trends, one of which is decreasing fertility, have promoted the entry of increasing numbers of women into the labor force (Anderson, 1988; Hayghe, 1990; Moen, 1992). Beginning in the 1960s, women were having fewer children and completing their families at a younger age. Second, the women's movement, which gained momentum throughout the 1970s, challenged the gender gap with the concept of combining work and family roles (Cooney & Uhlenberg, 1991). In addition, rapid economic growth created a major expansion in teaching, nursing, clerical, sales, and service work, areas that employ large numbers of women (Anderson, 1988; Shank, 1988). The postwar marriage boom decreased the number of single women available to fill these positions. Consequently, employers began hiring married women (Coontz, 1992).

The trend of combining work and family roles was supported by inflationary cycles in the 1970s and again in the early 1980s, which propelled many wives into the labor force to keep real family income at a constant level (Anderson, 1988; Kessler-Harris, 1982; Mintz & Kellogg, 1988). As the necessity for dual incomes increased, it pulled more wives and mothers into work outside the home. Consequently, the proportion of "traditional" families (those with a breadwinning husband and a wife who stayed home with the children) declined gradually. By 1988, the traditional family accounted for only about one-fifth of all families compared with more than three-fifths in 1940 (Hayghe, 1990).

Women in the 45-to-54 age group led the influx into the labor force in the postwar period with the general support of society's shifting and positive attitudes (Shank, 1988). In the early 1960s, along with having fewer children and completing their families at younger ages, women of childbearing age began to enter the labor market in large numbers. This flood of young women into the labor market changed the long-standing pattern of female participation rates by age. Historically, women's labor force participation patterns have taken an M shape: they are highest when women are in their early 20s before having children, drop off as women leave the labor force to raise children, but increase again as some women return to work after their children enter school. This pattern typified women's participation in the 1950s.

Since the 1970s, there has been a strong tendency for women to return to work soon after the birth of a child. Curves plotting labor force participation of women now look very similar to those of men, with an inverted U pattern as both women and men enter the labor force sometime after age 16 and remain until they retire. This curve has replaced the historical M that showed women between the ages of 20 and 45 taking extended time out to remain at home with their children (Bianchi & Spain, 1986; Employee Benefit Research Institute, 1988; Smith, 1979). The sharpest sustained increases in the participation rates of women occurred between 1975 and 1980. By 1987, the percentage of the female population in the labor force for 45- to 54-year-old women averaged 67%, compared to 74% for 35- to 44-year-olds, and 72% for 25- to 34-year-olds (Shank, 1988).

During the 1960s and 1970s, as a new generation of young women emerged from college and universities and sought jobs, ideas about the nature and extent of women's connection to market work also began to change. Not only were most women in the labor market, but the vast majority were full-time, career-oriented workers (Shank, 1988; Sweet & Bumpass, 1987). This reversed an earlier correlation between a husband's income and the likelihood his wife would work. For the first time, wives with more education were more likely to work. Women were delaying marriage and motherhood to complete their education and to establish themselves in the labor force (Bianchi & Spain, 1986; McLaughlin et al., 1988). Furthermore, growth in the female labor force began occurring in traditionally male occupations such as managerial positions, the professions, and nontraditional blue-collar work (Anderson, 1988; Kessler-Harris, 1982; Thornton & Freedman, 1983).

As work outside the home has become the norm for women, differences in their employment patterns by marital status and the presence and age of children have greatly diminished. For example, in 1957, labor force participation rates between "young married" and "never married" women differed by nearly 57%. Although 84.4% of single women aged 25 to 34 worked or looked for work, only 27.6% of the married women in this age category did so. In 1987, the labor force included the mothers of 60% of all school-age children, and nearly two-thirds of all employed mothers had children younger than age 14 (U.S. Bureau of Labor Statistics [BLS], 1989c). In addition, 57% of those with children under age 6 and more than half of all women with children under age 1 were in the labor force. By contrast, in 1950, just 12% of women with children under age 6 were in the labor force (BLS, 1989a; Hayghe, 1990). Employment during pregnancy has also risen, from 44% in 1961–1965 to 65% in 1981-1985 (BOC, 1987, 1992b). In June 1992, 58.5% of married women were in the labor force, and 45.3% of all workers were women (BOC, 1975, 1981; U.S. Department of Labor [DOL], 1992).

Current Trends for Working Women

Most of the economic, social, and demographic factors that have contributed to the growth in the number of females in the labor force are expected to continue to the year 2000. Labor force projections indicate that by 2005, female labor force participation will be 62.6% to men's 76.1% (BLS, 1989c). White women are projected to be the largest group of labor force entrants, followed by Latino and African American women (Ries & Stone, 1992).

The inroads women have made into the labor market are also reflected in the number of businesses owned by women. In 1989, women owned 31.3% of all businesses in the United States (U.S. Small Business Administration [SBA], 1992). Although the greatest growth was in the services and in finance, insurance, and real estate industries, in virtually every category the number of female-owned companies at least doubled between 1977 and 1989. Their firms, however, accounted for just under 13% of all receipts generated—nearly 4 out of 10 had total receipts of less than $5,000. This was because of the type and size of business that women owned; 90% are sole proprietorships with few or no employees (Ries & Stone, 1992; SBA, 1992).

Current Trends for Working Men

Despite the entry of men of the baby boom generation (i.e., those born from approximately 1946 until about 1964) into the labor force, the proportion of males in the labor force has actually fallen. In 1948, 87% of men were in the labor force, compared with 33% of women. By 1983, 76% of men and 53% of women were in the labor force (Bianchi & Spain, 1986; Owen, 1986; Smith, 1979). Not only had the proportion of employed males declined, but the hours worked per employed male had also dropped. Together, these trends indicate a considerable substitution of female for male labor (Owen, 1986).

The explanation for changes before 1940 is that most of the drop in measured working hours resulted from a decline in the full-time workweek toward a standardized 40 hours. Because males tended to be overrepresented in industries and occupations with above average workweeks, the move to standardize hours meant a more than proportionate decline in the male workweek (Owen, 1986). The standard workweek also changed over the years; at the turn of the century, a standard workweek was approximately 53 hours (Employee Benefit Research Institute, 1994). Full-time workers are currently defined by the U.S. Bureau of Labor Statistics (BLS) as those who work 35 or more hours per week.

The declines in men's labor force participation after 1975 are largely attributable to their spending more time getting an education, earlier retirement, and longer life spans (Smith, 1979). Rates for men aged 25 to 54 have remained about 95%, but they have declined from 71% to 43% for those 55 and over. This decline in men's rates reflects, among other things, the increased number of workers covered by Social Security, private pension plans, and disability benefits, allowing for earlier withdrawal from the labor force than was possible in the past (Bianchi & Spain, 1986; Fullerton, 1991). Men's labor force participation is projected to rise in the first part of the 1990s but then to fall steadily, reflecting the fact that baby boomers will be approaching their retirement years (Fullerton, 1991).

From the 1940s to the 1960s any conflicts between work and family obligations were resolved by women. They either worked before children were born and/or after they were school age. Taking part-time work and moving to shift work or a less demanding job were other strategies used by employed mothers

(Moen, 1992). But from the 1970s on there has been no standard pattern of meshing work and family obligations. Women work when they must by combining a variety of ad hoc personal strategies. Prevailing social attitudes about child care as the responsibility of women only (as though fathers and society in general received no benefits from them growing up to be contributing adults) has hindered institutional supports to ease the strains of working parents (Lopata, 1993).

As discussed in the sections that follow, changes in women's and men's employment patterns have prompted a few public initiatives and policies supportive of working families. Those that do exist are outlined in the section that follows.

PUBLIC POLICY FOR EMPLOYED PARENTS

The idea that employers' practices and the benefits[3] connected with employment should be responsive to family needs surfaced in the late part of the 1970s and became a major issue at the White House Conference on Families in 1980. The basic objective of the conference had been to develop an agenda to strengthen and support families. The primary recommendation to come out of the conference was a call for "family-oriented personnel policies—flexitime, leave policies, shared and part-time jobs, [and] transfer policies" (White House Conference, 1980).

Findings about the interconnectedness of work and family from the studies of Rosabeth Moss Kanter (1977) and others have made inroads into policy statements of labor, social, and family policy analysts as well as some corporate leaders (Walker, 1991), but the White House conference recommendation has never been fully implemented. By the mid-1980s it was acknowledged that most accommodations to family and work lifestyles continued to be made by individual family members. But pressure was growing for change at the workplace as well (Cook, 1989; Kahn & Kamerman, 1987; Kamerman, 1983). This mood was reflected in the literature during this period, as researchers began to focus on "the spillover from family to work" (Crouter, 1984). Certainly, the new interest in home-based work is affected by public policies related to employment. Such policies shape the nature and location of work, as well as employee benefits or other work-related arrangements such as child care and work time.

Comprehensive Family Employment Policy

As more and more women entered the labor force, child care, elder care, leave proposals, and policy discourse on working families accelerated (Levitan & Gallo, 1990). More than 100 child care bills were introduced in the 100th Congress (i.e., during 1987–1989) by members of both political parties. They ranged from federal grants to states to expand day care facilities to tax incentives that would encourage employers to help meet employees' child care needs. No action was taken, but the stage was set for further debate in the 101st Congress (i.e., 1990–1992). Again, no specific child care bills were passed, but Congress did include child care assistance in the 1991 Omnibus Budget Reconciliation Act.[4] This was the first federal legislation enacted to address child care since World War II, when Congress voted to establish child care centers to help young mothers involved in war production (Swoboda, 1990).[5]

Before passage of the Family and Medical Leave Act of 1993 (FMLA), the focus of federal legislation relative to employer-provided leave was on prohibiting discrimination among employees in the provision of such benefits as were offered. Until FMLA, employers were not required to follow a standard leave policy. Leave benefits were the consequence of either state-mandated disability insurance, collective bargaining agreements, or voluntarily provided employee benefits.

For example, the Pregnancy Discrimination Act (PDA) of 1978 requires employers who offer disability insurance plans to treat pregnancy and childbirth as any other disability, with the same employee benefit program. Employers usually meet this mandate by paying for short-term disability insurance plans that allow women to take paid leave and provide insurance for pregnancy and childbirth. If states mandate short-term disability insurance, they also must include coverage for pregnancy and childbirth.

The 1993 Family and Medical Leave Act became effective on August 5, 1993, just 6 months after it was signed into law by President Clinton. It requires private-sector employers with 50 or more employees[6] and most public-sector employers to grant an eligible employee up to 12 weeks of unpaid leave, with guaranteed reemployment, for a serious medical condition of the employee or the employee's spouse, child, or parent, or to care for a newborn or newly adopted child. With the exception of highly compensated employees,[7] who under certain circumstances are not guaranteed reemployment, an employee is entitled to be restored to the position of employment held when the leave commenced or to be restored to an equivalent position with equivalent benefits, pay, and other terms and conditions of employment. While on leave, employees continue to receive the same group health coverage they had while employed.

Family leave legislation was long in coming as it had been bitterly contested by political conservatives and the U.S. Chamber of Commerce, who charged such policies would "bankrupt" small businesses. It had been passed by Congress twice only to sustain a presidential veto prior to its final enactment.

Child Care

Most child care assistance is designed for employed parents and is supported at the national level by favorable tax policy. Tax credits, including the Earned Income Credit (EIC) targeted at low-income families, are available for eligible parents. At the workplace, employers are involved primarily through the provision of dependent care assistance programs (DCAPs). Little has been done to help mothers who are kept out of the labor force because of the unavailability of child care. In one study, 1.1 million young mothers attributed their inability to seek or hold a job to the unavailability and unaffordability of quality child care (Cattan, 1991). For the most part, jobs continue to be structured as though the labor force consisted primarily of men, not workers with child care responsibilities (Moen, 1992).

Tax credits. The government uses two types of income tax credits to support child care. In the first, under Section 21 of the Internal Revenue Code (IRC), tax credits are available to those with qualified child care expenses that are not covered by or paid for by an employer-sponsored DCAP. An income tax credit is allowed for eligible children when both spouses work full-time, when one spouse is a student and the other is employed, or to single parents who are employed or students.

The Family Support Act of 1988, effective for the 1989 tax year, reduced the amount of child care expenses eligible for the tax credit by the dollar value of child care provided through a dependent care spending account and excluded from the taxpayer's income.[8] Prior to passage of the Family Support Act, taxpayers could use one form of tax relief (i.e., either tax credit or income exclusion) up to its maximum, then use the other for any remaining expenses. The 1988 law greatly reduced the ability to use both a tax credit and a DCAP.

The second type of tax credit for child care is the Earned Income Credit (EIC), a major program administered by the IRS to provide assistance to the working poor. For 1994, a tax credit became available to workers with earned incomes below $24,010 who have a "qualified child" and file a "joint" or "head of household" income tax return.

Dependent Care Assistance Programs. The Economic Recovery Tax Act of 1981 (ERTA) provided tax incentives for employees as well as for employers for employer-sponsored programs that provide assistance for care for children and other qualified dependents. If these dependent care assistance programs are provided by an employer, neither the employee nor the employer pays taxes on the value of the DCAPs. The costs are deductible by the employer if they constitute an ordinary and necessary business expense. No employee can shelter more than $5,000, and eligible expenses are limited to dependents under age 15 and elderly or disabled dependents. A DCAP may be, but is not required to be, one of the benefits offered in a flexible benefits plan.[9]

Flexible spending accounts are a popular method of funding DCAPs through employer contributions, employee salary reductions, or both. The employee makes a pretax contribution to the spending account, thus reducing the amount of salary subject to income and Social Security tax. Employees determine at the beginning of the year how much to contribute toward this spending option. A "use it or lose it" provision prohibits the carryover or refund to the employee of any money left in the plan account at the end of the year; these funds become available to the employer for program management.

Flexible Benefits Plans

Flexible (or flex) benefits, flexible compensation, and cafeteria plans are terms used interchangeably to describe benefit plans that permit employee choice. As a result of the Revenue Act of 1978, eligible employees are permitted to choose among two or more benefits consisting of cash and qualified benefits or among two or more benefit options paid for by employer contributions, purchased through pretax salary reduction arrangements, or both.

Parental Leave

Parental leave allows an employed parent to stay home to care for a child beyond the period of short-term disability following childbirth or adoption and guarantees that the employee will be reinstated in the same or an equivalent job with no loss of previously accrued pension benefits or seniority rights. Such parental leave may be paid or unpaid, and applies to the father as well as the mother of a newborn or adopted child (DOL, 1990).

EMPLOYERS' RESPONSES TO WORKING FAMILIES

Some corporations have established family-supportive policies with the assumption that assistance with child care and leave policies reduces turnover rates and thus lowers retraining and recruitment costs (Bower, 1988; Friedman, 1986, 1987; Meirs, 1988). A recent study by the Department of Labor (DOL) of collective bargaining agreements in effect after July 1990 found that just over 50% contained one or more work and family provisions, including maternity and parental leave, reimbursement for adoption expenses, child care, leave for family illness, employee assistance programs, elder care, and prohibitions against discrimination because of a worker's or potential employee's marital status (DOL, 1992). However, it is larger businesses that are taking the lead in adopting family-supportive personnel policies and benefits, not small businesses where 90% of the U.S. work force is employed (Marshall, 1991; Moen, 1992).

Child Care Programs and Policies

Surveys conducted by the BLS in 1989 indicate that only 5% of the employees of medium and large private-sector firms[10] were eligible for child care assistance. The smaller the establishment, the less likely it is to offer assistance with child care (DOL, 1988). Nor are work-family benefits generally available for hourly workers because wages and other benefits usually take priority at the bargaining table (Starrels, 1992).

The 1990 National Child Care Survey, which studied employed mothers with children under the age of 13,[11] found that flexible work options were more common than were child care benefits. Although the differences in availability of flexible work options for women living in different regions of the country were not great, women in urban areas were most often eligible for both flexible work options and child care benefits. Fewer than 10% of employed mothers had the option of working at home although 20% could choose flexitime. On-site child care was available to only 11% of the employed mothers (Hofferth, Brayfield, Deich, & Holcomb, 1991b; Miller, 1992).

Flexible Work Options

Flexitime, part-time work, job sharing, personal leave policies, and other personnel policies are just some of the strategies working families have used to meet the dual demands of work and family (Galinsky & Stein, 1990; Huth, 1989). Flexible work schedules can be any adjustment in the hours worked that differs from a fixed, five days a week schedule. The type and availability of flexible work schedules vary substantially between companies and even within a particular company and include flexitime, seasonal hours, compressed work-weeks, part-time employment, and job sharing (Axel, 1985; Mamorsky, 1987).

Flexitime. These work arrangements allow employees to vary the hours their workdays begin and end, the number of hours worked per day, or the total number of hours worked each week or pay period. Most plans nearly always have a required core time each day or days of the week that employees must be on-site. These programs range from highly organized systems to informal arrangements between a supervisor and an employee (Bernstein, 1988; Rosow & Zager, 1983). Flexible scheduling sometimes involves alternating the length or timing of the workday throughout the year, taking advantage of annual changes in daylight times. Seasonal hours usually can be offered to all workers, including those on production lines at a particular work site (Axel, 1985).

In 1991, only one out of every eight workers, or 15.5% of the labor force, operated on a flexitime schedule. Flexitime was more commonly used by men (13.2%) than by women (11.1%). More than twice as many (22.1%) managerial and professional workers were on flexitime than were those in service occupations (10.5%), who may be low-paid and already have rotating shifts (BOC, 1993).

Compressed workweek. Another form of flexible scheduling is a compressed workweek in which several long workdays are put in on a fixed or rotating basis. Many federal government agencies offer employees the option of working 9 hours a day for 8 days in a 2-week period, followed by one 8-hour day so they can have an extra day off every other week. Although compressed work schedules may be difficult to accommodate into family life and child care arrangements, some employees enjoy them for the long weekends or periodic rest days (Staines & Pleck, 1986).

Part-time workers. This group includes those who are employed on a temporary basis and those who work part-time on a continuous or so-called permanent basis (Axel, 1985). Temporary part-time work helps employers meet their peak-time or seasonal needs, but part-time employees generally get low wages, low job status, and no benefits. Part-time workers are most often found in retail sales and service industries. Except for the loss of benefits such as health insurance and paid vacations and a somewhat lower job status, permanent part-time employment may afford the worker advantages similar to those of flexitime. The employer's gains or losses from using part-time workers are similar to the advantages and disadvantages of flexitime (Employee Benefit Research Institute, 1993; Nollen, 1982).

Job sharing. Employees who job share have a structured arrangement that merges the efforts of two or more (part-time) workers into one job (Stackel, 1987). Employees involved in the sharing are interchangeable. The incidence of workers actually using this scheduling practice is low relative to other flexible schedule options.

Extended Personal Leave

Such arrangements with one's employer can serve to meet family caregiving responsibilities and may be another way to create a more flexible work environment. In 1988, for the first time, the BLS studied parental leave provisions in the private sector. By 1989, unpaid maternity leave was available to 33% of the employees in medium and large firms. Unpaid leave for new fathers was available to 16% of the employees of medium and larger firms in 1988 and 18% in 1989 (BLS, 1989a).

Where available, both maternity and paternity benefits averaged 4 months in duration (BLS, 1989d). Small establishments usually offered neither maternity nor paternity leave. Unpaid maternity leave was available to 16% and unpaid paternity leave to 7% of these workers. Paternity benefits were far less common, despite a flurry of attention to the subject in the media. A 1991 survey of the four most family-friendly companies in the country by the Families and Work Institute estimated that no more than 10 men employed by these four companies had taken paternity leave in the past 2 years (Staff, 1993).

Work and family initiatives to accommodate the meteoric rise in the number of women in the labor force, particularly those with young children, have taken a number of forms: creating or subsidizing child care, preferential tax treatment for employers and employees, offering flexible working hours, and family and personal leave. But the reality for most working parents is that work, school, businesses, and service providers still behave as though there is a full-time housewife available to chauffeur children, take charge of home repair, and serve as consumer at all times (Lopata, 1993; Moen, 1992). The consequence of this is that families are finding their own ways of adapting to what appears to be an inflexible social and economic structure.

ROLE OF HOME-BASED WORK IN CHANGING WORK ENVIRONMENTS

Because families have been the ones accommodating themselves to work conditions, they proved to be inventive in experimenting with ways to make family life and income maintenance mesh. One innovation that received widespread attention was working at home with the sanction of one's employer and immediate supervisors. Another, which was largely innovated by families themselves and which provided them even more control, was self-employment. Home-based work encompasses these two innovations for many persons. Interest in this option as a primary avenue to meet the simultaneous demands of income assurance and family life was rising in the 1980s. The return to home-based employment also creates new economic development opportunities for small-town and rural America by generating new jobs to fuel economic growth (Deming, 1994; Edwards & Edwards, 1994a).

Estimates of the numbers of people currently working at home, projections of future trends, and the characteristics of homeworkers vary widely (Kraut, 1988; Pratt, 1987). One of the earliest counts of homeworkers was based on the 1980 census of the population estimate that 1.3 million people work at home on their primary job (Kraut & Grambsch, 1987). An American Telephone and Telegraph (AT&T) marketing study estimated that 23 million people, representing 26% of the U.S. labor force, performed job-related, income-producing work at home (AT&T, 1982). A taxpayer usage study of Internal Revenue Service income tax returns estimated that 5.1 million businesses were conducted at home (Grayson, 1983). An estimate based on a 1985 Current Population Survey (CPS) put the number at 17.3 million people who do some work at home for their primary employer and 8.4 million people who work at home at least 8 hours per week (Horvath, 1986). Deming (1994) found that only about 8 million, or 40%, of the 20 million workers who do some work at home are paid specifically for this work, and when paid they are mostly self-employed. These prevalence rates are discussed in detail and a prevalence rate for the nine-state study is reported in Chapter 3.

The variability in the estimates of who works at home results from diverse definitions of homeworking and from the inclusiveness of the definition. The AT&T estimate counted anyone who performed any work for any job at home as a homeworker. The estimate by the Bureau of the Census (BOC) counted only those who worked at home a majority of their time for their primary employer without specifically determining whether the worker was compensated, and it imposed an arbitrary cutoff of 8 hours per week before a respondent was considered for further analysis (Horvath, 1986). The IRS estimate was based on business units rather than individuals because individuals potentially could have multiple businesses (Grayson, 1983).

In the literature, the terms *home-based work, at-home income generation,* and *homework* are frequently used interchangeably, which influences who is counted. The definition of home-based work used in the study discussed in this book is any income-generating activity that is performed in the home or on the land immediately surrounding the dwelling or work that is based in the home for which there is no other regular work space. According to this definition, home-based workers can be the sole owners or partners in a home-based business as well as individuals who earn a wage working at home for someone else. Thus, the study includes building contractors who perform their tasks at a site away from their dwelling but whose dwelling functions as the only office for their business; providers of services such as family day care, veterinarians, cosmetologists, and mechanics who work in their homes and garages; marketing and sales representatives; consultants; artists and craftspeople; truck gardeners; and a host of others who devote a portion of their dwelling to activities that generate income.

The 1985 and 1991 CPS surveys conducted by the BOC included as home-based work, work taken home that was related to one's primary employment (Horvath, 1986). Deming (1994) later added a question to the 1991 survey related to whether or not workers were compensated for their work at home. The criterion that included taking work home from a primary job was not used in the nine-state study reported here. A college professor who spent 8 hours a week grading papers and preparing lectures at home would have been included in the CPS survey but excluded from the present study. A professor who spent 8 hours a week consulting for paying clients would have been excluded from the CPS but included in this study. In any case, being compensated or paid for the work was one of three essential eligibility criteria of the nine-state study. The other two were minimum levels of hours per year and length of time in home-based work before the interview.

Defining home-based work to include all paid activities for which the home is the center, not just homeworking efforts associated with a primary job, allows examination of routines used by families whose members are engaged in multiple jobs, both home-based and not, to garner sufficient income for survival. Limiting the definition to those whose primary work was home-based would have precluded analyses of such strategies. Similarly, limiting the definition of home-based work to the primary work performed by someone whose travel time to work was either zero or variable would also exclude second jobs that are done at home after hours.

SUMMARY AND CONCLUSIONS

Home-based work continues to garner public and political attention through the tax treatment of home office space, the determination of the status of an employee or independent contractor, and the implementation of local zoning ordinances. Also, the rising number of contingent workers raises questions of financial security, career development, and extent of benefit coverage.

Based on this historical, as well as contemporary, overview of employment, it is clear that home-based work has always existed to a greater or lesser extent depending on the composition of families and communities, labor legislation, and the demands of the economy on human structures. At the beginning of our country's history, home-based work was fully integrated into family life as well as communities. Industrialization pulled workers from the home and made them dependent on wages from employers and other benefits such as health care. Economic cycles and other historical events such as wars were often related to ups and downs in the work lives of individuals.

More current trends in men's and women's employment rates, the rise in self-employment, the downsizing of corporations and industries, and the levels, types, and general availability of technology all contribute to the prevalence of home-based employment today.

Public policies and employers' policies both affect the employment choices and circumstances of families and individuals. The lack of a comprehensive public family employment policy further frustrates workers as they attempt to balance the demands of work and family. Employers' slow response to the incompatibilities of work and family has caused many family members or employees to turn to home-based work. Health insurance coverage is also a major consideration of employment and may actually influence where and how individuals work. The choice of home-based work may mean forgoing important benefits unless other family members' jobs provide them.

Finally, although national data do not allow for precise analysis of trends in home-based work, few doubt that it is on the rise. Deming (1994) has suggested that "as the country moves into the 'information age' and away from the industrial economy that concentrated the work force in centralized work sites, opportunities for workers to bring the work site back into the home will no doubt grow" (p. 19). The persistence of home-based employment or work may have much to do with its universal nature, flexibility, and adaptivity in offering individuals, families, and communities choices within the employment world.

NOTES

1. Home office deductions were originally covered by Section 280-A of the Tax Reform Act of 1976.

2. An employer must generally withhold income taxes, withhold and pay Social Security and Medicare taxes, and pay unemployment taxes on wages paid to an employee. An employer

does not generally have to withhold or pay any taxes on payments to independent contractors. To help determine whether an individual is an employee under the common law rules, 20 factors have been identified that indicate whether sufficient control is present to establish an employer-employee relationship (Stevens, 1994). The degree of importance of each factor varies depending on the occupation and the context in which the services are performed. It does not matter that the employer allows the employee freedom of action, so long as the employer has the right to control both the method and the result of the services. If an employer treats an employee as an independent contractor and the relief provisions discussed earlier do not apply, the person responsible for the collection and payment of withholding taxes may be held personally liable for an amount equal to the employee's income, Social Security, and Medicare taxes that should have been withheld. The 20 factors indicating whether an individual is an employee or an independent contractor are as follows:

1. *Instructions.* An employee must comply with instructions about when, where, and how to work. Even if no instructions are given, the control factor is present if the employer has the right to give instructions.

2. *Training.* An employee is trained to perform services in a particular manner. Independent contractors ordinarily use their own methods and receive no training from the purchasers of their services.

3. *Integration.* An employee's services are integrated into the business operations because the services are important to the success or continuation of the business. This shows that the employee is subject to direction and control.

4. *Services rendered personally.* An employee renders services personally. This shows that the employer is interested in the methods as well as the results.

5. *Hiring assistants.* An employee works for an employer who hires, supervises, and pays assistants. An independent contractor hires, supervises, and pays assistants under a contract that requires him or her to provide materials and labor and to be responsible only for the result.

6. *Continuing relationship.* An employee has a continuing relationship with an employer. A continuing relationship may exist where work is performed at frequently recurring although irregular intervals.

7. *Set hours of work.* An employee has set hours of work established by an employer. An independent contractor controls his or her own time.

8. *Full-time work.* An employee normally works full-time for an employer. An independent contractor can work when and for whom he or she chooses.

9. *Work done on premises.* An employee works on the premises of an employer or works on a route or at a location designated by an employer.

10. *Order or sequence set.* An employee must perform services in the order or sequence set by an employer. This shows that the employee is subject to direction and control.

11. *Reports.* An employee submits reports to an employer. This shows that the employee must account to the employer for his or her actions.

12. *Payments.* An employee is paid by the hour, week, or month. An independent contractor is paid by the job or on a straight commission.

13. *Expenses.* An employee's business and travel expenses are paid by an employer. This shows that the employee is subject to regulation and control.

14. *Tools and materials.* An employee is furnished significant tools, materials, and other equipment by the employer.

15. *Investment.* An independent contractor has a significant investment in the facilities he or she uses in performing services for someone else.

16. *Profit or loss.* An independent contractor can make a profit or suffer loss.

17. *Works for more than one person or firm.* An independent contractor gives his or her services to two or more unrelated persons or firms at the same time.

18. *Offers services to general public.* An independent contractor makes his or her services available to the general public.

19. *Right to fire.* An employee can be fired by an employer. An independent contractor cannot be fired so long as he or she produces a result that meets the specifications of the contract.

20. *Right to quit.* An employee can quit his or her job at any time without incurring liability. An independent contractor usually agrees to complete a specific job and is responsible for its satisfactory completion or is legally obligated to make good for failure to complete it.

In doubtful cases, the facts will determine whether or not there is an actual employer-employee relationship. For the IRS to determine whether a worker is an employee, employers must file Form S-8, Determination of Employee Work Status for Purpose of Federal Employment Taxes and Income Tax Withholding, with their local district director.

3. Employee benefits include any form of compensation other than direct wages provided by employers. They usually are paid for by the employer but may require a contribution from the employee. Although the characteristics of individual plans vary greatly from employer to employer, most include provisions for voluntary as well as mandatory benefits. Benefit plans generally are designed by employers and may supplement or build on government social programs. Employers are required by law to make contributions to the Social Security Old Age, Survivors and Disability Insurance program as well as to Medicare and to federal, state, local, and private-sector workers' compensation funds. In addition, they must pay federal and state unemployment insurance taxes. Voluntary benefits include life insurance, health insurance, retirement plans, long-term disability insurance, and vacation and sick leave pay for time not worked. Far less prevalent are family-supportive benefits for child care and family leave (Saltford & Heck, 1990).

4. The Omnibus Budget Reconciliation Act was passed by Congress on October 27, 1990, just before adjournment, and signed by President Bush on November 5, 1990.

5. Although Congress had passed the Comprehensive Development Act to deal with child care and child development issues nearly 20 years earlier, in 1971, President Nixon vetoed this proposed legislation.

6. The law does not apply to employers with work forces that are dispersed over multiple work sites at least 75 miles apart, each of which has fewer than 50 employees.

7. For the purpose of this act, highly compensated employees are salaried employees in the highest paid 10% of an employer's work force, employed by the employer within 75 miles of the facility at which the employee works. IRC Code 414 (q) does not apply as the definition for the purposes of the act.

8. Taxpayers who claim the child care credit are required to list the name, address, and Social Security or other taxpayer identification number of the child care provider on their tax forms.

9. To qualify for tax-free status an employer can provide information and referral services, an on-site child care center, or financial assistance through direct payment to a child care provider or reimbursement to an employee. If offered, the program must be available to all employees and cannot favor those who are officers, owners, or highly compensated. An employer must prepare a written plan setting forth eligibility requirements and method of

payment. Eligible employees must be notified regarding the availability and terms of the plan. On or before January 31, the employer must provide each participant with a written statement indicating the amounts paid or expenses incurred by the employer in providing dependent care assistance to the employee during the previous calendar year.

10. The BLS defines private-sector medium and large firms as those with 100 or more full-time employees. Small establishments include those with fewer than 100 full-time employees.

11. The National Child Care Survey, the first study of its kind in over a decade, was administered between October 1989 and May 1990. The survey collected information from a nationally representative sample of U.S. households with children under the age of 13. Data reported here are from a subsample of 2,600 employed women who participated in the study. The survey was jointly sponsored by the National Association for the Education of Young Children and the Head Start Bureau of the Administration on Children, Youth, and Families in the U.S. Department of Health and Human Services.

Chapter 3

The Workers at Work at Home

*Ramona K. Z. Heck, Rosemary Walker, and Marilyn M.
Furry with the assistance of Kathryn Stafford,
Mary Winter, Diane M. Masuo, Joan E. Gritzmacher,
Suzanne Loker, and Elizabeth Scannell*

INTRODUCTION

Alvin Toffler, in his 1980 book *The Third Wave*, advanced the idea of the
electronic cottage. Since then the popular press has used Toffler's term to
promote the rebirth of cottage industries. This popular literature would have us
believe that many home-based workers are telecommuters sitting at home with
their computer modems connected to a mainframe (Christensen, 1988b), or that
they are young mothers who have solved a multitude of problems by being able
to care for their children while they work for pay at home (Horvath, 1986).
Findings from the nine-state study presented in this book suggest that neither
scenario portrays reality.

Advanced technologies have moved the United States from an industrial
economy to an information society. One advantage of this systemic change is
more potential for flexibility in the workplace. The kinds of paid employment
that can be accomplished at home have greatly expanded.

At the time of the nine-state study, one work-at-home sourcebook reported over
1,000 work-at-home opportunities with as many as 500 corporations indicating a
work-at-home option for employees who use computer technology for their jobs
(Arden, 1988). A survey by Electronic Services Unlimited, reported by the *Chicago
Tribune*, projected that by the end of the century, home employment will make up
12% to 13% of the work force, and that by the year 2025, home-based workers
will outnumber commuting workers (Kleiman, 1988).

Results from the nine-state study provide baseline data on home-based
workers and their work. Who was really working at home and what kind of

work they performed were major topics examined in this study. After briefly reviewing previous research on prevalence and profiles of home-based workers and their work, this chapter presents findings to describe selected characteristics of home-based workers. Next, the nature of home-based work is characterized, including the major dimensions of home-based work space. Then, the intrusiveness of home-based work on the family is examined and the management behavior of home-based workers is explored. Finally, the subjective outcomes of working at home are described.

Descriptive analyses of home-based workers in the United States have been imperfect because of methodological problems or limitation in scope. One major problem has been the definition of home-based work (Pratt, 1987); in all but the 1991 Current Population Survey (conducted in 1991), questions were not asked about whether the worker was compensated for the work done at home.

The latest figures vary depending on how "work at home" is defined. In February 1993, a national survey conducted by LINK Resources reported that 39 million or 31.4% of adults, including after-hours homeworkers, worked either part-time or full-time at home (Sloane, 1993). Deming (1994) reported that in May 1991 approximately 20 million nonfarm employees were engaged in some work at home as part of their primary job, accounting for 18.3% of those employed (Table 3.1). Only 40% or 8 million of these were considered homeworkers because they were compensated for the work they did at home; of those who were paid or were self-employed, only about half or 4 million worked at home for 8 hours or more per week.

Around the time of the nine-state study, estimates of the number of nonfarm home-based workers in the United States varied from 8.4 million in 1985 (in a survey where respondents were not asked whether or not they were paid) (Horvath, 1986) to 25 million in 1988 (in a study which defined homeworking telecommuters as anyone doing any work at home as part of his or her job) (Ambry, 1988; Silver, 1989).

Four nationally representative data sets have been used to profile home-based workers and their work although the definition of home-based work varied substantially from study to study.

1991 Current Population Survey

Women were more likely to work entirely at home, although men and women work at home at similar rates. Sixty percent of those who worked at home were not compensated for their work; of those who were, most were self-employed, and only about half worked at home for 8 hours or more per week. White-collar managers and professionals or salesworkers were in the majority.

Children had less effect on the likelihood of parents working at home than previously thought. About 23% of the homeworkers were mothers, and married men without children were more likely than married fathers to be homeworkers.

Table 3.1
Prevalence of Home-Based Workers

Worker type	Current Population Survey, 1990		Nine-state projection, 1990	
	Number	*Percent*	*Number*	*Percent*
Total	19,967	100.0		
Total paid	7,432	100.0	9,017	100.0
Self	5,553	74.7	6,727	74.6
Wage	1,879	25.3	2,290	25.4
Paid > 8 hours	3,651	100.0 (49.1)[a]	6,077	100.0 (67.4)[b]
Self	3,078	84.3	4,528	74.5
Wage	573	15.7	1,550	25.5
Paid > 35 hours	1,070	100.0 (14.4)[a]	3,091	100.0 (50.9)[b]
Self	976	91.2	2,147	69.4
Wage	94	8.8	944	30.6

Note: Numbers in thousands and based on 94,312,000 households in the United States in 1990 in U.S. Bureau of the Census, (Current Population Series P-20, No. 458). *Household and family characteristics: March 1991.*

[a]For the 1990 CPS: paid > 8 hours were 49.1% of total paid 3651/7432; paid > 35 hours were 29.3% of paid > 8 hours 1070/3651; paid > 35 hours were 14.4% of total paid 1070/7432; wage paid > 35 hours were 15.4% of wage paid > 8 hours 94/573. [b]1989 Nine-state study: paid > 8 hours were 67.4% of total paid 6078/9017; paid > 35 hours were 50.9% of total paid > 8 hours 3091/6078.

1985 Current Population Survey

The 1985 Current Population Survey defined home-based workers broadly as farmers and individuals who took work home as part of their regularly scheduled work on a primary job. No question was asked about compensation for the work done at home. The study's author estimated that there were 18 million home-based workers in 1985; 17.3 million of them were nonfarm.

Full-time employed home-based workers in the 1985 Current Population Survey tended to be unincorporated business owners, whereas part-time workers were wage and salary employees. A larger proportion of home-based workers were men (55%), although two-thirds of those working exclusively at home were women. Female workers were most numerous in the services industry, where they were employed full-time as wage earners. Most of the homeworkers were between 35 and 44 years old; however, older workers, particularly those over age 65, were disproportionately overrepresented in homework. Of five selected nonfarm occupations, the largest number of workers was in managerial and professional specialties, followed by workers in technical, sales, and administrative support.

1984 Panel Study of Income Dynamics (PSID)

Using household data obtained from the 1984 PSID, Heck (1988) provided a profile of home-based workers. The sample studied consisted of 6,744 workers. Home-based work was defined as employment situations in which the worker either did not travel to the place of employment or the amount of time spent traveling varied. The likelihood of being involved in home-based work was positively related to age, absence of children, presence of children under age 6, being self-employed, and being a farmer. Decreased participation was associated with minority status, higher total family labor income, having a high school education or less, and working longer hours.

1980 Census

According to the 1980 census, there was a home-based clerical work force of 181,000 people who were predominantly white and self-employed and had experienced difficulty finding work outside the home (e.g., mothers, the elderly, the disabled, and rural residents). The 1985 update (Horvath, 1986) by the U.S. Bureau of Labor Statistics (BLS) documented an increase to 246,000 clerical workers, and Kraut and Grambsch (1987) have pointed out that 85.8%, or 211,000, of those jobs were part-time.

PREVALENCE RATE FOR HOME-BASED WORK

The estimated prevalence of home-based work varies widely depending on the definition used. In the nine-state study, home-based work was defined as paid work performed in or from the home. The sampling frame was based on a two-stage process in which households were screened for specific additional criteria including (a) a minimum of 312 hours of home-based work per year by at least one person in the household, (b) participation in home-based work for the year before the survey, and (c) home-based work other than production agriculture.

Only 6.4%, or 1,109,284, of the households in the nine states had a home-based worker who met the study criteria. Just under 10% (9.6%), or 1,645,831, of all households in the nine states had at least one member engaged in any activity that generated income at home. Therefore, 536,547 additional households in these nine states reported a member engaged in any home-based work.

Based on the count of 94,312,000 households in the United States in 1990 (U.S. Bureau of the Census [BOC], 1991b), the estimated prevalence rates from the nine-state study can be used to extrapolate the count of home-based workers for the entire country. Using the more restrictive study criteria, the resulting projected number for 1990 was 6,077,578 households with at least one family member engaged in home-based work (Table 3.1). Likewise, the prevalence rate based on the more liberal definition of any home-based work yielded an estimate for 1990 of 9,017,224 households with at least one member engaged in any home-based work. These estimates are specific to the nine-state study criteria. Because the study omitted three major metropolitan areas, these figures underestimate the prevalence rate for the general population.

SELECTED CHARACTERISTICS OF HOME-BASED WORKERS

A profile of the person who does work at home was built from the information obtained from a representative sample of 899 households in which at least one household member was engaged in at least one home-based employment situation. The respondent in the nine-state survey was the household manager, defined as the person who takes care of most of the meal preparation, laundry, cleaning, scheduling of family activities, and overseeing of child care. The household manager was considered to be the household member best able to report accurately about issues on the work-family interface. In 53.6% of the households studied, the household manager was also the home-based worker. When the home-based worker was another household member, the household manager provided information about the worker.

The characteristics reported here refer to the entire sample of 899 home-based workers. In instances when there were multiple home-based workers in a household, the person working the highest number of hours was designated as the worker of interest, unless the household manager was also a home-based worker. In that case the household manager's home-based work hours were used if they met the minimum criterion of 312 hours per year. For further information and definitions, see Appendix A and Stafford, Winter, Duncan, & Genalo (1992).

Gender

There were more male (58.1%) than female home-based workers (41.9%) (Table 3.2). These findings on gender closely match earlier studies on home-based work (Heck, 1988; Horvath, 1986), which found that men homeworkers outnumbered women. A national work-at-home study conducted in 1987 and 1988 by LINK Resources, a New York consulting firm, however, found more women working at home, as did a 1985 BLS survey (Horvath, 1986; Sloane, 1993). Part of the inconsistency among these findings is related to differences in the definition of home-based work that was used in each case.

Age

The average age of 899 home-based workers was 43.6 years (Table 3.2). Only 10.0% of the home-based workers were under 30 years old, and 12.0% were

Table 3.2
Characteristics of Home-Based Workers, $N = 899$

Characteristic	Number	Percent	Mean	Median
Gender				
Male	522	58.1		
Female	377	41.9		
Age			43.6	41.0
Under 30	90	10.0		
30–39	321	35.7		
40–49	214	23.8		
50–59	166	18.5		
60 and over	108	12.0		
Education			13.9	13.0
Elementary or some high school	53	6.0		
High school diploma	295	32.8		
Some college	269	29.9		
College degree	183	20.4		
Some graduate school	99	11.0		
Marital status				
Married	762	84.8		
Nonmarried	137	15.2		
Number of children				
None	396	44.1		
1	159	17.5		
2	211	23.5		
3 or more	133	14.8		
Child under 6 years				
Yes	240	26.7		
No	659	73.3		
Homeownership				
Own home	785	87.3		
Do not own	114	12.7		
Years in community			19.8	15.0
0–5	181	20.1		
6–10	149	16.6		
11–20	228	25.4		
Over 20	341	37.9		
Place of residence				
Town or city > 2,500	485	53.9		
Town or city < 2,500	174	19.4		
Rural nonfarm	177	19.7		
Farm	63	7.0		

over 60. Similarities and differences in age structure have been found in other studies. For example, most workers in the studies by Becker (1984) and Heck (1988) were over 35 years old. Horvath (1986) hypothesized that home-based work may be an appealing option for people over age 55 who find daily commuting very tiring. In this same BLS study, however, most home-based workers were between 35 and 44 years old.

Education

The link between education and home-based work is probably stronger now than in previous years because of the increasingly complex, technological nature of our economy. Educational attainment of home-based workers is one of the key factors that determines the occupation they can and will pursue. Examination of the education variable indicated that the majority of the home-based workers had more than high school education. Home-based workers in the nine-state study, on average, had 13.9 years of formal education (Table 3.2), with a median of 13.0. Of the home-based workers, 32.8% had a high school diploma, 29.9% had some college, 20.4% had a college degree, and another 11.0% had additional formal education beyond a four-year college degree.

Overall, it appears that home-based workers in the nine-state study were more educated than workers in the traditional or centralized workplace. Differences in educational attainment were found between the nine-state study and other studies. Heck (1988) found that those involved in home-based work generally had a high school education or less. The home-based workers in the nine-state study had, on average, 1.9 more years of education beyond high school than home-based workers in other studies. In the study by LINK Resources, however, home-based workers, who were mostly women, were college educated (Sloane, 1993).

Marital Status and Number of Children

Home-based work is often viewed as an ideal way to combine employment and family and most home-based workers (84.8%) were married at the time of the survey (Table 3.2). In the nine-state study, however, 44.1% of home-based workers had no children, and 73.3% did not have children under age 6 in the house. Heck (1988) found that not having children was positively related to the probability of home-based employment, perhaps because it gave the worker periods of time when he or she could focus, uninterrupted by family demands.

Homeownership

A probable influence on the low mobility of the 899 home-based workers was their homeownership status. A large proportion of these workers, 87.3%, lived in a home owned by family members. In 1989, 63.9% of the households in the nation were homeowners (BOC, 1992a), almost 23 percentage points lower than the homeownership rate in the nine-state study.

Years in the Community and Location of Residency

Home-based workers were not highly mobile. The average length of time they had lived in their community was 19.8 years (Table 3.2) and 37.9% of the workers had lived in the same community for over 20 years.

Slightly over half (53.9%) of these home-based workers lived in a town or city with a population over 2,500 (Table 3.2). Another 39.1% of workers lived and worked in rural communities and towns with populations under 2,500. Farm households accounted for 7.0% of the sample. One reason for this low number of farmers was the nine-state study's criteria. To be eligible for this study, farmers had to have home-based work other than the production of crops and livestock. They had to engage in retail sales or "value-added" agriculture, such as weaving cloth out of wool sheared from sheep they had raised or making maple syrup from sap they had collected.

HEALTH INSURANCE COVERAGE ISSUES

Overview of National Trends

The 1992 presidential election spotlighted health care issues. The aging of the U.S. population, the escalation of health care costs, and the increasing number of persons without health insurance have made paying for health care a national concern (Foley, 1992). Many people employed outside the home, particularly those working for large firms, have some access to health insurance coverage through their employer (Foley, 1992). But increasingly, health insurance premiums formerly paid by employers are now negotiated each year as part of a "compensation" package rather than being an expected employee benefit. Members of Congress and some state legislatures are debating a variety of health care options. Home-based workers seem particularly vulnerable to problems with insurance coverage because many are self-employed or have a tenuous relationship with their employers.

Research Results on Health Insurance from the Nine-State Study

Access to health insurance may or may not be a problem for home-based workers. The nine-state study revealed that 89.3% of the home-based workers in the sample had some form of health insurance coverage (Table 3.3). The extent or type of coverage is not known because the survey instrument did not

Table 3.3
Sources of Health Insurance Coverage for All Home-Based Workers, *N* = 899

Source of coverage	Number	Percent
Job-related coverage		
Coverage through home-based work		
Business expense for owner	71	7.9
Wage earner is covered through employer but worker pays	14	1.6
Wage earner is covered through employer who pays	50	5.6
Coverage through another job		
Policy through another job of home-based worker	108	12.0
Policy through another family member's job	288	32.0
Retirement medical coverage (including Medicare)	53	5.9
Non-job-related coverage		
Individual/personal policy (private)	173	19.3
Combination including private policies	47	5.2
No health insurance coverage	96	10.7

Note: Numbers and percents may not add to 899 and 100%, respectively, because of rounding errors.

include questions to elicit such information. Nor did the survey ask detailed information about who paid the premium. Consequently, the researchers know relatively little about differential access to tax deductions for health expenses.

Sources of coverage. Respondents were asked to identify which, if any, potential sources of coverage their households used to obtain health insurance. These sources were (a) business expense, (b) wage worker is covered through employer's policy but worker pays premium, (c) wage worker is covered through employer's policy and employer pays, (d) coverage through another job of home-based worker, (e) coverage through another family member's job, (f) retirement medical coverage including Medicare or other similar support programs, (g) individual or personal policy, and (h) some combination of the above that included private policies.

As a rule, group health insurance is less expensive than a private individual policy, and the primary means of access to group coverage is through employment or a job. Sixty-five percent of home-based workers in the nine-state study obtained their health insurance coverage through job-related means. Only 24.5% obtained coverage through a source other than their jobs including individual policies (19.3%) or a combination of policies which included an individual policy (5.2%). Looked at this way, access does not seem to be a problem.

A quick glance at Table 3.3 would lead one to believe that a home-based worker's best friend was a family member with health insurance benefits because 32.0% of the sample received coverage through another family member's policy. Closer examination, however, reveals that 15.1% of the home-workers in the sample obtained coverage through policies related to their home-based work, another 12.0% through another job of the home-based worker, and 5.9% through retirement benefits. When added to the number obtaining coverage through sources other than a job (i.e., the sum of 19.3%, 5.2%, 12.0% and 5.9% is 42.4%), home-based workers most often (42.4% versus 32.0%) obtained health insurance coverage by relying on themselves. If these households had had to rely on the home-based work alone for their access to group health insurance, the great majority would be without coverage. About 10.7% of the sample had no health insurance coverage.

Multivariate research model of health insurance. The likelihood of a home-based worker having health insurance coverage paid for by any of the payment mechanisms listed above was examined using a multivariate research model[1] that included the characteristics of the worker and the work. A multivariate analysis has the advantage of revealing the specific effect of a particular variable while holding all other variables constant. Throughout the discussion of the results from the nine-state study, keep in mind that effects for individual independent variables in the multivariate analyses should be interpreted at the margin, meaning that as the value of an independent variable increases, the effect is on the dependent variable, holding all other independent variables constant.

This multivariate analysis was performed on the weighted sample of 899 workers, and the results are presented in Table 3.4. Age was positively related to the likelihood of having health insurance coverage. This means that the older the home-based worker, the greater the likelihood that health insurance coverage had been obtained through some payment mechanism. Older workers are likely to need more stable and consistent health insurance coverage than younger workers; older workers may also have been involved in home-based work longer and have set up mechanisms to assure their health insurance coverage. Rural residency was negatively related to the likelihood of having health insurance coverage. Because health insurance coverage for 44.0% of the workers was financed through their other jobs or the job of another family member, rural residents may be at a disadvantage. They may be constrained by the local job market because such additional or extra jobs are less available.

Compared to workers in agricultural products and sales,[2] workers in mechanical and transportation, crafts and artisans, and contracting categories were less likely to have health insurance coverage. Workers in such occupations may be more likely to operate as independent contractors and, therefore, must obtain and finance health insurance coverage on their own. They are also less likely to have professional associations, employer-related programs, or the special status or rates available to business owners.

Finally, home-based workers involved in seasonal work were more likely to have health insurance coverage. Seasonal work usually occurs for short periods of time and is intermittent in nature. With this as a known job parameter, these workers may have greater incentives and thus a greater likelihood to obtain their health insurance through another job or from a job held by another family

Table 3.4
Odds of the Worker Having Health Insurance, *N* = 899

Variable	Significant effects
Worker characteristic	
Male	
Age	+
Education	
Rural residence	-
Work characteristic	
Business owner	
Home-based work income	
Occupation	
Professional and technical	
Marketing and sales	
Clerical and administrative support	
Mechanical and transportation	-
Crafts and artisans	-
Managers	
Services	
Contracting	-
Agricultural products and sales	omitted variable
Seasonality	+
Other employment	
Constant	
Chi-square = 39.41, significant at .001 level	

Note: Effects were statistically significant at the .10 level or less.

member. Seasonal work may be supplementary to other jobs that include insurance benefits.

NATURE OF HOME-BASED WORK

Selected and Salient Aspects of Work

Ownership status. Ownership status was one dimension of home-based work examined. As a business owner, the home-based worker is responsible for all business activities and management, including production, marketing, selling, and record keeping. The intrinsic and extrinsic rewards of business ownership are numerous and include the potential for profits and personal satisfaction, but there are also the obvious risks of financial insecurity, business demands, and family conflicts. Home-based work that is either contracted or done for a piece-rate wage should have fewer risks than business ownership. Yet the evidence indicates that wage earners may face as many barriers as do home-based business owners. Wage earners' financial rewards and personal independence are controlled by the employer (Christensen, 1989; Lozano, 1989).

In this study 74.6% of the home-based work was done by workers who owned businesses, and the remaining work was done by wage earners who were paid by an outside employer (Table 3.5). In most of the studies on home-based work, a majority of workers were self-employed (Christensen, 1987; Heck, 1988; Horvath, 1986). Other variables used to describe the nature of home-based work or home employment were the amount of income generated, hours worked, number of years in home-based work, and seasonality of the work.

Income from home-based work. The income figures derived from the nine-state study refer to the calendar year of 1988. The means for the income variables were as follows: gross annual income from home-based businesses was $53,164; net annual income from home-based businesses was $15,628; net annual wage income received from home-based work was $24,300; and annual

Table 3.5
Selected and Salient Aspects of Home-Based Work, *N* = 899

Characteristic	Number	Percent	Mean	Median
Ownership status				
Business owner	670	74.6		
Wage worker	229	25.4		
Net annual home-based work income	899	100.0	$17,835	$11,000
Home-based work hours (annual)			1,819	1,800
Home-based work hours (per week)			36.4	31.2
Less than 20	312	34.7		
20–29	89	9.9		
30–39	73	8.1		
40 or more	425	47.3		
Employment status				
Part-time	443	49.3		
Full-time	456	50.7		
Duration			9.1	6.0
Less than 5 years	352	39.2		
5–9 years	215	23.9		
10–14 years	144	16.0		
15 years or more	188	20.9		
Seasonality				
Yes	122	13.6		
No	777	86.4		
Other employment				
Yes	235	26.1		
No	664	73.9		

household income from all sources was $42,263. The mean average net income from both kinds of home-based work was $17,835, which was the average of net incomes of both business owners and wage workers (Table 3.5).

For comparison purposes, the mean before-tax household money income for the United States in 1988 was $34,017 (the median was $27,225) (BOC, 1991c). The mean annual wages and salary in 1988 totaled $19,251. Per employee in 1988, the mean annual before-tax wage income was $21,649 (with an average weekly wage of $416) (BLS, 1989b). Finally, the mean annual nonfarm self-employment net income was $15,241 (BOC, 1991c).

The comparative income figures are most similar for the self-employed home-based worker and other self-employed workers who are not home-based. Otherwise, the various income levels of home-based workers in the nine-state study tended to be somewhat higher than for similar worker groups who were not home-based. For wage workers, it may be that the large group of marketing and sales home-based workers drove the income averages up. In addition, the benefits of working at home may include lower transportation costs, lower child care costs, and lower clothing costs. When additional expenses are considered in making income comparisons, the income figures appear to leave home-based workers in a favorable income position relative to other workers.

Moreover, on average, home-based work contributed 39.7% of the total annual household income. Thus the home-based work under study was an important element of the overall income pool for the household with a member engaged in such work.

Home-based work hours. Information needed to ascertain the commitment to home employment was generated from hours worked per week and the employment status variables. Respondents were asked the total number of hours devoted to home-based work during 1988. The total annual hours were divided by 50, assuming 50 weeks as a workyear. The distribution of hours worked per week is found in Table 3.5. The largest number, or 47.3%, of the home-based workers had performed 40 or more hours per week of home-based work. Another 34.7% committed fewer than 20 hours per week to generating income at home.

Employment status. Employment was defined as full-time and part-time. An average workweek of 35 or more hours was considered full-time, working less than 35 hours for an average workweek was classified as part-time. About one-half, 50.7%, of home employment was full-time, while 49.3% was part-time work.

Duration. On average the home-based worker in the nine-state study had engaged in home-based work for 9.1 years. This duration parallels the finding that workers had lived in their communities for an average of 19.8 years. Such longevity may be associated with the need to have established a client or business base and may be related to the deliberate planning and desires of home-based workers to pursue independent work lives. This finding may also be related to the study's sampling design, which excluded those who had been involved in home-based work for less than a year. Only those households whose home-based worker had established some longevity were included in the nine-state study; thus the average longevity rate of the home-based workers surveyed was deliberately skewed toward longer periods.

Seasonality. Seasonal work is work performed only during specific months or at a certain time of the year. Snow removal, outside contracting, sales of vegetables and fruit plants, and lawn care services are examples of seasonal home-based work. In this nine-state study, only 13.6% of home-based workers reported that their work was seasonal.

Other employment. Some home-based workers (26.1%) had other employment besides the home-based work. Because nearly half of the sample workers were part-time, their home-based work was a secondary source of income.

Job Titles and Occupations

According to a traditional perspective, arts and crafts occupations are ones in which individuals primarily work at home (Littrell, Stout, & Reilly, 1991). Home knitting (Loker, 1985) was studied as a specific job appropriate for home-based work. Child care, contracting, and sales also have been considered ideal at-home employment (Arden, 1988).

The variety of job titles in the nine-state study expands assumptions about suitable home-based work. For example, engineers, teachers of Lamaze, scuba, and aerobics, beekeepers, artificial inseminators, coordinators for home patient care, swimming pool builders, graphic designers, book reviewers, and disc jockeys are just some of the occupations given by home-based workers. Responses to the question "What does the home-based worker do?" provided an extensive list of occupations. In the nine-state study, this question was asked of all 1,591 respondents originally included in the screening stage of the interviews. All job titles relevant for the 899 study participants are included in Table 3.6.

The jobs were classified based on the U.S. Department of Commerce's (1980) *Standard Occupational Classification Manual.* Nine categories were used: (a) professional and technical, (b) marketing and sales, (c) clerical and administrative support, (d) mechanical and transportation, (e) crafts and artisans, (f) managers, (g) services, (h) contracting, and (i) agricultural products and sales.

The range of job titles within each occupational category is worthy of mention because past research has highlighted particular at-home jobs. For example, as the computer revolution continues, telecommuting will encourage and enhance the home-based opportunities for both employers and employees (Kroll, 1984; McGee, 1988; Olson, 1983). Artisans, craftspersons (Littrell et al., 1991), and home knitters (Loker, 1985) have been studied as examples of workers whose jobs are suited to being done at home. Beauticians, builders, and real estate and insurance sales are other examples of jobs traditionally thought of as natural home-based opportunities.

Table 3.6 shows examples of job titles for each of the occupational categories. For example, the professional/technical classification includes consultants; engineers; teachers of aerobics, swimming, and music; graders of English; and community representatives. The mechanical and transportation category includes piano tuners and repairers; structural and electrical inspectors; and bus drivers. Many of these job titles have identical counterparts in jobs outside the home.

Table 3.7 lists the distribution of occupations among the nine categories. The occupations most often represented were marketing and sales (24.3%), contracting (14.9%), and mechanical and transportation (13.2%). These three categories accounted for more than 50% of all the workers.

No one occupational group was dominant. Marketing and sales had the highest number of workers, with 24.3% of the sample. Typically, these jobs involved selling an employer's product or service from a home telephone or by door-to-door sales. The established direct selling companies Amway, Avon, and Tupperware were represented, along with an extensive list of other products and services. English riding accessories, satellite dishes, sauna equipment, water distillers, and wind surfing gear were some other products not often associated with a home business but, in this study, were named as being marketed and sold.

Contracting such as masonry, electrical, and sign painting engaged 14.9% of workers, and 13.2% did mechanical or transportation work. Twelve percent (12.1%) of the occupations were in services that included home child care, elder care, and processing vegetables for McDonald's. Other occupations included crafts and a variety of endeavors related to the arts, such as composing, film producing, graphic designing, and creating greeting cards; and professional work in education, finance, government, health, law, religion, and science.

The list of specific job titles in Table 3.6 clearly documents the variety of occupations pursued by home-based workers. Some computer job titles were found in the professional and technical category and in the clerical and administrative support group, although in the total sample of 899 home-based workers, less than 1% of the job titles were computer related. Contrary to the forecasts of the early 1980s (Toffler, 1980), computer technology did not seem to play a significant role in the home employment chosen by the workers in the nine-state study. Bacon (1989) also reported that the telecommuting revolution predicted a decade ago has not happened. On the other hand, data from the nine-state study did not permit analyses of the type or amount of technologies used in connection with home-based work regardless of the job title or occupational category.

The category of agricultural products and sales had a minimal number of home-based activities probably because only farm work that was "value added"

Table 3.6
Job Titles by Occupations, *N* = 1,591

Professional and technical. Computer consultant, veterinarian, rehabilitation therapist, land surveyor, lawyer, vice-president, manager, consulting engineer, optician, architectural engineer, freelance designer, management consultant, accountant, interior designer, minister, computer programmer, financial consultant, transportation consultant, consultant for Asian businesses, legal consultant, marketing consultant, therapy consultant, energy consultant, architect, investment analyst, safety engineer, portfolio manager, acoustical engineer, proprietor of a company, civil engineer, dietitian, translator, stockbroker, psychologist, doctor, draftsman, engineer, planner, sea captain, health care consultant, nurse, art consultant, landscape architect, agriculture consultant, education consultant, admissions representative, marketing survey analyst, consulting psychologist, public relations, economic consultant, hydrology consultant and civil engineer, field director for Girl Scouts, teachers of piano, art, music, math, aerobics, Lamaze, swimming, driving, scuba, percussion, college tutor, dance, interpreter for the deaf, grader of English, elected state legislator, town supervisor/selectman, township clerk, city council

Marketing and sales. Avon, Amway, Sasco, Mary Kay, Shaklee, door-to-door, network marketing, batteries, gun care products, firearms, golf equipment, telemarketing, crystal, home party, ice cream, food concessions, auto/truck parts, fuel oil, used cars from yard, cars, welcome wagon, Snap-On Tools, antique dealer, distributor of shelving, buys and sells junk metal, sports card dealer, telecommunications equipment, monuments, floor covering, cruises, dog food, undercover wear, cutlery, mailing lists, precious metals and coins, computers and software, oil products, stocks and bonds, T-shirts, flea market, water distillers, sauna equipment, snowmobiles, satellite dishes, fishing tackle and lures, encyclopedias, wind surfing gear, Tupperware, Herbal-life, LeVoy's Fashions, World Book, bait, rural paper route, used English riding accessories. Agents for real estate, insurance, auto leasing, coin broker, direct market, mail order book store, sales director, advertising sales, auctioneer, mail order business, sales consultant, runs a newspaper agency, art dealer, finds referees, medical recruiter, financial service, contract equipment to federal/state government, industrial supplies, import sales, publishing business, sales manager for entertainment company, division manager or sales representative, printing broker, land developer, sales consultant/travel, greeting cards, sales representative, manufacturers representative, music company sales manager, computer systems, trade shows, bulk mailing service, preschool programs, shops: bicycle, bait, body, clothing, archery, grocery, gift, boots

Clerical and administrative support. Secretary, bookkeeper, makes computer labels, computer work, inventory-computer, office manager, real estate appraiser, rural mail carrier, postmaster, tax preparer, typist, locate people, checks truckers' logs, freelance proofreading, condenses law journal articles, insurance billing, freelance legal and medical records, crop insurance adjuster, freelance court reporter, data processing, market researcher, phone service for home health care agency, administrative assistant, book research company, audit checker, town clerk, credit information checker, fire investigator, tax collector for school district, insurance adjuster, payroll officer, reports news to radio station, pays insurance claims, medical transcription, coordinator for home patient care, truck dispatcher

Mechanical and transportation. Truck drivers, sand and gravel, backhoe/bulldozing business, trash hauling, wood cutter, gravel bank, hauls scrap iron, drives Leadfoot Express, motor route for newspaper, anhydrous ammonia applicator, hot oil truck, clears land, fuel oil delivery, bus driver, car crusher, oil transporter, lumber, locks, guns, lawnmowers, small engines, aquarium maintenance, appliances, electrical, computer, typewriters, kerosene heaters, refrigeration, radio & TV, telephones, boats, hot air balloons, solar panels, household, motorcycle, farm equipment, sewing machine, knives, air conditioning, makes rubber seals, grass cutting, welder, builds race cars, building service repair, soldering, auto technician, auto bodywork, piano tuning

Table 3.6
"continued"

and repair, cleans windows and upholstery, constructs feeder building, makes playground equipment, vacuum system installer, pipe organ technician, stagehand, engine rebuilding, oil well pumper, attach handles to ski ropes, portable welder, structural and electrical inspector

Crafts and artisans. Crafts, potters, clock maker, blacksmith, horse-shoer, picture framer, furniture maker, quilt maker, pattern designer, clothing and costume designer, needlework, smocker, woodworker, ceramics, silk flowers, tole painting, knitter/designer, sewing/seamstress, makes leis, taxidermist, antique refinisher, windsock and kite making, cross stitch designer, makes magnetic signs, upholstery, weaver, crocheting, makes fishing rods, paints T-shirts, glazing photos on china, stained glass, calligraphy, chair caning, knife maker, photo refinisher, liquid embroidery, designs and builds cradles, Christmas wreaths, ice carver/designer, molded fiberglass/marble, metalsmith, makes jewelry, china painting, tool and die maker, flower arranger, doll maker, basket maker, windmill designer, children's clothing designer, makes window coverings, machine knitter, author, artist, songwriter, composer, photographer, disc jockey, freelance writer, musician, entertainer, videotaping, inventor, runs an opera house, creates greeting cards, film producer, illustrator, newspaper columnist, book reviewer, recording studio, art and photo consultant, vocal soloist, graphic designer, new product developer, audio/visual producer, studio artist, acoustic technician

Managers. Manager of commercial laundry, water testing, garbage collection, special events coordinating, cleaning business, trailer manufacturer, car waxing, motor home storage, party planner, restaurant district manager, housecleaning supervisor, district manager of food products company, income property, owns and runs a trailer court, owns and maintains apartment building, manages apartments/condos, owns a bed and breakfast/vacation rental business, runs a resort, property maintenance, motel manager, landlord, real estate manager, campground, rental property manager, tavern owner

Services. Beautician, suntanning business, dog groomer, fitness studio, barber, yoga therapist, model, beauty consultant, massage therapist, fashion wardrobe consultant, color analysis, hairdresser, day care, child care, foster care, elder care, private duty nurse, home health aide, adult foster care, home parents, housekeeper, house/office cleaning, carpet cleaning, snow removal, ironing, industrial cleaning, handyman, carpet installer, security work (e.g., concerts), processes vegetables for McDonald's and schools, caterer, wedding cake baker

Contracting. Contractors, construction (i.e., road and other), carpentry, well driller, house painter, excavation, concrete, roofing and siding, drywaller, plumbing and heating, wallpapering, masonry, electrician, cable construction/installation, electrical wiring, home renovator, gutter installer, swimming pool builder, heating (i.e., air conditioning business, welding, electrical, plumbing work), sidewalk contracting, estimator for building work, ceramic tile and carpets, floor coverings, builder, sign painter, snow removal, home maintenance

Agricultural products and sales. Hay, fruits, vegetables, herbs, maple syrup, Christmas trees, sprouts, foliage, flowers, eggs, alfalfa seed, greenhouse/nursery, raspberries, tomato and flower plants, strawberries, pumpkins, Indian corn, dried flowers, peaches, cherries, apples and cider, African violets, feed, farm, cockatiels, horses, rabbits, cats, pigs, horse trainer, artificial inseminator, beekeeper, dairy inspector, chickens, beef farm, bovine embryo, dogs, boards/trains dogs, boards horses, logger, sod layer, lawn care service, tree service, lawn sprinkler system, mows cemetery, cow hoof trimmer, fisherman, slaughterhouse, meat processing, grain elevator

Note: Unweighted data from initial screen interview.

Table 3.7
Home-Based Work Occupations, $N = 899$

Occupation	Number	Percent
Professional and technical	107	11.9
Marketing and sales	218	24.3
Clerical and administrative support	53	5.8
Mechanical and transportation	118	13.2
Crafts and artisans	105	11.6
Managers	31	3.5
Services	109	12.1
Contracting	134	14.9
Agricultural products and sales	24	2.7

was eligible for this study. For example, farm households that sold produce, eggs, herbs, and other farm products at a roadside stand or made candy and jams from their own fruit qualified for the study.

HOME-BASED WORK SPACE

Location of Home Work Site

A little over one-third (37.3%) of the home-based workers had carved out a home work space in an office/workroom/study, or attached cottage, business, shop, or studio office (Table 3.8). A basement, laundry room, or recreation room was the second most popular *first* work site (i.e., primary site for work) for home-based work, used by 17.8% of workers. Each home-based worker could have reported up to a total of four work sites in the nine-state study. If the worker had a third and/or fourth work site, most popular locations out of the top four first sites were work sites that were separate from home and family activity areas. Respectively, these locations were, again, basements, laundry rooms, or recreation rooms, followed by detached buildings or outdoor work areas.

Living rooms and kitchens were most often used as tertiary and quaternary sites for home-based work; these rooms were less likely to be the first or second site. These patterns indicate that although home-based workers may make a deliberate effort to keep work and family life spatially separate, timing and/or activities of one sphere tend to spill over into the other for at least some families occasionally. These tertiary and quaternary sites tend to be the most shared spaces for family activities.

Table 3.8
Primary and Exclusive Home Work Space Used by Home-Based Workers, $N = 899$

Work space area	Primary work space				Exclusive work space			
	First site		Second site		First site		Second site	
	Number	Percent	Number	Percent	Number	Percent	Number	Percent
Office/workroom/study, attached cottage, shop, studio, attached business	335	37.3	126	14.0	295	32.9	50	5.6
Basement, laundry room, recreation room	160	17.8	41	4.6	101	11.2	2	0.2
Detached building, outdoor work area, yard, garden, yard for auto mechanic, enclosed shop	119	13.2	0	0.0	54	6.0	0	0.0
Garage/enclosed porch, apartment used for storage, screened porch, storage room, attic	98	10.9	30	3.3	40	4.4	11	1.3
Living room/family room, den, foyer, hallway	50	5.5	76	8.5	—	—	—	—
Bedroom (empty bedroom for exclusive use)	55	6.1	37	4.2	5	0.6	8	0.9
Kitchen	45	5.0	62	6.9	—	—	—	—
Dining room	37	4.1	68	7.5	—	—	—	—
Small work space in home living areas (last 3 rooms)	—	—	—	—	7	0.8	1	0.1
No other primary or exclusive home work site	—	—	458	51.0	397	44.1	827	91.9

Exclusive Home Work Site

Slightly over one-half, or 55.9%, of the home-based workers had exclusive work sites. The two most popular exclusive work sites were also the two most popular work sites for home-based workers in general (Table 3.8). Exclusive home-based work space did not include areas of the home where necessary family activities were carried out, such as the kitchen and living room. Although home-based work has the advantage of being performed in the home, it appears that work and family activities are conducted in fairly distinct and separate arenas within and associated with the home. This pattern may indicate a need to keep work and family spheres separate even though both are home-based. Such a need may arise from the differential roles, responsibilities, and rights assumed in the two different spheres.

INTRUSIVENESS OF HOME-BASED WORK

When family activities and income-generating activities occur within the same space, there may be the maximum amount of flexibility in arranging work and family schedules. There is also the potential, however, for the family to limit work activities (Rowe & Bentley, 1992) and for the work to intrude on family life. The degree to which the work intrudes on family life and factors associated with high levels of intrusiveness are discussed in this section.

Measures of Intrusiveness

Four different measures are included in an index designed to assess the degree to which the home-based work intrudes into the everyday lives of the workers and their families: how often telephone calls are received at home, whether work occurs in a space in which other activities are occurring at the same time, whether clients are seen in the home, and whether there are conflicts over the use of a family vehicle for the home-based work (Table 3.9).

Each item was assessed on a scale that was coded 0 for least intrusion, 1 for a medium amount of intrusion, and 2 for the most intrusion. Receiving telephone calls once a week or less was coded 0; receiving calls two or three times a week was coded 1; and receiving calls daily received a 2. If it was reported that there was a space for the exclusive use of the home-based work, such as an office or workshop, the household was coded 0; households in which activities occurred in the same space never or seldom were coded 1; and those reporting that such activities occurred sometimes, often, or always were coded 2. Seeing clients at home less than once a month received a 0; seeing clients at home one to four times a month received a 1; and seeing clients two or more times a week at home was coded 2. If no vehicle was used for both the home-based work and the family, the household received a 0; households in

Table 3.9
Components of the Intrusiveness Index, $N = 899$

Source of intrusion	Number	Percent
Receiving telephone calls at home		
Weekly or less	169	18.8
2–3 times a week	203	22.5
Daily	527	58.7
Work conducted in space where other activities are occurring simultaneously		
Never, work space is exclusive	502	55.9
Never or seldom	191	21.3
Sometimes, often, or always	206	22.9
See clients at home		
Less than once a month	407	45.2
1–4 times a month	212	23.6
2–3 times a week or more	280	31.2
Conflicts occur over the use of a vehicle		
Never, none is used for both work and family	267	29.7
Vehicle used for both, no conflicts occur	582	64.7
Vehicle used for both, conflicts occur	50	5.6

which a vehicle was used for both purposes but no conflicts occur received a 1; and those in which conflicts occur received a 2.

Research Results on Intrusiveness from the Nine-State Study

More than half of the sample (58.7%) reported receiving telephone calls daily. More than half of the households reported no conflicts over space; almost half reported seeing clients at home less than once a month. Although almost two-thirds (64.7%) had a vehicle used for both the household and the home-based work, there were no conflicts over the use. Only 5.6% reported conflicts over the use of a single vehicle.

The four items were summed to form a single intrusiveness index with a potential range of 0 to 8. Sixteen households (1.7%) reported no intrusion and so had a score of 0; at the other end of the scale, 2.8% had a score of 7; no household received a score of 8. The mean is 3.68, the standard deviation is 1.5, and the median is 4.

Not surprisingly, individuals who perform a personal service (e.g., beauticians, child care providers, and home health aides) reported the most intrusion (Table 3.10), followed by mechanical and transportation workers and managers. Those doing clerical or administrative activities reported the least intrusion. Workers receiving the most remuneration from the business reported the least

Table 3.10
Level of Intrusiveness of the Home-Based Work Related to Selected Characteristics of the Worker, the Household, and the Work, $N = 899$

Characteristic	Number	Mean	F-ratio
Worker characteristic			
Gender			24.90*
Female	377	4.0	
Male	522	3.5	
Marital status			.01
Married	762	3.7	
Nonmarried	137	3.7	
Household size			10.05*
1–2 persons	308	3.4	
3–4 persons	400	3.7	
5 or more persons	191	4.1	
Homeowner			2.11
Yes	785	3.7	
No	114	3.5	
Location of residence			1.24
Farm, nonfarm, town or city < 2,500	414	3.8	
Town or city > 2,500	485	3.6	
Work characteristic			
Respondent was the home-based worker			14.20*
Yes	482	3.9	
No	417	3.5	
Ownership status			
Business owner	670	3.8	19.00*
Wage worker	229	3.3	
Net home-based work income			
Less than $4,799	281	3.9	4.04*
$4,800–$19,999	302	3.6	
$20,000 and higher	316	3.6	
Occupation			
Professional and technical	107	3.6	6.07*
Marketing and sales	218	3.5	
Clerical and administrative support	53	3.2	
Mechanical and transportation	118	3.8	
Crafts and artisans	105	3.4	
Managers	31	3.8	
Services	109	4.6	
Contracting	134	3.6	
Agricultural products and sales	24	3.4	
Employment status			
Part-time	270	3.9	6.22*
Full-time	629	3.6	

* Statistically significant at the 0.05 level or less.

intrusion; those with the lowest incomes (i.e., under $4,800 annually) reported the most intrusion.

The households of wage workers (e.g., shoe sewers, home knitters, home health aides, apartment managers, and electrical inspectors) scored lower on the intrusion index than households of business owners; female workers had higher intrusion scores than male workers. Not surprisingly, respondents who were also the home-based worker reported higher levels of intrusion than respondents who were not the home-based worker. Large households reported the most intrusion, probably because the potential for conflicts over a vehicle and space within the home was higher when there are more people in the household. There was no difference in the level of intrusiveness on the basis of rural/urban location and homeownership.

MANAGEMENT OF HOME-BASED WORK

This section describes specific activities that are identified as components of the management of paid work and relates these factors to a family management model. Only the 482 home-based workers who were also the household managers were studied. Because of the need for agreement and consistency in performing management activities, it was assumed that this subgroup would be able to evaluate the overlap and permeability of the boundary between work and family. Chapter 5 discusses the nature of family management.

Studying Managerial Behavior

Prior to this research project, no effort had been made to delineate managerial processes that are unique to home-based workers in their paid work activities. It is generally assumed, however, that effective management is a major determinant of the achievement of such desired paid work outcomes as the creation of products and the provision of services. Although the outcomes are self-evident, the proof that the behaviors producing the outcomes are part of a conscious, goal-driven managerial process has been elusive for family resource management researchers.[3] To address this deficiency, a multiple-item scale was developed to assess the management of the income-generating activities.[4]

Research Variables for Managing Paid Work

The Deacon and Firebaugh (1988) management framework, discussed more extensively in Chapter 5 and elsewhere (see note 4), provided the basis for the 10 statements comprising the management scale. This scale was administered to the 482 home-based workers who were also managers of their households.

Deacon and Firebaugh (1988) posited that demands and resources are inputs to the managerial system. The internal structure of the managerial subsystem, called throughput, consists of two main components, planning and implementing; thus planning and implementing the use of resources to meet demands are the purposes of managerial activity. Planning consists of standard setting and action sequencing; demand clarification and resource assessment are separate components of standard setting. The plan is implemented by actuating and controlling behaviors. Controlling involves checking conformity to a plan and making adjustments when needed. The output of management is responses to demands and changes in resources.

Emphasis was given to the throughput components of management in the scale developed for this project. Table 3.11 lists the specific statements to which the workers who were household managers responded. The management concept thought to be represented by the statements is also listed in Table 3.11. The leading question was "Which number (1 = not at all; 3 = somewhat; 5 = exactly) most closely describes you and how you work?" Higher scores, after recoding for three questions, indicated management behavior more closely aligned with the underlying conceptualization than not. For example, the statement "Each week you decide how much work you will do" relates to goal setting. Goal setting is one type of demand represented in the Deacon and Firebaugh model (1988).

Research Results on Managerial Behaviors from the Nine-State Study

The frequency of responses to the home-based work management scale is given in Table 3.12. About 70% of the worker-managers ($n = 482$) indicated that the statements representing resource assessment (69.6%) and demand responses (72.0%) exactly described their behavior. In fact, for nine of the statements, the distribution of responses tended to cluster toward the high (exactly) values. The exception was the statement pertaining to goal setting to which there was a wide distribution of responses.

For each respondent the scores on each of the items were added to compute a total score. The individual's potential overall score could range from 10 to 50. As shown in Table 3.12, the total scale mean was 40.3. The reliability of the scale, represented by alpha, was reasonable and sufficient given the number and correlation of items composing the scale (Kim & Mueller, 1981).

Mean scores across individuals were calculated for each item (Table 3.12). The item means for two statements relating to resource assessment and demand responses were the highest (4.5 and 4.6, respectively) and had the smallest standard deviations (< .90). These findings suggest that the statements associated with the concepts are salient to the workers and that the concepts are crucial elements of a work management model. The item mean

Table 3.11
Family Management Concepts Related to Questionnaire Items for Home-Based Work Management, $n = 482$

Management concept	Questionnaire item
Input	
Demands	
Goals (setting)	Each week you decide how much work you will do.[a]
Events	
Resources	
Throughput	
Planning	
Standard setting	Before starting a job, you have a firm idea about how to judge the outcome.
Demand clarification	When planning a job, you think the plan through so that your goal is clear before you actually begin doing the job.
Resource assessment	Before starting a particular job, you figure out what you need, like tools, supplies, time, etc.
Action sequencing	Although you are flexible, you make work schedules.
Implementing	
Actuating	When there is work to be done, you wait until the last minute.[b]
Controlling	
Checking	As you work, you check whether things are going as planned.
Adjusting	You change how you are doing a task when the results are not as planned.
Output	
Demand responses	When you finish a job, you think about whether the results meet your standards as well as your client's or employer's.
Resource changes	When finished, you ask whether people and equipment have been used to the best advantage.

Note: Management concepts refer to definitions used in *Family Resource Management: Principles and Applications*, 2nd ed., by R. E. Deacon and F. M. Firebaugh, 1988, Boston: Allyn and Bacon.

[a]Actual statements are listed. Each statement was responded to by only those household managers who were the home-based worker *in reference to their home-based work*. Leading question was "Which number (1 = not at all; 3 = somewhat; 5 = exactly) most closely describes you and how you work?" *Statements were not given in the order listed*. A parallel and similar series of statements were used for the family work management scale discussed in detail in Chapter 5. [b]This statement was reverse coded in descriptive statistics and the factor analysis results.

Table 3.12
Frequency of Responses to Home-Based Work Management Scale by Home-Based Workers Who Were Also Household Managers, *n* = 482

Management concept	Home-based work scale					Mean	Standard deviation
	Not at all		Somewhat		Exactly		
	1	*2*	*3*	*4*	*5*		
Input							
Goals	23.1%	5.6%	26.9%	9.1%	35.3%	3.3	1.5
Planning							
Standard setting	3.7	1.4	19.0	31.8	44.1	4.1	1.0
Demand clarification	3.9	1.0	20.5	20.4	54.2	4.2	1.0
Resource assessment	1.1	2.8	11.8	14.8	69.6	4.5	0.9
Action sequencing	9.5	4.6	24.2	18.4	43.3	3.8	1.3
Implementing							
Actuation	6.9	5.0	31.0	15.6	41.4	3.8	1.2
Checking	2.1	2.3	26.9	25.8	42.9	4.0	1.0
Adjusting	2.7	1.7	18.2	23.9	53.6	4.2	1.0
Output							
Demand responses	1.9	0.5	6.8	18.8	72.0	4.6	0.8
Resource changes	9.8	4.7	22.2	25.8	37.6	3.8	1.3
Total scale mean						40.3	5.9
Alphas for additive scales			.71				
Standardized item alpha			.73				

Note: Sum of percentages for all five scores per item may not equal 100% due to rounding.

for the goal statement is also of interest because it had the lowest mean (3.3) and the largest standard deviation (1.5). Almost one-fourth (23.1%) of the respondents indicated that the statement pertaining to setting goals was "not at all like me." Based on their responses to the other statements, it is difficult to believe that these workers who seem highly involved in managerial behavior do not have goals. Thus the researchers were left with the possibility that the statement intended to capture the goal-setting concept is unsatisfactory. It may also be the case that home-based workers do not think in terms of the wording used in the statement pertaining to goals—"deciding how much work to do" each week.

SUBJECTIVE OUTCOMES OF HOME-BASED WORK

Introduction

In the model developed for the study of home-based working families, Owen, Carsky, and Dolan (1992) included two major outcomes for the worker: money income and satisfaction, the latter consisting of work satisfaction and family satisfaction. They discussed the notion of psychic rewards from work (i.e., the feelings associated with being a productive member of society) which are important to workers in addition to the money income generated by the work.

Beach (1987) emphasized the value home-based workers place on autonomy and flexibility, the ability to control their work schedule and to restructure work time to accommodate family needs. Perhaps workers are willing to trade off a portion of money income to gain the psychic rewards of autonomy and flexibility. Aronson (1991) discussed the nonpecuniary advantages of self-employment, such as greater control over work performance, flexibility in time use, and absence of institutional restraints. Hoover (1986) reported that rural female entrepreneurs started their businesses based on their interests or hobbies and the ability to stay home to care for their children. Burdette (1990) found that approximately one-third of the female business owners cited income or financial benefits as the primary reason for being in business. Thus it seems that a variety of reasons may motivate individuals to work at home and that both money and certain satisfactions may accrue to the worker.

Advantages and Disadvantages of Home-Based Work

To pursue this area of inquiry, the home-based workers/household managers ($n = 482$) were asked open-ended questions about the advantages and disadvantages of generating income at home. They could give two responses to each question. The researchers then recoded the responses based on common themes found among the various replies.

Advantages. Three advantages were cited most frequently as either a first or second reply. Flexibility was the most frequently cited advantage mentioned by 40.7%, followed by care for family (32.9%), and saving time and avoiding hassle (9.7%). A chi-square statistical procedure was performed to ascertain whether an association existed between any of the three advantages and gender–ownership status (which denotes four subgroups of female owners, female earners, male owners, and male earners; see Chapter 4 for additional analyses), the presence of children under 6 years, and the presence of children under 18 years. Mentioning flexibility as an advantage was significantly associated with gender–ownership status but not with either of the family composition variables. Male earners were more likely than other groups to cite flexibility as an advantage. None of the independent variables was associated with saving time as an advantage.

Three of the independent variables were associated with whether or not care for family was mentioned as an advantage. Female owners and female earners were more likely than others to identify care for family, as were workers with children under 6 years and those with children under 18 years.

Disadvantages. Three disadvantages (*n* = 482) were mentioned most often: can't get away from work (21.3%), family interrupts work (12.8%), and work interferes with family (11.8%). Workers with no children under 6 or 18 were more likely than others to mention "can't get away from work" as a disadvantage. The gender–ownership status variable was not associated with this disadvantage. Whether "family interrupts work" was mentioned as a disadvantage was not associated with gender–ownership status or with having children under 6 years; it was, however, associated with having children under 18 years of age. In other words, no matter whether the respondent was male or female, an owner or an earner, having children under 18 increased the likelihood that family life interrupts work. Similarly, "work interferes with family" was more likely to be mentioned by workers with children under 18, whereas no association existed with gender–ownership status or having young children.

The results focusing on the disadvantages of home-based work have some interesting implications. It seems that workers with children face some challenges at the work-family interface, a topic to be discussed at length in Chapter 5. There are times when their families interfere with work and other times when the work interferes with family. Recall that in the management of work section, the one component of management with which workers were least likely to identify was the one related to goal setting. Perhaps there are times when, even though working, the worker is concerned primarily not with work output, but with consideration of competing family responsibilities.

These disadvantages, work and family interfering with each other, may also be advantages from another perspective—the worker can attend to work and family concomitantly or separately when it is appropriate. In fact, the presence of children may at times force the worker to engage in a mental process in which work and family are deliberately separated. Those without children under 18 do not need to make this mental separation; thus their complaint is that they have trouble getting away from their work.

Attitudes about Work and Money

The workers/home managers (*n* = 482) were asked the question "Overall, would you say you like this work a lot, some, a little, or not at all?" Because very few respondents selected the latter two responses, they were combined to represent "not much." Overwhelmingly, the worker-managers liked their work a lot (83.1%). About 11.7% answered "a little," and 5.2% said "not much." Women and men were equally likely to enjoy their work. An association was found between the "like to work" variable and ownership status, however. Earners disproportionately responded "not much" which may reflect a loss of autonomy not experienced by owners.

Four choices were available for the statement that began with "Thinking of home-based work and how much money you make." The choices were as follows: make good money for the time you put in; make adequate money for the time; just meet expenses; lost money last year. Of 482 worker-managers, a very few (5.8%) reported they lost money and 18.1% said they just met expenses. Nearly half of the workers/home managers (48.5%) reported making adequate money, and about one out of four (27.5%) responded that they made good money for the time involved. Gender was not associated with responses to this variable, but ownership status was. Earners were more likely than owners to respond "good money."

The relationship between income and attitudes is shown in Table 3.13. It is clear that the home-based workers' attitudes toward their work were related to the income generated from that work. The higher the income from the work, the more likely the worker was to report that he or she liked the work and expected that feelings about the work will be even better in the future. Gammas of .40 indicated that the level of income generated was strongly related to the worker's current attitudes about income from the work and expectations about income over the next three years. Almost half (46.7%) of those with high incomes reported making "good money for the time spent"; fewer than one-fifth (17.9%) of those in the low-income category reported such attitudes. Similarly, more than four-fifths (82.5%) of those with high incomes thought income would increase, as compared to less than half (48.5%) of those with low incomes.

Specific Subjective Outcomes of Home-Based Work

As increasing numbers of workers acclimate to a home-based work setting, it becomes increasingly important to examine not only economic outcomes such as net business income but also the nonmonetary aspects of employment such as satisfaction levels. Aronson (1991) suggested that self-employment behavior over time cannot be fully or adequately explained by examining only wages. Nonmonetary aspects of these work arrangements such as the desire for autonomy and independence may play major roles. The same might be said of home-based employment.

Although literature on satisfaction with home-based work is lacking, related research that has examined job satisfaction and small businesses is relevant. An

Table 3.13

Relationship Between Income from the Home-Based Work and Attitudes Toward the Work Among Respondents Who Were Also the Home-Based Workers, *n* = 482

Attitude	Income from home-based work			
	Low	*Medium*	*High*	*Gamma*
Respondent likes the work				.25
A little or somewhat	20.3%	17.3%	8.3%	
A lot	79.7	82.7	91.7	
The way the respondent feels about the work will				.35
Get worse	11.5	4.1	0.1	
Stay the same	62.4	58.5	51.3	
Get better	26.1	37.4	48.6	
Thinking about how much money made from the home-based work, the respondent				.40
Lost money or met expenses	34.9	15.3	13.6	
Made adequate money for time spent	47.2	55.2	39.8	
Made good money for the time spent	17.9	29.5	46.7	
In the next three years, the respondent expects that the money from the home-based work will				.40
Decrease	24.6	14.5	2.1	
Stay the same	26.9	25.8	15.4	
Increase	48.5	59.8	82.5	

extensive literature review conducted by Lacy, Shepard, and Houghland (1979) found that job satisfaction was positively related to satisfaction with other aspects of life such as marriage, family leisure, health, and place of residence. Orpen's (1978) findings suggested that work satisfaction had a stronger effect on nonwork satisfaction than the reverse and that there is a causal relationship between job and life satisfaction. Pleck, Staines, and Lang (1980) found that work and family interfered with each other and were negatively related to job satisfaction, family, adjustment, and overall well-being. About one-third of the respondents in the study by Pleck, Staines, and Lang experienced "a lot of" or "some" interference.

Three subjective outcome variables were examined in the nine-state study: satisfaction with quality of life, income adequacy, and control over everyday life. Results showed that 48.0% of household managers in households with home-based employment were satisfied with their quality of life (Table 3.14). The next highest percentage, those who were very satisfied, was 29.2%. Thus it appears that most home-based workers, 77.2%, are satisfied

Table 3.14
Frequencies and Percentages for Subjective Outcome Variables, *N* = 899

Variable	Number	Percent
Life quality		
Very dissatisfied	4	0.5
Dissatisfied	22	2.5
Mixed	178	19.8
Satisfied	432	48.0
Very satisfied	262	29.2
Income adequacy		
Not at all adequate	27	2.9
Can meet necessities only	110	12.3
Lets you afford some but not all the things you want	461	51.3
Lets you afford about everything you want	140	15.6
Lets you have what you want and lets you save too	161	17.9
Life control		
No control at all over your life	1	0.1
Very little control	18	2.0
Some control	195	21.7
Quite a bit of control	436	48.5
Almost complete control	249	27.7

or very satisfied with their quality of life. The majority of household managers, 51.3%, responded that the family's income let them afford some but not all the things they wanted (Table 3.14). Only 2.9% felt their income was not at all adequate. Of the household managers, 48.5% felt that they had quite a bit of control (Table 3.14). Overall, respondents felt that they were in control of their everyday lives.

The majority of households with home-based workers were satisfied with their quality of life and control over life although they perceived their incomes to be only moderately adequate. These findings provide information for policy makers about the income adequacy of various types of home-based employment. The majority of households who pursue such work felt their incomes were fairly adequate and they were satisfied with other important areas of their lives. Home-based employment can be viewed as a viable alternative to the centralized employment markets for some households.

SUMMARY AND CONCLUSIONS

Prevalence and a Profile of Home-Based Workers

Counting home-based workers shows that this group of workers is an important segment of the labor force. Just under 10% (9.6%) of all households in the nine states had at least one member engaged in any activity that generated income at home. Using the more restrictive nine-state study definition, 6.4% of the households were considered homeworking. These rates are consistent with other national estimates. Home-based work is currently a significant alternative for a growing number of workers; most commentators suggest that this trend will continue.

In the nine-state study, the average home-based worker was male, older, and had more than a high school diploma. He was married (i.e., at the time of the survey) with children, owned his own home, and had lived in the same urban area community for some time. This profile suggests that home-based workers are more mature workers who have not only a family but a community base that likely supports their choice of working at home.

Health Insurance

The great majority of home-based workers have health insurance (89.3%), but only 15.1% obtain coverage through their home-based work. Most (49.9%) obtain their coverage through a second job or a former job. The great majority who obtain coverage this way do so through a family member's job. Looked at another way, 42.4% obtained coverage themselves through their home-based work, other jobs they held, or sources unrelated to jobs.

Age was positively related to the likelihood of having health insurance coverage, while rural residency was negatively related. Relative to workers in agricultural products and sales, workers who held occupations in mechanical and transportation, crafts and artisans, and contracting were less likely to have health insurance coverage. Home-based workers involved in seasonal work were more likely to have health insurance coverage.

Nature of Home-Based Work

The typical home-based worker made a net income of $17,835 in 1988, was involved in a marketing and sales occupation, and had been engaged in this type of work for 9.1 years. This worker was most likely a self-employed business owner who worked 1,819 hours per year (i.e., about 36 hours per week, assuming a 2-week vacation per year) in full-time, nonseasonal work.

No one occupational group was dominant, although marketing and sales had the highest number of workers with 24.3%, followed by contracting (14.9%), and mechanical and transportation (13.2%). In fact, these three occupations accounted for more than 50% of all the workers in the sample. Very few job titles were computer related. However, the type and amount of technologies used in the home-based work could not be analyzed given data limitations.

Home-Based Work Space

Separate and distinct work space was the preferred location for the primary work sites of home-based workers. Only when third and fourth work sites were ranked did the typically shared spaces for family activities become important. Slightly over one-half, or 55.9% of the home-based workers had exclusive work sites. Exclusive home-based work space was most often a separate office, workroom, or study or an attached cottage or business shop, studio, or office.

Intrusiveness and Management of Home-Based Work

More than half (58.7%) reported receiving telephone calls daily, and 55.9% reported no conflicts over space because the home-based work space was exclusive. Almost half (45.2%) reported seeing clients at home less than once a month, and almost two-thirds (64.7%) had a vehicle used for both the household and the home-based work, but reported no conflicts over the use. Less than 6% (5.6%) reported conflicts over the use of a single vehicle.

Individuals who perform a personal service reported the most intrusion, and those doing clerical or administrative activities reported the least intrusion. Income level appears to be inversely related to the level of intrusion experienced; those with the lowest incomes reported the most intrusion.

The home-based workers identified specific management concepts such as standard setting and adjusting but less frequently identified goal setting relative to their home-based work.

Subjective Outcomes

The demands and needs of work and family compete side-by-side in the home-based working situation. The priorities and responses of home-based workers to this enmeshed and complex phenomenon are only partially revealed. Most liked their work, citing flexibility, ability to care for family, and saving time and avoiding hassle as major advantages. On the other hand, the home-based worker felt disadvantaged in not being able to get away from the work and noted that interruptions and interferences were reciprocated between the work and the family.

NOTES

1. All multivariate research models in this book refer to regression procedures, either as ordinary least squares (OLS) regression or a logistic regression depending on the nature of the dependent variable in the model. The OLS regression was used in the case of a continuous dependent variable such as income. If the dependent variable was binary in nature, meaning it

had a value of either 0 or 1, a logistic regression procedure was used. For further discussion of either procedure, see standard statistical references such as Kmenta (1986).

2. Agricultural products and sales was the category used consistently in all multivariate research models or regressions as the occupation group to which the other eight occupation categories were compared if the effect was significant. Although one category in any series of groupings used as independent variables must be omitted from any regression procedure for statistical reasons, the choice of which category to omit is often arbitrary. In the case of the multivariate research models in this book, agricultural products and sales was chosen because it had the lowest frequency of home-based workers.

3. See Heck, Winter, and Stafford (1992) for a discussion of the study of family managerial behavior.

4. Earlier scales were developed by Newton (1979) and Garrison and Winter (1986).

Chapter 4

The Hidden Hum of the
Home-Based Business

*Rosemary Walker and Ramona K. Z. Heck with the
assistance of Marilyn M. Furry, Kathryn Stafford,
and George W. Haynes*

INTRODUCTION

Economic, technological, demographic, social, and political factors have contributed to an increasing number of individuals working at home (Aronson,
1991). The unstable economy of the 1970s and 1980s coupled with strong
foreign competition pushed U.S. businesses toward a leaner labor force working
longer hours to maintain quality and remain viable in a world market (Coates,
1988; Gumpert, 1984). To remain competitive, corporations are scrutinizing
their operations to lower costs, and many are engaging in "downsizing"
maneuvers as a result. This trend has recently been paralleled by an increase in
telecommuting and at-home work programs. Dun and Bradstreet estimates this
shift has created a 15% to 20% real estate cost saving over the next five years.
The current average real estate cost of one employee per year is $4,500, and
adding in other fixed costs such as secretarial support and equipment can raise
the cost to $10,000 (Bers, 1993).

Concomitantly, the U.S. economy has been transformed from an industrial
base to an information and service base. Advanced telecommunications equipment such as personal computers, laser printers, high-speed modems, and
facsimile machines has made it possible to move service-related work away
from centralized work sites to homes (Christensen, 1988b; Edwards & Edwards, 1994b; Pratt, 1993).

Other forces supporting the reemergence of home-based work are changes
in family structure and the allocation of work and family roles between men
and women (Giele, 1984; Pleck, 1977). Several authors have suggested that

home-based work provides an effective way to balance the demands of paid employment and family responsibilities, particularly for women (Edwards & Edwards, 1991, 1994b; Horvath, 1986; Kraut & Grambsch, 1987; Voydanoff, 1987).

All of these trends, coupled with the elimination of legal restrictions (see Chapter 2 for a more detailed discussion) on work at home, have contributed to an increase in the number of home-based workers. Although federal laws and regulations have been essentially removed, some state, city, and local legal restrictions remain and others are changing more slowly. For example, in the cities of Chicago and Los Angeles, home-based work is prohibited by local zoning laws (Edwards & Edwards, 1994a); these laws may be rationalized relative to the management and use of public utilities or the amount of traffic on neighborhood streets.

Although wage and salary employees continued to dominate the work force, between 1975 and 1987, self-employed workers in nonagricultural settings increased steadily both in absolute numbers and as a percentage of all workers (Aronson, 1991). Caucasian men and women were largely responsible for this increase (U.S. Small Business Administration [SBA], 1993). However, by 1990 women and African Americans were disproportionately adding to the trend toward self-employment.

Only recently have researchers provided demographic and earnings comparisons between self-employed persons and wage and salary employees in the overall work force (Aronson, 1991; Casson, 1991). The information available in the nine-state study of home-based workers provides an opportunity to make similar comparisons between self-employed persons and wage and salary employees in the home-based work segment of the labor force.

This chapter reviews the literature on self-employment and provides results from the nine-state study of 899 home-based workers, with a special focus on the 670 business owners. Comparisons are then made between business owners and their wage worker counterparts relative to demographic and work characteristics, income, health insurance coverage, and use of at-home work space. The next section explores the differences between the two groups by gender. Then the business practices of home-based business owners are examined. Finally, outcomes are studied relative to the effects of employees and unpaid helpers on the owners' incomes and work efforts, and the influence of important variables on the owners' satisfaction with quality of life, income adequacy, and control of life.

Self-Employment

In 1993, about 10.3 million (10,335,000) Americans were self-employed (U.S. Bureau of Labor Statistics [BLS], 1994). Trends in self-employment have been examined closely since the early 1970s (Blau, 1987; Steinmetz & Wright, 1989).

Over this period, the nonagricultural segment showed a steady increase, while agricultural self-employment has shown a steady decline since 1980 (U.S. Bureau of the Census [BOC], 1993, Table No. 647). Despite the decreasing importance of agricultural self-employment, the self-employment and small-business segments of rural areas are vital and stable components of rural economies (Lin, Buss, & Popovich, 1990; Miller, 1985, 1989, 1990, 1991; Mokry, 1988).

Although self-employment has historically provided a mechanism for individual workers to exchange their labor and expertise for monetary rewards, scholars have only recently begun to study this employment alternative. Recent studies focused on a broad conceptualization of entrepreneurial activities and provided demographic and earnings comparisons between self-employed persons and wage and salary employees (Aronson, 1991; Casson, 1991). Characteristics examined included gender, age, race and ethnicity, educational levels, occupational distribution, hours worked, and income.

Men continue to outnumber women in the ranks of the self-employed, but women are a faster-growing segment of this group (Cromie, 1987; Devine, 1994; Hagan, Rivchun, & Sexton, 1989; Hisrich & Brush, 1986). In 1990, 1 out of 15 employed women was self-employed as a main job (Devine, 1994). Furthermore, Devine has suggested that a woman's self-employment decision is closely related to her other roles in life, and over her life span as an individual and as a household member.

Self-employed persons are generally substantially older than wage and salary workers (Becker, 1984; Fuchs, 1982; Quinn, 1980) and have more education (Aronson, 1991; Evans & Leighton, 1989; Fredland & Little, 1981). The occupational distribution of the self-employed shows larger numbers among white-collar occupations and skilled crafts.

Income and hours worked among the self-employed range widely. Significant numbers of individuals may be found in both high- and low-income classes. On average, they earn less per hour than their wage-earning counterparts and tend to work longer hours for lower wages (Aronson, 1991). About 14% of all business owners earn less than the minimum wage. Self-employment can, however, generate capital gains as well as wage earnings. These capital gains and the longer hours worked may account for the finding of some studies that the self-employed tend to receive a higher rate of return on educational investments despite their lower earnings per hour (Evans & Leighton, 1989). These findings also suggest that business owners may experience nonmonetary benefits, expect relatively higher future incomes, or place a high value on being their own bosses and having autonomy (SBA, 1993). The self-employed often supplement earnings with other income. Among older workers, self-employment is usually not the sole or even major source of income but a supplement to retirement income (Becker, 1984).

A more detailed understanding of self-employment emerges from studies that analyze major subgroups such as business owners and home-based workers.

For example, self-employed incorporated businessmen earn slightly more than their wage counterparts. Haber, Lamas, and Lichtenstein (1987) studied business owners using the Survey of Income and Program Participation (SIPP). They found that business owners accounted for 11.9% of workers in nonagricultural industries during the last half of 1983, or 60% more than reported as self-employed. About 70.8% of businesses were sole proprietorships; 18.3% were incorporated businesses. The nature of business ownership exhibited differences by gender. Men were more likely to work full-time at businesses than women, but women were more likely than men to be engaged in casual and side businesses. Although underreporting of business earnings appeared to be an issue, annual earnings ranged from about $3,700 for female sole proprietors to $24,000 for male owners of incorporated businesses. In addition to the employment of the business owners themselves, these small business owners employed, at a minimum, 28.5 million workers or slightly over 25% of all workers. This percentage may be somewhat misleading because some workers hold multiple jobs.

Sole proprietorships represent important aspects both of self-employment and of wage and salary employment. Of the 20 million businesses that filed tax returns in 1990, approximately 70% were sole proprietorships. Most of these businesses employed nine or fewer employees, and nearly half employed four or fewer employees (SBA, 1991). Although many business enterprises operate on a small scale, their importance to the economy and in the creation of jobs is well documented (Birch, 1987; Brock & Evans, 1986; Brown, Hamilton, & Medoff, 1990; Solomon, 1986).

Previous Research on Home-Based Businesses

According to the limited information in the literature, home-based businesses, in comparison with businesses that are not home-based, (a) more often start as sole proprietorships, (b) obtain less start-up capital, (c) operate with fewer employees, (d) have lower costs of doing business, and (e) generate less business income. Pratt (1993) described these home-based businesses as "an informal shaping of hobbies and casual activities into business dress" (p. 7) and their owners as women with young children who self-select home employment to spend more time with their families.

A general profile of home-based workers, including self-employment, was provided by Heck (1988, 1991), using household data obtained from the 1984 Panel Study of Income Dynamics (PSID). This sample consisted of 6,744 individual workers. Controlling for other factors, the likelihood of being involved in home-based work was positively related to being self-employed. In fact, of the home-based worker subsample, approximately two-thirds were self-employed.

COMPARISON OF OWNERS AND EARNERS IN THE NINE-STATE STUDY

In the nine-state study, the relative magnitude of the home-based business owners to wage earners is dramatic. The majority (74.6%) of home-based workers in the sample were business owners. The remaining 25.4% were working at home for someone else and were labeled earners. Clearly, home-working households are most likely to be operating a home business, thus the focus of this chapter.

The Worker and the Work

Table 4.1 provides a comparison of these two groups on some variables of interest. Both owners and earners were predominantly male. The average age of the owners was 44.3 years, about 3 years older than the average age of earners (41.5 years). In contrast, the earners' average years of education were slightly higher than that of owners. Owners were members of larger households than were earners.

Table 4.1
Descriptive Statistics of Selected Variables by Ownership Status, $N = 899$

Variable	Owners $n = 670$[a]	Earners $n = 229$[a]	Significance[b]
Female (%)	41.7%	42.7%	n.s.
Age (years)	44.3	41.5	< .005
Education (years)	13.7	14.4	< .001
Married (%)	85.0%	83.9%	n.s.
Household size	3.4	3.1	< .05
Household income	$41,417	$44,742	n.s.
Net home-based work income[c]	$15,628	$24,300	< .001
Home-based work income as percent of total household income[c]	35.8%	51.4%	< .001
Home-based work hours[c]	1,779.6	1,936.3	< .01
Duration	9.5	8.2	= .05
Seasonality (%)	17.9%	4.7%	< .001
Other employment (%)	28.4%	19.5%	< .05

Note: Throughout the table, n.s. denotes nonsignificance.

[a]Weighted numbers, percentages, and means. [b]Based on results of chi-square tests and analyses of variance. [c]Figures given in annual terms.

Average total household income of all the workers was over $42,000 and did not differ significantly by ownership status. The average home-based work income of earners was $24,300, significantly higher than the average for business owners, which was $15,628. Likewise, a significantly higher proportion of the earners' average family income came from home-based work than did that of owners.

At least part of the difference in income can be explained by the large difference in the average number of home-based work hours engaged in by the two groups. Earners worked on average more than 1,900 hours per year compared to less than 1,800 hours for owners. Earners averaged about 1½ fewer years in their present home-based work than did owners. A larger proportion of owners than earners were engaged in seasonal work. Finally, owners were more likely than earners to have another job in addition to the home-based one.

Multivariate Research Model of Ownership

To determine the characteristics associated with being an owner rather than an earner, a multivariate analysis[1] was performed on the weighted sample of 899 workers. Repeated once for the readers' convenience, remember that a multivariate analysis has the advantage of revealing the specific effect of a particular variable while holding all other variables constant. Throughout the discussion of the results from the nine-state study, effects for individual independent variables in the multivariate analyses should be interpreted at the margin, meaning that as the value of an independent variable increases, the effect is on the dependent variable, holding all other independent variables constant.

Results, shown in Table 4.2, indicate that the following characteristics of workers increased the likelihood of ownership: being older, being a single parent, and having a larger than average household size. Not owning a home decreased the likelihood of ownership.

Work characteristics that contributed to an increased likelihood of ownership were having higher than average income from work that was not home-based, engaging in home-based work in the professional and technical occupations or in clerical and administrative support (i.e., both compared to agricultural products and sales[2]), working seasonally, and having other employment. Persons working in mechanical and transportation or in contracting occupations (i.e., compared to agricultural products and sales) were less likely than others to be owners.

Health Insurance

National concern about the increasing costs of health care has focused attention on the importance of health insurance coverage. Home-based workers seem especially vulnerable to not being covered by health insurance for several reasons. Those who are self-employed in small, marginal businesses cannot afford to pay the higher premiums charged for individually purchased policies (Hall & Kuder, 1990). At least some wage workers who are home-based, particularly those working for piece-rate wages, are in very competitive industries that have eliminated or reduced such fringe benefits as health insurance coverage.

As noted in Chapter 3, surprisingly few home-based workers were not covered by health insurance (10.7%). Table 4.3 shows the source of coverage by ownership status. Even a brief perusal of the table reveals differences in

Table 4.2
Factors Related to the Likelihood of Business Ownership, $N = 899$

Variable	Significant effects
Worker characteristic	
Male	
Age	+
Education	
Single parent	+
Household size	+
Children under 6	
Nonhomeowners	-
Years lived in community	
Farms	
Rural areas	
Towns < 2,500	
Work characteristic	
Net income from other employment (annual)	+
Occupation	
Professional and technical	+
Marketing and sales	
Clerical and administrative support	+
Mechanical and transportation	-
Crafts and artisans	
Managers	
Services	
Contracting	-
Agricultural products and sales	omitted
Total work hours (annual)	
Duration	
Seasonality	+
Other employment	+
Constant	
Chi-square (25, $N = 899$) = 269.00, significant at .001 level	

Note: Effects were statistically significant at the .05 level or less.

Table 4.3
Sources of Health Insurance Coverage by Ownership Status, $N = 899$

	Owners $n = 670$		Earners $n = 229$	
Source of coverage	*Number*	*Percent*	*Number*	*Percent*
Job-related coverage				
Coverage through home-based work				
Business expense for owner	71	10.6	—	—
Wage earner is covered through				
employer but worker pays	—	—	14	6.1
Wage earner is covered through				
employer who pays	—	—	50	21.8
Coverage through another job				
Policy through another job of home-				
based worker	89	13.3	19	8.3
Policy through another family				
member's job	232	34.6	56	24.5
Retirement medical coverage				
(including Medicare)	44	6.6	9	3.9
Non-job-related coverage				
Individual/personal policy (private)	155	23.1	18	7.9
Combination including private policies	3	0.4	44	19.2
No health insurance coverage	76	11.3	20	8.7

Note: Numbers and percents may not add to 670, 229, and 100%, respectively, because of rounding errors.

source of coverage between home-based business owners and wage earners. Only 10.6% of the owners were covered through their home-based work while 27.9% of the wage earners were. Obtaining health insurance through another job, whether their own or another family member's, was a much more prevalent means of obtaining coverage for owners than for wage earners. The percentage of owners obtaining health insurance this way was almost half again as large as the percentage of wage earners, 47.9% for owners versus 32.8% for wage earners. The percentage of business owners who obtained health insurance through some kind of retirement program was larger than the percentage of wage earners who obtained it this way, 6.6% versus 3.9%.

Both groups obtained health insurance through individual policies at about the same rate and relied more heavily on another family member's job as a source of coverage than they did on a second job for the home-based worker. Moreover, both groups also had relatively few people uncovered, although more owners were uncovered than wage earners. Both groups also rely heavily on themselves and their family members to piece together health insurance coverage. Although the majority of both groups obtain coverage through employment, a minority of both groups relied soley on the home-based work to provide health insurance coverage.

Only a small percentage of either group received health insurance through retirement provisions (including Medicare), although the coverage through retirement provisions was more common for owners than for earners because a larger proportion of the owners were in the older age categories. Even if not yet 65, they may have retired early from, for example, the military, and had both medical benefits and the stamina to start or manage a business. This health care finding also illuminates the age issue for this study. One reason for the high proportion of older home-based workers may be that these businesses are second careers for employees who have retired from one job. The carryover of medical benefits allows these workers to take the risks associated with being in business. People who know that their health care costs are covered through insurance may be financially able to start or expand a business.

Multivariate Research Model of Health Insurance

To answer which variables increased or decreased the likelihood that a worker was covered by health insurance, a multivariate analysis was performed. The results, shown in Table 4.4, indicate that whether the worker is an owner or an earner makes a significant difference. Owners who were older or in seasonal businesses were more likely to be covered, although rural owners or those in three occupational groups, namely mechanical and transportation, crafts and artisans, and contracting, were less likely to be covered. In contrast, occupational type had no influence on the likelihood of coverage for earners, but rural residency had a positive effect. Being male, having more education, and being older had independent positive effects on an earner's likelihood of being covered.

Home-Based Work Space

In households where home-based work occurs, the spatial link between work and family life is obvious. Fusing domestic and work settings, critics have contended, is disruptive (Ahrentzen, 1990). An alternative view is that blending work and family space enhances family and spousal interaction (Beach, 1988, 1989).

To learn more about the use of home space for work, the researchers asked a series of questions about what areas of the house were used for the work. One to four different sites could be identified. Other questions focused on which spaces, if any, were used exclusively for the home-based work.

Location of home work site. Table 4.5 presents the distribution of owners and earners by primary and secondary home work sites. Office/workroom/study

Table 4.4
Significant Effects of Worker and Work Characteristics on Likelihood of Health Insurance Coverage by Ownership Status, *N* = 899

Characteristic	Owners $n = 670$	Earners $n = 229$
Worker characteristic		
Male		+
Age	+	+
Education		+
Rural residence	-	+
Work characteristic		
Net home-based work income		
Occupation		
Professional and technical		
Marketing and sales		
Clerical and administrative support		
Mechanical and transportation	-	
Crafts and artisans	-	
Managers		
Services		
Contracting	-	
Agricultural products and sales	omitted	omitted
Other employment	-	
Seasonality	+	
Constant		
Chi-square (both significant at .001 level)	39.41	64.06
Degrees of freedom	16	16
Number of observations	670	229

Note: Effects were statistically significant at the .20 level or less.

was designated most frequently as the primary area by both owners and earners; 60.7% of earners and 29.3% of owners worked in such a space. The difference between these rates for earners and owners is remarkable—owners were about one-half of earners—given a presumed need by business owners for an area to conduct their business activities. Clearly, these home businesses were not laid out in the familiar "storefront" arrangement of businesses that are not home-based; possibly the nature of the home business work activity is flexible and adaptable to varied work sites in or near the home. For a first site, the second most frequently chosen area by both groups was the basement; this time, the earners' use was about one-half that of the owners. As the third choice for a first work site, 17.1% of owners used a detached building for work; only 1.9% of earners worked there. Each of the living areas of the house (bedroom, living room, kitchen, and dining room) was used as a primary work site by less than

Table 4.5
Distribution of Primary Home Work Space by Ownership Status, $N = 899$

Work space area	First site				Second site			
	Owners, $n = 670$		Earners, $n = 229$		Owners, $n = 670$		Earners, $n = 229$	
	Number	Percent	Number	Percent	Number	Percent	Number	Percent
Office/workroom/study, attached cottage, shop, studio, attached business	197	29.3	139	60.7	108	16.2	17	7.6
Basement, laundry room, recreation room	137	20.4	23	10.0	39	5.9	2	0.8
Detached building, outdoor work area, yard, garden, yard for auto mechanic, enclosed shop	114	17.1	4	1.9	0	0.0	0	0.0
Garage/enclosed porch, apartment used for storage, screened porch, storage room, attic	89	13.3	9	4.0	30	4.5	0	0.0
Bedroom	45	6.8	9	4.1	21	3.1	17	7.3
Living room/family room, den, foyer, hallway	37	5.5	13	5.7	56	8.3	21	9.0
Kitchen	31	4.6	14	6.3	43	6.4	19	8.2
Dining room	20	3.1	17	7.3	57	8.4	11	4.9
No second home work site	—	—	—	—	316	47.2	142	62.2

Note: Numbers and percents may not add to 670, 229, and 100%, respectively, because of rounding errors.

7% of the owners and less than 8% of the earners. In sum, owners tended to choose among three to four rather separate work sites in or near the home although the majority of the earners chose one first site, namely a separate office/workroom/study.

Secondary sites (i.e., worker worked in two places in or around the home) were more common to owners than earners; 47.2% of the owners and 62.2% of the earners said they had no second work area. The most common secondary site mentioned by owners was an office/workroom/study. In contrast, the earners' most common secondary site was the living room.

Most of the owners and earners did not use a third or fourth work site. In fact, of the owners, only 24.0% specified a third site and 10.1% specified a fourth site. The most frequent locations mentioned were living/family rooms for the third site and kitchens for the fourth site. Of the earners, only 12.0% mentioned a third site and 7.8% mentioned a fourth site. When earners did use these third and fourth sites, they too most frequently selected living/family rooms as the third choice and kitchens as the fourth choice. These third and fourth sites tend to be the spaces most likely shared with family activities. Thus for a small proportion of homeworking households, the work sphere spatially overlaps at times with the family sphere.

Exclusive home work site. Fifty-five percent (55.7%) of the owners and 56.3% of the earners had areas that they used exclusively for their home-based work. Table 4.6 shows the distribution of the sites for the 373 out of 670 owners and 129 out of 229 earners who designated exclusive work sites. The most common exclusive site for owners and earners was an office/workroom/study, followed by the basement. A detached building was designated as an exclusive site by 8.1% of the owners, but no earners had such an arrangement. Most owners and earners did not have an additional exclusive work site, although 6.6% of the owners designated the office/workroom/study as a secondary exclusive space.

Although owners and earners differed in the exact work areas used, a high percentage of both groups avoided using the main living areas of the house as primary or secondary work sites. Additionally, more than half of each group set aside space that was used exclusively for work, and these exclusive work sites were nearly always away from the main living area. This pattern of space use would seem to indicate a desire of owners and earners to separate spatially the spheres of work and family.

GENDER–OWNERSHIP STATUS COMPARISONS

Previous research on this sample of home-based workers established associations between ownership status and income, occupation, and work experience (Masuo, Walker, & Furry, 1992). Likewise, Rowe and Bentley (1992) found that gender was related to income, occupation, and hours worked.

Table 4.6
Distribution of Exclusive Home Work Space by Ownership Status, $N = 899$

Work space area	First exclusive				Second exclusive			
	Owners, $n = 670$		Earners, $n = 229$		Owners, $n = 670$		Earners, $n = 229$	
	Number	Percent	Number	Percent	Number	Percent	Number	Percent
Office/workroom/study, attached cottage, shop, studio, attached business	190	28.4	105	45.9	44	6.6	6	2.6
Basement, laundry room, recreation room	87	13.0	14	6.1	2	0.3	0	0.0
Detached building, outdoor work area, yard, garden, yard for auto mechanic, enclosed shop	54	8.1	0	0.0	0	0.0	0	0.0
Garage/enclosed porch, apartment used for storage, screened porch, storage room, attic	38	5.7	2	0.9	11	1.6	0	0.0
Empty bedroom	3	0.4	2	0.9	3	0.4	6	2.6
Small part of room	1	0.2	6	2.6	1	0.3	0	0.0
No exclusive first or second home work site	297	44.3	100	43.7	609	90.9	218	95.2

Note: Numbers and percents may not add to 670, 229, and 100%, respectively, because of rounding errors.

Preliminary investigations exploring differences in work income, number of hours worked annually, hours worked at home, and years of work experience by gender and ownership status showed an interaction on several of the dependent variables. This means that gender and ownership status are not two distinct variables operating independently but rather they operate in combination to define four distinct groups of workers: female owners, male owners, female earners, and male earners.

Table 4.7 shows the means of some important dimensions of work by gender–ownership status category. Analysis of variance was the statistical procedure used to ascertain that significant differences existed between the category means for each of the work characteristics.

Income

Net income from home-based work varied significantly by gender–ownership status category. The average incomes ranged from a low of $7,691 for female owners to a high of $34,467 for male earners (Table 4.7). Although the average income of male business owners was significantly lower than that of male earners, it was significantly higher than that of female owners or earners.

Work Hours

The average annual number of hours worked was 1,672, but this figure varied significantly by gender–ownership status category. Male earners averaged 2,390 hours, about 600 hours more than male owners and more than 1,000 hours greater than either female earners or owners (whose numbers of hours were similar).

Although all of the jobs investigated here fit the definition of home-based work, each job might be composed of many different tasks, only part of which are done in the worker's home. For example, many salespersons might perform their sales functions by going from one house to another or from one retail store to another, using their homes to make and receive phone calls, do book work, and so forth. In other words, they work *from* their homes. In fact, 75.0% of the workers spent some of their working hours away from home. These hours might be spent at any one of several outside work sites such as a client's home or office, a vehicle, or a farmer's market.

One of the often cited advantages of at-home income generation is the possibility of combining paid work with family responsibilities at the same site, presumably a combination usually more relevant to women than to men. Thus it was originally hypothesized that women rather than men would work in jobs that allowed them to spend more hours of work at their homes and that their hours worked at home as a percentage of total work time would be higher than

Table 4.7
Means of Work Characteristics by Gender–Ownership Status Category, $N = 899$

Characteristic	Female owners	Male owners	Female earners	Male earners	Overall	F-ratio
Net home-based work income	$7,691$_a$	$21,298$_b$	$10,680$_a$	$34,467$_c$	$17,835	68.72*
Hours worked	1,350$_a$	1,750$_b$	1,317$_a$	2,390$_c$	1,672	32.56*
Hours worked at home	1,238$_a$	864$_b$	805$_b$	920$_b$	979	9.83*
Percent of work time spent at home[a]	85.1%$_a$	52.9%$_b$	63.9%$_c$	38.7%$_d$	62.1%	65.34*
Duration	8.8$_a$	10.3$_b$	5.2$_c$	10.4$_b$	9.3	8.90*

Note: Means with different subscripts differ significantly at the .05 level or less. Three degrees of freedom existed for all ANOVAs.

[a]Variable definition excluded 83 missing values.

*Statistically significant at the .001 level or less.

those of men, regardless of ownership status. The average number of hours worked at home was 979 (Table 4.7). Female owners worked considerably more hours at home (1,238 hours) than did any of the other groups. This seems to be consistent with a nine-state study result cited later in this chapter that the service and crafts and artisans occupations were dominated by female owners; these occupations are related to tasks that are done primarily at home (e.g., home day care providers).

In contrast, female earners, on average, worked the fewest hours at home. They were overrepresented in the marketing and sales occupations, which involve a low number of at-home hours and a high level of out-of-home activities. The conclusion is that, contrary to the hypothesis, gender alone is not the determining factor here but rather that the gender–ownership status combination is relevant.

The percentage of work time spent at the home site for female owners and female earners is higher than the overall average of 62.1%. In contrast, male earners spent only 38.7% of their work time at the home site.

Duration

On average, the workers had been engaged in these jobs for more than 9 years. Duration varied by gender–ownership status category. To qualify as a participating household, the worker had to be engaged in home-based work for at least one year; thus these results do not include workers just getting started in working at home. Female earners had worked at their jobs slightly more than 5 years, significantly less than workers in the other groups. In contrast, both male earners and male owners had an average of more than 10 years of experience.

Seasonality

A significant association was found between seasonality of work and gender–ownership status. Overall, only 14.5% of the workers were in seasonal jobs. Male owners were most likely to work seasonally; 19.5% of them did. In contrast, only 3.2% of male earners worked in seasonal jobs. Nearly 7% of female earners and 16% of female owners worked seasonally.

Occupation

Table 4.8 shows the distribution of the nine occupations by the gender–ownership status categories. The row percentages across the four categories add to 100%. Overall nearly one out of four (24.3%) workers was in marketing and sales. Although this was the occupation with the most even distribution across the four gender–ownership categories, female owners and male owners were underrepresented. The field of contracting was dominated by male owners, who

Table 4.8

Distribution of Occupation by Gender–Ownership Status Category, *N* = 899

Occupation	Female owner *n* = 279	Male owner *n* = 391	Female earner *n* = 98	Male earner *n* = 131	Overall *N* = 899
Professional and technical	16.7%	55.0%	8.2%	20.1%	11.9%
Marketing and sales	19.3	25.8	25.0	29.9	24.3
Clerical and administrative support	33.6	16.8	41.3	8.3	5.8
Mechanical and transportation	5.5	82.2	0.6	11.6	13.2
Crafts and artisans	60.2	35.0	3.8	0.9	11.6
Managers	44.5	20.0	0.6	34.9	3.5
Services	93.4	0.6	6.0	—	12.1
Contracting	2.5	88.6	1.0	8.0	14.9
Agricultural products and sales	53.5	31.6	—	15.1	2.7
Overall	31.0	43.5	10.9	14.6	100.0

Chi-square (24, *N* = 899) = 633.6, significant at .001 or less.

compose 43.5% of the sample but 88.6% of those engaged in contracting. Male owners were also overrepresented among mechanical and transportation workers. The service occupation consisted mainly of female owners (93.4%). Male owners and male earners, constituting 55.0% and 20.1%, respectively, of the professional and technical group, were overrepresented. Among crafts and artisan workers, female owners predominated, representing 60.2% of the workers. In the managerial category, female earners and male owners were underrepresented. Whereas only 2.7% of the total sample worked in agricultural products and sales, these workers were most likely to be female owners (53.5%).

Male owners dominated contracting, mechanical and transportation, and professional and technical occupations. Nearly all workers in services were female owners. Only marketing and sales seemed to have a fairly even distribution among worker types.

Some contrasting impressions emerge from these results. Compared to female earners, female owners have more years of experience, spend more working time at the home site, and earn considerably less income. Some of the characteristics of their work are presumably intertwined with the occupations in which they work. One wonders to what extent their working is motivated by nonpecuniary interests such as flexibility in time use or the absence of institutional restraints. Perhaps owners may choose to work less than full-time to allow for an array of activities in other work and nonwork arenas. Many female owners may fall in the "hobbies and casual activities [shaped] into business" category to which Pratt (1993, p. 7) alludes.

Clearly, of all the groups, male earners work the most hours, spend the lowest proportion of time at home, are the least likely to work seasonally, and earn the most income. The outcome of their work efforts does seem to include pecuniary rewards.

RUNNING THE BUSINESS AND PRODUCING OUTCOMES

Businesses can be organized as sole proprietorships (i.e., sole owners), partnerships, or corporations. A sole proprietorship is owned by a single individual, which presumably limits the size of both human and financial capital available to the firm. Owners may incorporate for a variety of reasons, such as to reduce personal legal liability, to lower marginal tax rates, or to make themselves eligible for unemployment insurance. The act of incorporating suggests that the business owner has a certain level of sophistication about the business environment and a seriousness about the profit motive that may not be characteristic of owners who do not incorporate. Partnerships can divide the many responsibilities of ownership (e.g., planning, producing, marketing, selling, distribution, and bookkeeping) between two or more people. The partners can specialize in specific functions and thus develop efficient operations.

When asked about the organizational form of their businesses, the 670 business owners reported that 82.4% were sole proprietorships, 10.4% were partnerships, and the remaining 7.2% were corporations. The high proportion of sole proprietorships among home-based businesses was similar to the 80% of all businesses in existence in the United States organized as sole proprietorships (Kolb, 1987).

Capital Investment by Home-Based Business Owners

A common assumption is that business owners borrow capital to start and run their businesses. Borrowing money to start or run the home-based business was not common among these owners, however; only 20.5% of them did so (Table 4.9), and, conversely, 76.4% of male and 83.8% of female business owners did not borrow money to start or run their home-based business. An association was found between business borrowing and occupation with owners in three occupations (agricultural products and sales, marketing and sales, and mechanical and transportation) that were more likely than others to have had outside financial help. Owners in the services and contracting occupations were less likely than others to have borrowed.

Table 4.9
Selected Home-Based Work Variables by Ownership Status, *n* = 670

Variable	All owners		Sole ownership		Partnership		Corporation	
	n	*Percent*	*n*	*Percent*	*n*	*Percent*	*n*	*Percent*
Financial behavior								
Borrowed money								
Yes	136	(20.5)	104	(19.1)	20	(28.2)	12	(25.7)
No	526	(79.5)	441	(80.9)	50	(71.8)	36	(74.3)
Bank account for business								
Yes	404	(61.2)	301	(55.4)	58	(81.8)	46	(97.5)
No	257	(38.8)	243	(44.6)	13	(18.2)	1	(2.5)
Promotion mechanism								
Word-of-mouth								
Yes	621	(93.6)	510	(93.6)	63	(89.6)	48	(100.0)
No	42	(6.4)	35	(6.4)	7	(10.4)	—	—
Newspapers								
Yes	195	(29.4)	156	(28.7)	27	(38.5)	11	(24.0)
No	468	(70.6)	389	(71.3)	43	(61.5)	36	(76.0)
Yellow pages								
Yes	119	(18.0)	79	(14.5)	26	(36.9)	15	(30.9)
No	544	(82.0)	446	(85.5)	44	(63.1)	33	(69.1)
Direct mail								
Yes	90	(13.6)	68	(12.5)	12	(17.8)	9	(19.5)
No	573	(86.4)	477	(87.5)	57	(82.2)	39	(80.5)
Catalogs and trade journals								
Yes	63	(9.6)	45	(8.3)	11	(15.1)	8	(15.9)
No	600	(90.4)	500	(91.7)	59	(84.9)	40	(84.1)
Some other way								
Yes	194	(29.3)	144	(26.5)	33	(47.8)	16	(32.9)
No	468	(70.7)	400	(73.5)	37	(52.2)	32	(67.1)

Note: Numbers may not add to 670 owners, 552 sole ownerships, 70 partnerships, and 48 corporations due to missing values and rounding errors.

Financial Practices

The 670 business owners were queried about their business practices. More than 60% (61.2%) had business bank accounts that were kept separate from personal or family accounts, as shown in Table 4.9. Nearly all owners organizing as corporations maintained separate business bank accounts (97.5%). An association was found between having a separate account and occupation. Owners in the contracting category were more likely than those in other occupations to have separate bank accounts. Owners in services and crafts and artisans were less likely to keep separate accounts for their businesses.

Sales Promotion and Product Distribution by Owners

Home-based business owners were asked about the various methods they used to promote their products or services. More than 9 out of 10 (93.6%) relied on word-of-mouth or referrals, a traditional and inexpensive means. Newspapers (29.4%), yellow pages (18.0%), direct mail (13.6%), and catalogs or trade journals (9.6%) also were used. A variety of other promotional strategies included signs on billboards, radio and television ads, and distribution of business cards and flyers. Clearly, many of the owners were aware of a variety of promotion techniques as well as the positive value of good customer relations that result in word-of-mouth advertising.

Eighty-eight percent (88.1%) of the owners sold most of their products or services in the same state in which they lived. A similar percentage of the owners bought most of their supplies in their home state. This information has implications for the owners' possible business expansion efforts and the states' interests in economic stability and development. The owners seem to be supporting the businesses of their states and boosting their states' economies when they purchase supplies. Increasing revenues and profits through out-of-state expansion is a feasible possibility for the 193 businesses that have a product to sell, although most of them do not sell out of state. If state leaders are interested in economic development, some home-based business owners who sell products may be ripe for extending their vision beyond local markets. There would seem to be opportunities for growth that would benefit the states as well as the individual businesses. Therefore, investment in marketing would help home-based businesses to expand beyond local boundaries.

Product Sales Markets and Methods

The 193 owners who sold products (i.e., not services) were predominantly in two occupations: crafts and artisans (35.7%) and marketing and sales (38.7%). They were queried about their methods of distribution. Most of them (58.4%) sold their products only in retail markets in contrast to the few (16.4%) who used only wholesale markets for distribution. Twenty-five percent (25.2%) sold in both retail and wholesale markets.

A variety of marketing methods were employed, and some product sellers used several methods. Direct sales to consumers who come to the owner's home was the most popular method (42.2%). Bazaars, fairs, and shows (16.0%), direct sales away from the owner's home (14.5%), consignment (13.1%), sales representatives (9.5%), and mail order catalogs (7.6%) were other marketing methods used by the home-based business owners. Because of the diverse nature of occupations and jobs represented by these owners, the wide variety of marketing methods is appropriate and to be expected.

The Gender Factor in Net Income and Hours Worked

In the overall labor force, substantial differences exist in the occupational distributions and earnings of men and women (Blau & Ferber, 1986). Previous studies have found similar gender differentials among home-based workers (Kraut, 1988; Rowe & Bentley, 1992), but the researchers here wanted to study the differential determinants of incomes and hours worked of the women and men owners.

The independent variables used in the multivariate research model were those characteristics of the home-based worker or work that had been shown to be related to working at home for pay (Heck, 1992; Horvath, 1986) or to influence gender differentials in wage rates, income, or business success (Bergmann, 1986; Blau & Ferber, 1986; Fuchs, 1971; Haber, Lamas, & Lichtenstein, 1987; Kalleberg & Leicht, 1991). The variables were age, education, presence of children under 6 years of age, rural residence, outside job, seasonal home-based business, years in home-based business (i.e., duration), and female-dominated occupation.

This final variable, female-dominated occupation, requires explanation. Responses to the question "What does the worker do?" were coded into 20 occupational categories, as shown in Table 4.10. The last column in the table gives the total number of businesses in that occupation. The middle column shows the percentage of businesses owned by a female. An occupation was considered to be female dominated if 75% or more of the owners were women. Thus the following occupations were female dominated: food service, beautician, human services, other services, service manager, and crafts.

Results of the regression analysis are shown in Table 4.11. Chow test results corroborate that the gender models for both dependent variables—net business income and hours worked—are different, indicating that the determinants of these two variables differ by gender. Having children under 6 years of age had no effect on the hours worked of either men or women but it had a negative effect on net business income for women and a positive effect for men. Thus if hours worked are held constant, the presence of young children produced monetary results for women that were far different from those of men. One explanation suggests that, given equal work hours, women with young children may be less productive in their business work than their male counterparts, for example, if they are interrupted by household and family demands. In contrast, in families in which business work is synonymous with "male work," the presence of young children may stimulate more intense work efforts by the owner and a stronger profit motive.

A difference between sole owners and owners who use other forms of business organization was expected, with the focus on entrepreneurial intent and efficiency. Sole ownership had a negative effect on females' net incomes and hours and on males' hours. The results seem to corroborate these differences in female- versus male-owned businesses, supporting the notion that perhaps female sole owners are

Table 4.10
Occupation by Percentage of Female Owners, *n* = 670

Occupation	Percent female	*n*
Food service	100.0	1
Beautician	100.0	26
Human services	100.0	67
Other services	90.0	6
Service managers	85.8	14
Crafts	78.8	68
Agricultural sales	63.7	16
Sales agents	63.0	31
Clerical	59.7	22
Teachers	59.0	17
Livestock sales	55.2	4
Manager of income	52.9	9
Other sales	38.6	53
Creators	29.8	31
Shopkeepers	15.0	9
Truck drivers	14.9	42
Professional	13.8	60
Contractors	6.4	124
Mechanics	0.0	65
Sales representatives	0.0	5

less likely than other business owners to be in business for the profit motive and more likely to be satisfied with deriving psychic income rather than money income. These results are reminiscent of Pratt's (1993, p. 7) conclusions that women select home-based employment so that they can spend more time with their families and that they shape their hobbies into "business dress."

Operating a business in a female-dominated occupation significantly reduced net income for females, as expected. It also significantly reduced the hours worked and net income for males. Thus it seems that operating a business that provides typical "female" labor-intensive services or low-capital-requirement products is not highly rewarded in our economy.

Experienced female home-based workers (i.e., women who had been working more years in their home-based work) tallied more annual home-based work

Table 4.11

Significant Effects of Research Variables on Owner's Net Business Income and Hours Worked by Gender, *n* = 670

Variable	Net annual business income		Annual hours worked	
	Female	*Male*	*Female*	*Male*
Worker characteristic				
Age	-		-	-
Education	+	+		
Child under 6 years old	-	+		
Rural residence				
Work characteristic				
Sole owner	-		-	-
Female-dominated occupation	-	-		-
Home-based work hours	+	+	omitted	omitted
Duration			+	
Seasonality				-
Other employment	-	-	-	-
Constant		-	+	+
F-ratio = (all significant at .001 level)	18.6	10.17	5.75	9.30
Adjusted R^2 =	.39	.19	.13	.16
Number of observations =	279	391	279	391

Note: Effects were statistically significant at the .10 level or less.

hours. Working another job in addition to working as a home-based business owner had a negative effect on hours worked and net income for men as well as women. Engaging in a home-based business that was seasonal had a negative effect only on the hours worked by men.

In summary, some of the major determinants of two important dimensions of work, income and hours worked, are different for women and men. Researchers have reported the same finding for years in studies of overall labor force employees. Similar conclusions related to business owners have been based on sparser evidence (Aronson, 1991; Moore, 1983). In this random nine-state study in which the sample contained 670 home-based business owners the same gender differences persist.

Do Owners Have Help?

Little is known about employees of home-based businesses, although it is usually assumed that each firm's work force is small. Additionally, some writers have implied that family members are often exploited as unpaid, stand-by labor (Rosenblatt, de Mik, Anderson, & Johnson, 1985). This study provides a unique opportunity to study the effect of paid and unpaid helpers on the work outcomes of 508 sole owners in families.

Nine worker types. Information was available concerning whether or not the owner hired paid workers, contracted some work done (e.g., accounting), or used unpaid helpers. The paid, contractual, or unpaid workers could be family members, other relatives, or nonrelated persons. Thus nine categories of workers/helpers were possible: family members who were paid, unpaid, or contractual; other relatives who were paid, unpaid, or contractual; and nonfamily persons who were paid, unpaid, or contractual.

Multivariate research model of worker types. The outcomes of interest were net annual business income, total annual work hours, and hourly wage rate. Desirable outcomes for owners were assumed to be increased incomes and wage rates but reduced work hours.

It was hypothesized that the type of worker would influence owner outcomes. For example, family workers would likely improve business outcomes because they had a vested interest in the success of the business, particularly if they worked on a paid or contracting basis. Other relatives were viewed as more tangential, with less access to the benefits accruing from the business and therefore likely to have a negative effect by reducing optimal business outcomes or benefits. It was hypothesized that unrelated workers, who make up the majority of the work force, would be positively associated with optimal business outcomes (i.e., high incomes, low hours, and high wage rates).

Regression analysis was used to determine the effect of the nine worker types and other socioeconomic characteristics on the three outcomes of the 508 sole proprietors. Based on previous research, selected variables were included in the analysis as controls and were categorized as owner or business characteristics. The business owner characteristics included gender, age, education, single parent, family size, presence of children under 6 years of age, nonhomeowner, years lived in community, and residence in towns of less than 2,500 population, rural areas, and farms. The gender of the owner was a binary variable that assumed the value of 1 if the owner was a male and 0 if a female. Both the age and education of the owner were measured in years. Marital status was a binary variable that assumed a value of 1 if the owner was a single parent and 0 if married. Family size counted the total number of individuals present in the household. Children under 6 was a binary variable, assuming the value of 1 if one or more children under 6 years of age were present in the family and 0 otherwise. Nonhomeowner was a binary variable that assumed a value of 1 if no person in the household owned the dwelling and 0 otherwise. The variable for towns less than 2,500, rural areas, and farms equaled 1 if the owner resided in such a place and 0 if not.

Business characteristics included net annual business income, occupational rank, total annual work hours, duration of the business, and seasonality of the business. Occupational rank was an ordinal variable that represented one of nine occupational types: 1 = professional and technical, 2 = marketing and sales, 3 = clerical and administrative support, 4 = mechanical and transportation, 5 = crafts and artisans, 6 = managers, 7 = services, 8 = contracting, and 9 = agricultural products and sales. Duration referred to the length of time the owner had been in the business. Finally, seasonality was a binary variable, assuming a value of 1 if the business was seasonal in nature (e.g., landscaping service) and 0 if not.

Results of the multivariate analysis are presented in Table 4.12. Only the significant work force characteristics will be discussed. The significant F-ratios imply that the model explained the range in values for all three business outcomes under study. The following worker types had positive effects on owners' net business incomes: contracting family worker, unpaid family helper, and paid and contracting unrelated workers. In contrast, unpaid related helpers had a negative effect.

Contracting workers, related and unrelated, increased the total annual work hours of the owners. These workers may know less about the business than family members and thus require more of the owner's time in explanation and supervision. Unpaid family helpers and paid unrelated workers had, by contrast, positive effects on the hourly wage of owners. It seems that supervising unpaid unrelated helpers may be more burdensome than any contributions they might make.

As a group, family workers and helpers did not affect the total annual work hours of the owners; nor did they appear to serve as a substitute for the owner's work hours. In general, they had no effect or a positive effect on business incomes and owner wage rates.

Both unpaid related and unpaid unrelated helpers had negative effects, suggesting that not all workers increase business outputs and some reduce outputs. These findings are important in increasing our understanding of how home-based businesses achieve certain output levels. If high levels of output are desired, clearly owners need to select their work force carefully.

Subjective Outcomes of Owners

Katona (1975) suggested that psychological, subjective variables such as perception and satisfaction are important factors in determining consumer behavior. Campbell, Converse, and Rodgers (1976) concluded that satisfaction reflects the perceived gap between one's aspiration and achievement; furthermore, one's assessment of satisfaction could range from fulfillment to deprivation. Previous research has differentiated between objective and subjective variables, both as predictors and as outcomes in a family resource management model (Walker, Bubolz, & Lee, 1991; Walker, Lee, & Bubolz, 1989). Objective variables were measured in widely understood and standardized units such as dollars of income, hours of work, or years of education. Subjective measures

Table 4.12
Significant Effects of Worker Types and Other Control Variables on Net Business Income, Hours Worked, and Hourly Wage Rate of Sole Proprietors, $n = 508$

Variable	Net annual business income	Total annual work hours	Hourly wage rate
Main effect or work force characteristic			
Family members as workers and helpers			
Paid family worker			
Contracting family worker	+		
Unpaid family helper	+		+
Other relatives as workers and helpers			
Paid related worker			
Contracting related worker		+	
Unpaid related helper	-		
Nonfamily persons as workers and helpers			
Paid unrelated worker	+		+
Contracting unrelated worker	+	+	
Unpaid unrelated helper			-
Control variable			
Business owner characteristic			
Male	+	+	+
Age	+		+
Education	+	-	+
Single parent			
Family size		+	
Children under 6	+	-	
Nonhomeowners			
Years in community	-		
Towns < 2,500, rural areas, and farms	-		
Business characteristic			
Net annual business income	omitted	+	omitted
Occupational rank	-	+	-
Total annual work hours	+	omitted	omitted
Duration			
Seasonality		-	+
Constant	-	+	-
F-ratio = (all significant at .0001 level)	15.23	7.21	7.36
Adjusted R^2 =	.38	.21	.21
Number of observations =	508	508	508

Note: Effects were statistically significant at the .10 level or less.

were used in an attempt to determine how a person feels about income, hours of work, or years of education. A conceptual model of management and productivity in home-based work families was presented by Owen, Carsky, and Dolan (1992, p. 133). Output variables in the model included "psychic rewards" such as the satisfaction derived from work and from family life.

Multivariate research models were built for the three subjective outcomes of interest: life quality, income adequacy, and life control. Owners were asked how satisfied they were with the quality of their lives. Potential responses ranged from very dissatisfied to very satisfied. The income adequacy question tested their feelings about whether their incomes were not at all adequate; enabled them to buy some necessities; let them buy some but not all the things they wanted; let them buy everything they wanted; or let them have everything they wanted and also save. The potential responses to a question about control over one's life ranged from no control to almost complete control. For each subjective outcome the variable was recoded into a binary dependent variable. For example, if the worker was mixed, satisfied, or very satisfied with the quality of life, the variable was coded 1, and 0 otherwise. This means that the independent variables were used to explain the condition of being satisfied with one's quality of life.

Three types of influences were hypothesized to affect the subjective outcome measures: the owner's personal and household characteristics and the work characteristics. The personal and household variables were gender, owner's age, educational category, whether married or not, household size, family structure categories, whether someone in the household required care or not, and whether the residence was rural (i.e., towns with fewer than 2,500 people, rural, or farm) or urban. The work variables included the occupational categories, owner's annual hours worked in the business, whether employed full- or part-time, and years (i.e., duration) in the business.

A logistic regression was the statistical technique employed to determine the significant influences on owners' reports about the quality of their lives, reviews of income adequacy, and level of control they felt they had over their lives. Results are presented in Table 4.13. The significance of the chi-square statistic implies that the model explained the probability of realizing the outcome examined.

Regarding the personal and household variables, older owners were more likely than others to report that their incomes were adequate. Being a high school or college graduate related positively to the likelihood of feeling good about life quality. In contrast, compared to owners with postcollege educations, others felt their incomes were less adequate. Owners in adults-only families were more likely than full-nest families to feel positive about their life quality and the adequacy of their income. Compared to owners in cities, rural owners were less likely to feel positive about their life quality.

Working longer hours had a negative effect on feeling in control of one's life. Compared to agricultural products and sales, being an owner in any one of six

Table 4.13
Significant Effects on Subjective Outcomes of Owners, *n* = 670

Variable	Life quality	Income adequacy	Life control
Personal and household characteristic			
Male			
Age		+	
Education			
Less than high school		-	
High school graduate	+	-	
Some college or vocational school		-	
College graduate	+	-	
Postcollege	omitted	omitted	omitted
Married			
Household size			
Family structure			
Nonfamily			
Adult only	+	+	
Single parent			
Full-nest	omitted	omitted	omitted
Care for others			
Rural residence	-		
Work characteristic			
Occupation			
Professional and technical	+	+	+
Marketing and sales	+	+	+
Clerical and administrative support	+	+	+
Mechanical and transportation			+
Crafts and artisans	+	+	+
Managers		+	
Services	+	+	+
Contracting	+	+	+
Agricultural products and sales	omitted	omitted	omitted
Home-based work hours			-
Employed full-time			
Duration			
Constant		-	
Chi-square (24, *n* = 670) = (all significant at .0001 level)	61.95	94.77	69.93

Note: Effects were statistically significant at the .10 level or less.

occupations had a positive influence on all three outcomes; these were professional and technical, marketing and sales, clerical and administrative support, crafts and artisans, services, and contracting. Interestingly, being an owner in a managerial occupation increased the likelihood of a positive response for only one outcome, income adequacy. Owning a mechanical or transportation business increased the likelihood of feeling satisfied with control of life.

In summary, the owners were able to articulate various feelings they had about the quality of their lives, their income adequacy, and the degree of control they had over their lives. Various work as well as household and owner variables were significant predictors of these subjective outcome measures.

SUMMARY AND CONCLUSIONS

Comparison of Owners and Earners

This chapter had three broad objectives. The first was to compare owners and earners relative to selected characteristics of their personal and work lives. Seventy-five percent (74.6%) of the sample were owners. About 60% (i.e., 58.3% owners and 57.3% earners) of both groups were male. The owners earned, on average, about $8,000 less annual home-based income and worked significantly fewer hours than earners. A higher proportion of owners worked seasonally. The factors that increased the likelihood of being an owner were having higher income from sources other than the home-based work, engaging in home-based work in the professional and technical occupations or in clerical and administrative support (i.e., compared to agricultural products and sales), having other employment, and working seasonally.

Eleven percent (11.3%) of owners had no health insurance coverage compared to 8.7% of earners. Both groups relied on jobs for coverage to the same extent, 65.2% of owners and 64.2% of wage earners. While the majority of both groups relied on jobs for their health insurance coverage, home-based business owners were more heavily reliant on second jobs and former jobs (through retirement programs). Many more home-based wage earners (27.9%) were able to obtain health insurance coverage through their home-based work than were business owners (10.6%). The variables that affected the likelihood of coverage differed by ownership status.

Although owners and earners specified a variety of work sites at their residences, office/workroom/study was designated as the primary site by 60.7% of the earners and 29.3% of the owners. A higher percentage of owners than earners designated a second work space. Space reserved exclusively for home-based work was selected by 373 owners and 129 earners. Office/workroom/study was usually the preferred exclusive work space. The results indicated that both owners and earners attempt to separate their income-producing work from their family space.

Ownership Status and Gender

The second purpose of this chapter was to explore differences of owners and earners by gender, using four categories of worker types. The worker types, based on gender and ownership status categories, varied by income, hours worked, hours worked at home, percentage of time spent at home, and duration of the home-based work. Male earners earned the most income, worked the most hours, spent the lowest proportion of time at home, and were the least likely to work seasonally. Several of the occupations were dominated by male owners: professional and technical, contracting, and mechanical and transportation. Marketing and sales occupations were fairly evenly distributed among the four worker types. Nearly all workers in services were female owners.

Business Outcomes

The third purpose of this chapter was to explore selected aspects of the work and work outcomes of business owners. Borrowing money to start their businesses was not a common practice of either male or female owners. Although 82.4% of the businesses were organized as sole proprietorships, corporations were more likely than other forms to have a separate business bank account. A variety of sales promotion strategies were used by the owners. Most of them sold products and services within their own states and bought most of their supplies in state. Owners who sold products, rather than services, used a variety of marketing methods.

The determinants of the owners' annual home-based work income and hours worked varied by gender. For instance, having children under 6 years old had a negative effect on the incomes of females but a positive effect for men. The gender differences that are well known in research about outcomes (e.g., occupational segregation by gender) for the general centralized labor force reemerged in this sample of home-based business owners.

The influence of employee type on three owner outcomes was studied, holding constant other relevant variables. Nine categories of workers/helpers were identified based on relationship to the owner and whether the helper was paid, unpaid, or contractual. Contracting family workers, unpaid family helpers, and paid and contracting unrelated workers had positive effects on owners' net business incomes. In contrast, unpaid related helpers had a negative effect. Unpaid family members were not substituting for owners' work hours. Results indicated that some worker types increased desirable business outcomes; others were a drag on desirable outcomes.

The owners articulated various feelings they had about the quality of their lives, the adequacy of their incomes, and the degree of control they had over their lives. Significant predictors of these subjective outcome measures were found. For example, the likelihood of feeling positive about the quality of life and about income adequacy was higher for owners in adults-only families than for those in other family types. Compared to owners residing in cities, rural owners were less likely to feel good about the quality of their lives. Other than the effect of occupation, the personal and household characteristics played a more significant role in determining subjective outcomes, especially in the case of income adequacy. Compared to agricultural products and sales, mechanical and transportation workers, and managers had less consistent significant effects on subjective outcomes.

Dimensions and outcomes in home-based employment are similar to those in centralized employment. It may be largely the family-side impacts that make home-based employment so enticing to increasing numbers of workers. Toward that focus, Chapter 5 will explore in detail the internal workings of the households engaged in home-based work from the nine-state study.

NOTES

1. All multivariate research models in this book refer to regression procedures, either as ordinary least squares (OLS) regression or a logistic regression, depending on the nature of the dependent variable in the model. The OLS regression was used in the case of a continuous dependent variable such as income. If the dependent variable was binary in nature, meaning it had a value of either 0 or 1, a logistic regression procedure was used. For further discussion of either procedure, see standard statistical references such as Kmenta (1986).

2. Agricultural products and sales was the category used consistently in all multivariate research models or regressions as the occupation group to which the other eight occupation categories were compared if the effect was significant. Although one category in any series of groupings used as independent variables must be omitted from any regression procedure for statistical reasons, the choice of which category to omit is often arbitrary. In the case of the multivariate research models in this book, agricultural products and sales was chosen because it had the lowest frequency of home-based workers.

Chapter 5

Homeworking Families and How They Make It Work

Barbara R. Rowe and Ramona K. Z. Heck with the assistance of Alma J. Owen, Kathryn Stafford, and Mary Winter

INTRODUCTION

This chapter focuses on the "home" side of home-based work. Its intent is to explore what was learned in the nine-state study about the households and families in which home-based workers live. As noted researchers such as Rosabeth Kanter (1977) and Ann Crouter (1984) have pointed out, on the whole, studies of the work-family interface have concentrated on the influence of work upon the family and rarely the reverse. The discussion that follows hopes to fill in some of the informational gaps in how families influence work, especially when it is home-based.

The chapter is organized as follows: first, general work-family literature is reviewed. Then, an overview of the structure and composition of all households in the sample is presented. Additional literature is reviewed as needed within the remaining sections of the chapter. Next, an exploration of the effect of children on home-based work and the use of child care services is examined. Following these sections is a review of the different approaches to family functioning, a discussion of the nature of family management, and the relationship between family functioning and how the family manages. Finally, the adjustment strategies used by homeworking households are presented.

Previous Research on Work and Family Life

Since the late 19th century, work has been seen as something one does for a living, outside the home, an activity that rarely involves other family members.

Conversely, the family is usually associated with the home, separate from the workplace or from one's place of employment. In this view, families are generally expected to arrange their lives so that they do not interfere with work efficiency and to make any adjustments necessary to accommodate the bread-winner's (i.e., usually male) work role (Ferber & O'Farrell, 1991).

As more women, especially married women with children, have moved into the labor force, the concept of work and family as separate and distinct worlds has changed (Beach, 1989; Kanter, 1977; Voydanoff, 1987). Scholars from several disciplines are observing and reporting an interconnectedness between work and family life.

In 1983, Staines and Pleck concluded that among a national sample of employed adults, work performance was significantly related to family charac-teristics such as time spent in child care and family involvement, as well as to work characteristics including the number of hours worked, the inflexibility of job demands, and perceived time conflicts. Previously, Near, Rice, and Hunt (1980) had discovered that several characteristics of work, including occupa-tion, characteristics of the work, and even just being employed, were correlated with life satisfaction.

Although the majority of work-family studies have concentrated on the effects of work settings and workers' attitudes on families, less well-docu-mented is the extent to which family life influences work, for example, the limitations that marriage and motherhood may place on the extent and timing of women's labor force participation and occupational advancement (Sullivan, 1992). For men, the reverse is true. Having family responsibilities increases married men's work hours, income, and involvement with work (Lambert, 1990; Voydanoff, 1987).

Research on Home-Based Employment and Family Life

Other researchers are beginning to explore the ways in which families are combining various work and family roles. One strategy to integrate the worlds of work and family has been the current trend toward home-based work. The number of families who do income-producing or job-related work at home full- or part-time increased 12% between 1990 and 1991, and a 7% increase was predicted for 1992 (Aburdene & Naisbitt, 1992).

The argument that having separate settings for domestic and work activities results in harmonious and balanced relationships in modern families has caused concern about the trend toward home-based work. Fusing such settings together spatially, critics have contended, may be disruptive (Ahrentzen, 1990). Beach (1989) has argued that combining work and family space enhances interaction with family and spouse.

Investigating home-based work from the perspective of the family, as op-posed to the individual worker, is important because the overlap goes both ways.

Combining paid work and home life in the same space affects the entire family even if only one family member is directly involved. The work requires time and energy that previously may have been devoted solely to the family. It may require the use of family possessions such as the telephone and automobile. Space that was used for family activities may be taken over by the business. Family leisure time may have to take a back seat to work activities, including last-minute rearranging to fit a customer's schedule. Telephone calls about work may come at all hours of the day or night, including mealtimes, weekends, and holidays (Owen, 1984; Rosenblatt, 1987).

On the other hand, there is a chance that home and family will undermine the paid work; family responsibilities may take priority or the worker may never have large blocks of time free of family distractions, to concentrate. In either case, the spatial proximity of income-generating activities and household activities provided a unique setting for studying families who attempt to do both (Heck, Winter, & Stafford, 1992).

THE STRUCTURE AND COMPOSITION OF HOMEWORKING FAMILIES

A Typology of Homeworking Households/Families

To examine some of these issues, the composition of the households included in the sample was used to create a typology of homeworking households based on the marital status of the household manager and the presence or absence of children in the household. A functional definition of marriage, which defined marital status by the presence of a spouse or live-in partner, was adopted to allow inclusion of instances in which unmarried couples were living together.

Households were categorized as nonfamilies when the household manager was not married and there were no children in the household. This category also included single-person households and instances of unrelated adults sharing housing. Single-parent families included household managers who were not married but who lived with one or more children. Adult-only families were those in which the household manager was married but no children under age 18 were present in the household. Full-nest families contained a married household manager with one or more children ages 18 or younger in the household. The labels given the four family groups are consistent with those used in Ahrentzen's 1990 study of 104 home-based workers.

Demographic Characteristics of Homeworking Households/Families

Table 5.1 illustrates some of the demographic characteristics of these home-working households. Most of the home-based workers were living in full-nest

Table 5.1
Household Characteristics, $N = 899$

Characteristics	Nonfamilies Percent	Single-parent families Percent	Full-nest families Percent	Adult-only families Percent
Family status	11.8	2.7	51.0	34.5
Number of children				
1 child		61.6	29.8	
2 children		23.1	43.2	
3 children		6.9	20.8	
4 children		4.9	4.3	
5 children		3.4	0.5	
6 children		0.0	0.7	
7 children		0.0	0.7	
		100.0	100.0	
Gender				
Women	40.1	60.3	44.7	36.4
Men	59.9	39.7	55.3	63.6
Homeowners	70.0	69.6	88.8	92.7
Location of residence				
Town or city > 2,500	57.2	55.3	52.5	54.9
Town or city < 2,500	21.0	30.5	17.9	19.9
Rural nonfarm	13.0	14.2	22.4	18.2
Farm	8.7	0.0	7.1	6.9
	100.0	100.0	100.0	100.0
Ownership status				
Business owner	69.3	82.5	73.4	77.3
Wage worker	30.7	17.5	26.6	22.7
Type of business				
Service providers	68.2	80.6	76.1	77.8
Product providers	31.8	19.4	23.9	22.2
	100.0	100.0	100.0	100.0
Occupation				
Professional and technical	19.7	23.3	10.4	10.0
Marketing and sales	31.8	19.4	23.9	22.2
Clerical and administrative support	2.0	0.0	6.9	5.1
Mechanical and transportation	19.4	1.6	11.7	15.6
Crafts and artisans	9.4	21.7	11.3	12.1
Managers	3.7	2.5	4.7	2.8
Services	8.0	20.1	14.0	8.9
Contracting	5.5	9.8	15.5	18.3
Agricultural products and sales	0.5	1.5	1.7	5.0
	100.0	100.0	100.0	100.0
	$\overline{X}$	$\overline{X}$	$\overline{X}$	$\overline{X}$
Age	46.2	44.5	38.1	51.7
Education	14.6	14.5	14.0	13.4
Years in community	23.0	19.5	16.1	24.8
Duration	11.1	6.6	7.0	12.1

families (51.0% of the households), followed by adult-only families (34.5%). Nonfamily households composed 11.8% of the sample and single-parent families, 2.7%.

Married home-based workers were 84.8% of the sample ($n = 762$), and slightly more than one-half of the households (55.8% or $n = 503$) had children. About 26.7% of the sample ($n = 240$) had children under age 6. The number of children per family ranged from zero to seven. Full-nest families were more likely to have two children living in the household (i.e., 43.2% of the group with children), and single-parent families usually had only one child (61.6%).

Overall, the home-based workers in these homeworking families were more likely to be male (58.1%) than female (41.9%). There was, however, a difference in the gender of the home-based worker by family type. In keeping with household trends overall, there were more female single-parent home-based workers ($n = 18$) than male ($n = 12$). The mean ages of homeworkers in single-parent and nonfamily households were 44.5 years and 46.2 years, respectively.

The majority of these families were homeowners (87.3% or $n = 785$) and had lived in their communities for about 19.8 years. Because home-based workers in adult-only families were older (mean age of 51.7 years), had lived in their communities longer (24.8 years), and had been engaged in home-based work for many of those years (12.1 on average), it was believed that these households had been full-nest families in the preceding life stage.[1]

There was very little variation in the education level of the home-based workers by family status. Nonfamily home-based workers had slightly more education (14.6 years); adult-only homeworkers, slightly less (i.e., 13.4 years).

Home-based workers can also be categorized by ownership status of the business into business owners and those working at home for a primary employer. In the overall sample, 74.6% of the home-based workers owned their businesses. Moreover, home business owners were more prevalent than wage workers in every family setting. Because many homeworkers may have subsidized a home business with their household budget, it seemed logical that nonfamily and single-parent workers, who had no other members of the household to supply their needs for income security and employer-related benefits such as health insurance, would choose home-based wage work (i.e., working for an employer), but that was not the case.

Work Characteristics of Homeworking Households/Families

The work performed by the home-based workers in these families was sorted into nine categories using the *Standard Occupational Classification Handbook*: professional and technical, marketing and sales, clerical and administrative support, mechanical and transportation, crafts and artisans, managers, services, contracting, and agricultural products and sales (U.S. Department of Commerce, 1980). These homeworking families were more likely to be in service-oriented fields such as consulting, teaching, or repairs than to be producing a product. Service providers composed 76.1% of the home-based workers living in full-nest families, 80.6% of the single-parent families, 77.8% of adult-only families, and 68.2% of nonfamilies. About one-third of the home-based workers in nonfamilies were in marketing and sales. The rest were concentrated in professional and technical and mechanical and transportation trades. Single-parent families were spread about equally among crafts, professional and technical work, marketing and sales, and service-oriented work. The largest percentage of home-based workers in full-nest and adult-only families were in marketing and sales (see Table 5.1).

The relationship between occupational choice and family structure may have been connected as much to responsibility for the care of young children or other family members as to education and job training. Marketing and sales jobs require interaction with other people and institutions in the performance of the work and may involve some overnight travel, whereas crafts and some professional and technical work can be performed almost exclusively at the home site.

Income levels. Stafford, Longstreth, Gritzmacher, and Smith (1986) reported that home-based working women differed from their traditional work site counterparts mainly in the income they earned. In their study, employed women who were home-based were slightly older, had more and older children, more job experience, and somewhat fewer hours of employment per week than women employed outside the home. The most substantial difference between the two groups was that home-based women workers earned only 57% as much as those who were not home-based.

In the nine-state study, incomes from home-based work were slightly larger for adult-only families ($18,670 in 1988) and smallest for single-parent families ($11,604). There was a significant difference in incomes from the home-based work in relation to the gender of the home-based worker and the category of family in which the homeworker lived. Male home-based workers earned, on average, $24,744 in 1988 while female home-based workers earned an average of $8,478. Women homeworkers in every family setting made less than men, but male members of full-nest families had much more net income from home-based work than did women. This family effect could reflect the larger number of hours spent in home-based work by men or the types of work they performed. Even when men and women worked in the same occupations, however, men earned more from home-based work. These differences could be because men and women price their goods and services differently or because the *forms* of home-based work they undertake are different. For example, selling cosmetics or cleaning supplies door-to-door would be categorized as sales in this study, as would being sales representative of a pharmaceutical company, but incomes from the two types of work would likely be very different.

Use of space by home-based workers. To examine the spatial overlap of home and paid work, homeworkers in the nine-state study were asked how often other activities took place in the work space concurrent with the home-based work. Women home-based workers in nonfamilies never experienced simultaneous activity; women in adult-only and full-nest families seldom did; but women in single-parent families often did. Men home-based workers in nonfamilies, adult-only, and full-nest families seldom experienced simultaneous activity, and male home-based workers living in single-parent families sometimes did but the differences were slight. Almost all homeworkers, regardless of gender or family structure, reported that their jobs involved at least some business transactions and contact outside the home at a work site or a client's home or office.

In all, the sample of homeworking households from the nine-state study is one dominated by full-nest or adult-only families. A majority of the home-based workers are married men living in full-nest families who own their businesses. They are homeowners and have lived in their present community for approximately 2 decades. These characteristics are similar to those consistently shown in studies of the self-employed. The self-employed are more likely to be male, to be older, to have additional years of formal education past high school, and to be married (Balkin, 1989). Family composition did seem to affect the amount of income earned from the home-based work as much as the gender of the home-based worker did. Spatial overlap and simultaneous activity levels also varied by family structure variables.

EFFECTS OF CHILDREN ON HOME-BASED EMPLOYMENT

Previous Research on Children and Home-Based Work

Home-based work is often mentioned as a strategy for mothers with young children to combine child care with paid work (Olson, 1983; Pratt, 1984).[2] In one of the few studies which incorporated analysis of the configuration of children in families where either or both of the parents performed work for pay within or from the home, Horvath (1986) found that three times as many women as men with very young children were involved in home-based work.

Most other previous research has examined the effects of children on centralized employment (Gramm, 1987). Hill and Juster (1985) and others[3] observed that the presence of children tends to reduce shared market work efforts by both husbands and wives. The presence of larger numbers of children is associated with decreased market work hours for men, and the presence of very young children reduces the market work hours of women (Gronau, 1977; Stafford & Duncan, 1985).[4] Women with child care responsibilities worked as many hours as women without those responsibilities, but fewer hours were in paid employment hours (Hill, 1985). Although overall market work hours have declined somewhat for men in the past decade, women have increased their labor force participation and maintained their level of market work hours (Juster, 1985a, 1985b; Robinson, 1985). The combination of these two trends has heightened the convergence of market work hours by men and women (Stafford, 1980). All of these studies were confined to the traditional and centralized market work sites at which men and women spend their respective market work hours.

Working at home may enhance flexibility in scheduling work (Horvath, 1986; Voydanoff, 1987); participants in this study cited it as a motivator for being in home-based work. Beach (1985) found that although work time was frequently interrupted by child, family, and household tasks, home-based workers, especially women, tended to adjust the demands of paid work to the needs of their families.

Research Results on Children from the Nine-State Study

Home-based employment did not appear to alleviate the time demands of work and family for the families in this study. In fact, the total annual work hours of the typical home-based worker in this study appear comparable to those of workers with similar family compositions in centralized workplaces.

To examine thoroughly the amount of time families in the sample were spending on their paid homeworking activities, it was necessary to sort them into families with only one home-based worker and those with multiple at-home income-generating activities. For example, a female home-based worker may have had two home businesses while her spouse was managing another. In 501 households only one individual generated income from working at home. In these 501 households, the number of hours spent in home-based work per year varied from a high of 1,861 for homeworkers in full-nest families to a low of 1,520 for single-parent homeworkers, who worked fewer hours than did those in any of the other household configurations. Single parents experience a shortage of many resources, especially time. When these hours were divided by the standard 40-hour workweek, most workers were found to be allocating at least 40 hours a week to home-based work and some workers were devoting considerably more hours.

The hours spent in paid work were examined for all the home-based workers in the sample using a multivariate research model.[5] The results showed that having a child 18 years of age or younger reduced home-based work by approximately 8 hours per week during the year or about 1 workday per week. The presence of a child under 6 years of age reduced total home-based work hours by about an *additional* 6 hours per week during the year. Parents of children under the age of 6, therefore, were losing about 14 hours or 1¾ workdays per week. Male home-based workers experienced fewer negative effects on their work hours than female home-based workers. Having children was negatively related to large-scale businesses. Having young children decreased a person's likelihood of owning a business and doing seasonal home-based work.

USE OF CHILD CARE SERVICES BY HOMEWORKING HOUSEHOLDS

Previous Research on Child Care and Home-Based Work

Only one empirical study has compared the relationship between the use of child care by home-based workers and that by women who were employed outside the home (Stafford et al., 1986). The researchers reported that employment location (i.e., home-based or not), price, and income significantly affected the demand for child care services by working women. Specifically, homeworking women used 224 fewer child care hours per year than women who were not home-based workers, the equivalent of about 4.5 fewer hours per week per year.

Ahrentzen (1990) and Christensen (1985, 1987, 1988b) discovered that working at home did not necessarily eliminate the need for outside child care, although it did solve some problems, such as caring for a sick child. Ahrentzen interviewed 104 telecommuters in five major metropolitan areas and found no differences in the number of hours worked at home among the different household types. These types included singles, households with at least two adults and no children, two adults plus children, and single parent plus children. As in the nine-state study of home-based work, there was a significant difference in average weekly work hours between men and women, with men working more hours per week (on average 43.2) than women (35.3). Child care and paid work activities were found to be incompatible by Christensen (1985), McLaughlin (1981), and Olson (1983). In these studies homeworkers worked while their children were cared for by others, were sleeping, or were in school.

Similarly, in her analysis of three panels of National Longitudinal Surveys, Pratt (1993) discovered that 38% of the home-based businesswomen interviewed had used child care arrangements in the 4 weeks just prior to the survey. She concluded very few women who work at home care for their children while they work. Part of the explanation may be that only 25% of the home-based business women in her study said their work activity is at home. The majority of the home-based business owners worked *from* the home, not always *in* the home. The type of child care arrangements used varied widely: 35% left their children in a nonrelative's home, 14% had their children cared for by a nonrelative in the home, and another 14% used a day care center. Other options were having children cared for in the home by their father or another relative (Pratt, 1993).

Although previous research on child care and home-based work is sparse, research on child care issues in general does exist. A few studies have examined the choice of child care arrangements for the children of employed mothers. These studies indicate that the choice and use of child care arrangements vary with characteristics of the mother's education and employment status, the family's race, ethnicity, and income, the age of the child, the geographic region, and the place of residence (Leibowitz, Waite, & Witsberger, 1988).

The use of family day care (which is defined as a private home other than the child's home, where an adult cares for children from infancy through school age on a regular basis) has remained constant over the past 25 years. During this same period, the use of center-based programs has increased, particularly among families in which the mother works outside the home. There has been a decline in the use of in-home providers and relatives (Hofferth, Brayfield, Deich, & Holcomb, 1991b). The National Child Care Survey, conducted in 1990 through telephone interviews of a nationally representative sample of U.S. families with children under age 13, found that parents continue to be the primary child care providers for most families. Thirty percent of all preschool children with an employed mother were cared for primarily by a parent, while 65% of the preschoolers of nonemployed mothers were cared for primarily by a parent. Center-based care was the primary care arrangement for 26% of the preschoolers with employed mothers. A surprising 15% of the preschool children of nonemployed mothers were in center-based care. Eighteen percent of the children of employed mothers were cared for by relatives either in the child's home or in a relative's home. Family day care was selected for 19% of the children of employed mothers. About 11% of the children of nonemployed mothers were cared for by relatives; less than 3% were in family day care (Hofferth, Brayfield, Deich, & Holcomb, & Glantz, 1991a).

A study by the U.S. Department of Health and Human Services (HHS) (1990) examined child care arrangements for preschool children relative to the characteristics of the children and their families. This study specifically concerned children 5 years of age or less, regardless of whether the mother was employed. Approximately 68% of U.S. children 5 years of age and under had been in child care at least once during their lives. The proportion who had ever received care increased with age.

Mothers' employment has been clearly related to the increased use of child care; however, one-fifth of the children of mothers not currently employed received some form of child care. A positive relationship between the mother's education and the percentage of children ever cared for in a regular child care arrangement has also been shown. Race and ethnicity have been related to child care use; blacks and Hispanics use less child care than whites. The geographic location of the family is also related to the availability of certain care arrangements (Dickinson, 1975; Duncan & Hill, 1975). Living outside a metropolitan statistical area (MSA) is associated with lower usage levels of child care, while parents living in the central city within an MSA use the least amount of child care of any type.

The ability to pay for care and the child's age have been found to limit the types of care the family may choose. Family income and mother's earnings are related to the choice of child care arrangements, and higher incomes are associated with increased use of child care (Lehrer, 1983). Leibowitz et al. (1988) found that the child's age is most likely to influence the choice of care arrangement. Infants and toddlers (i.e., children 2 years old and under) usually have been cared for in their own home or in someone else's home (O'Connell, 1990; U.S. Bureau of the Census, 1987; U.S. Department of Health and Human Services [HHS], 1990).

Research Results on Use of Child Care in the Nine-State Study

In this study of home-based work, the families with children who were designated as needing care constituted 41.5% of the 899 households interviewed. Of this group, approximately 37.9% used child care and the rest did not. The highest percentage of child care was used by home-based workers with children who were 2 and 3 years old. In this analysis, the usage variable was asked relative to each household rather than to each child receiving child care services.

The typical home-based worker with children who needed care was a 36-year-old male who was married with two children, had 14 years of education, and averaged $43,842 in annual family income from all sources in 1988. This home-based worker had lived an average of 15.5 years in a community with a population of 2,500 or more, had been engaged in his work for 6 years, and was likely to be a nonseasonal, self-employed businessman who did not hire employees or other services.

The use of child care services was further examined using a multivariate research model that included household, worker, and work characteristics. The results showed that being a single parent, having high family income, and having a 2-year-old child in the home were positively associated with the likelihood of using child care. Being an older worker, having a child who was 1 year or less or children 11 to 12 years old, and having a less professional occupation decreased the likelihood of using child care. Being a business owner decreased the likelihood of usage, but owning a business that hired employees or hired services increased the likelihood of usage.

At least two conclusions can be drawn from this analysis. First, because many workers did not use child care even when it was designated as needed, it could be inferred that home-based employment was used by some as a coping strategy to ease child care needs. Second, it is also clear that a large group of households engaged in home-based work did use child care and that not all parents could stay home to work and take care of children at the same time.

Home-based employment may not be amenable to every type of family structure and composition. Home-based workers and their families may be just as stressed at the end of a workday as workers in other types of employment. The demands of child care and employment appear to produce similar effects, such as reduced employment time, on most working families regardless of their work location. Reduced employment time may be desirable for working families as long as it is a conscious choice and not at the expense of needed income or career building. For parents who work at home, family time may be more desirable than more income.

In general, children affect paid work whether it is home-based or at a centralized workplace. The negative effects of children on the hours spent in home-based employment may not be overall negative effects when they are considered in combination with other factors. For example, the involvement of older children in the home-based work or the dovetailing of home-based employment with some of the demands of young children may be effective. Although the presence of children reduces the total hours of home-based work, when other factors are considered, this effect may be less negative than the effect of children on employment in a centralized work location.

FAMILY FUNCTIONING AND FAMILY TYPES

In this section, family functioning theory is reviewed and family functioning types are identified in the nine-state sample.

Changes in Family Life

If the 1950s were the golden age of the family, the 1970s and 1980s have been the age of study and scrutiny of the family. This has come about, in part, because of a struggle between two distinct and noncomplementary types of families. In the 1950s, the exemplary family was patriarchal in structure. It was symbolized by the TV families of "Ozzie and Harriet" and "Father Knows Best." This family type had one decision maker, typically the father, who was the family's connection with the world outside the family and its close neighborhood. He made all important decisions and set the parameters within which his wife and children could interact with the world.

Beginning in the 1960s two trends challenged this model family view. First was the increased labor force participation of married women in their childbearing years, which resulted in more action in the outside world by wives and mothers independent of controls set by husbands. The second change was an increased emphasis on the study of family life by its attendant practitioners who engaged in family intervention. Virginia Satir (1972) led a body of professionals studying family life in declaring that the "model" family of the 1950s was, in fact, pathological. The family life to strive for was one in which members were considered partners, with spouses as full partners and children's parity being based on age-appropriate autonomy and independence.

Considered as patriarchal and egalitarian, respectively, these two family types were the center of academic debate about which was the preferable manner in which to raise children and otherwise find the fulfillments of private life. In the meantime, they existed side by side within U.S. society.

In an attempt to bridge the debate over the preferable family, Kantor and Lehr (1975) undertook qualitative research on the way families lived out their everyday lives. They proposed that the purpose of family life was to fulfill psychological needs. They called these needs target dimensions and grouped them under the titles of power, affect, and content. The resources that families used to gain target dimensions are referred to as access dimensions: time, space, and energy.

To describe the families they found in their research, Kantor and Lehr (1975) used relatively new concepts introduced through systems theory. They labeled the older family model, in which the father had control, the closed family. The partnership model promoted by Satir was the open family. To these they added a third family type, the random one. In doing so they recognized a family type prevalent in both upper and lower socioeconomic classes and provided it with some legitimacy.

Although Kantor and Lehr (1975) used the concepts of systems theory, Constantine (1986) refined the work to a truly systemic model of family life. Based on his clinical work with families, he introduced other dimensions and family types to these three paradigms of family life and significantly systematized the explanation of family types.

A Systems Theory of Family Paradigms

Closed families. Simply defined, a closed family is one that seeks to maintain the status quo. It engages in activities and attends to ideals and values that maintain continuity with the past. Decisions, direction, and roles are delegated based on how things were done in the past and often replay structures of the members' families of origin. Analysis of the systems embedded in and around closed families shows that the family, not the individual or the community, is the most distinct unit, that is, the one with the most definite boundary. "Stability through tradition" is Constantine's phrase for the closed family.

Random families. Constantine (1986) described the random family as the opposite of the closed one. The random family revels in variety and change. It is oriented to the present and seeks the constant introduction of new experiences. Each member is in charge of his or her own direction and action and usually does not coordinate activities with those of other members. The individual has the most distinct boundary and interacts within and outside the family with equal freedom. "Variety through innovation" is the random family's motto.

Open families. The open family combines some aspects of both closed and random types. Its members seek to introduce some change into the enduring family unit. In doing so, the open family acknowledges ties with the past and incorporates experiences of the present to build a path to the future. Decisions and direction for the family are negotiated among all members. There is little role delineation inside the family, although there may be some delineation based on age. Individual members and the family unit have equivalent boundaries. Members value the family's identity as much as they do their own and consider each other's identity in determining actions and goals. "Adaptability through negotiation" is the hallmark of processes observed in open families.

Kantor and Lehr (1975) and Constantine (1986) have clearly stated that these family types are not absolute. Families display a mix of types in their everyday activities, but they are expected to display a propensity to one type or another. This propensity may be an overall preference for one type or another; it could also display itself in certain dimensions such as being rigidly random or tightly closed. The inclination of a family to be one type or another is expected to illustrate the standards for affective interaction within a family and to assist researchers in understanding the relationship among income-producing work, type and size of family, and various satisfaction measures.

Research Results on Family Types from the Nine-State Study

In 823 homeworking households that self-identified as families, a mix of family types was displayed. Respondents were asked to rate their family on how they used time and space (i.e., access dimensions) and what their decision-making style and family patterns (i.e., target dimensions) were. Responses to these items were analyzed to yield three scores for each family: a random score, an open score, and a closed one (Owen, Rowe, & Gritzmacher, 1992). Each family was assigned a family type based on these scores.

A family was classified as a relatively pure type of family (i.e., open, closed, or random) if it scored high on only one score. It was considered a mix of two types if it scored high on any two dimensions but not on the other. Finally, 149 families scored so close on all three scales that they did not display any typological distinction. Figure 5.1 is a pie chart that illustrates the relative size of the subpopulation for each family type that could be classified.

The ability to classify families by functioning type is useful to studies of home-based working families for several reasons. Family functioning may affect the satisfaction family members feel with different types of businesses. For example, it was hypothesized that families who value new experiences would be expected to enjoy a business that brings them into contact with new persons or situations, whereas families who value their privacy would rather limit contact with clients. Thus there may be better matches between certain family styles and businesses than others. It is expected that an open/random

Figure 5.1
Distribution of Family Types, *n* = 674

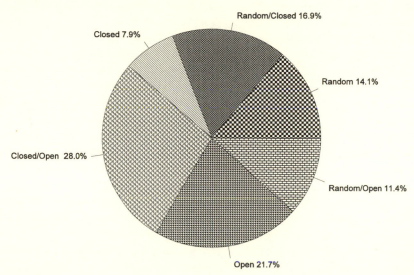

family might get more satisfaction from a retail business at home than would a closed family, for instance. In random families, members do not place restraints on the activities of any family member. Therefore, homeworking members of these families need not conform their work activities to family functioning types; however, they cannot depend on assistance from other family members.

FAMILY MANAGEMENT, ITS MEANING, AND SPECIFIC ACTIVITIES

The nine-state study of homeworking families also examined management strategies for the family unit. The purpose of this section is to discuss the nature of family management and describe specific activities that are identified as family management.

What Is Meant by Management

Management is a set of goal-directed activities that uses existing or obtainable resources to meet individual, family, or organization demands. Effective managerial behavior increases the likelihood of desired outcomes while poor managerial behavior diminishes the likelihood of achieving desired results. Family resource management provides a means of systematically describing the nature of families' purposeful actions to meet goals that take place within the family and near the home environs (Deacon & Firebaugh, 1988).[6]

Families produce goods and services that support their lifestyle and see to the needs of society by investing in each other's and the next generation's human capital. Although the production of these outputs is self-evident, establishing an empirical tie between management practices and outcomes has been problematic because there is disagreement on the scope of managerial behavior and on ways to identify such behavior when it occurs. Regardless of the scope, difficulty in measuring effectively that which is primarily a mental activity has been an immense challenge.

Previous research showing evidence of management. Three areas of research provide information on managerial activities of families. Time-use researchers have measured time spent in specific management activities—planning, scheduling, and budgeting (Berk, 1985; Juster & Stafford, 1985; Walker & Woods, 1976).[7] Other researchers have found evidence that families set goals and plan ways to reach these goals (Fitzsimmons, Larery, & Metzen, 1971).[8] Third, the range of family achievement levels suggests that families differ with regard to both goals and the management activities required to reach them (Williams & Manning, 1972).

Deacon and Firebaugh's family management framework. In general, management is a process of setting priorities, assessing resources, and organizing and directing resources to reach goals. Deacon and Firebaugh (1988) define the managerial subsystem as that part of the family's system that deals with planning and implementing the use of resources to meet demands. The internal structure of the managerial subsystem is called throughput and consists of two main components, planning and implementing. Planning consists of two parts, standard setting and action sequencing. Standard setting can be further broken down into demand clarification and resource assessment. Planning produces a plan that can be implemented by actuating and controlling behaviors. Controlling consists of checking conformity to a plan and adjusting when needed. The outputs of the management subsystem are met demands and resources that have been changed in some way. Families are faced with demands and resources that are, in part, derived from the larger environment. In the case of this research study, home-based work places demands on, as well as provides resources for, the families involved.

Heck and Douthitt (1982) and Heck (1983) developed a theoretical research model that delineated the managerial subsystem of the family which results in outputs that are met demands or used resources. The product output is viewed as a function of the inputs into the family's managerial subsystem and the throughputs or managerial activities engaged in by the family. Value-laden goals are fixed or given inputs into the managerial system.

Olson and Beard (1985) have offered methods of refining the measurement of management concepts for survey instrumentation. Eigsti (1984) has measured managerial behaviors within the family using a self-assessment instrument. These researchers have pioneered methods that attempt to gather reports of what people are thinking as well as what they are doing in family settings.

Research Results on Family Management and Specific Activities of Household Managers

One of the goals of the nine-state study was to be able to measure management, both of the household work and the home-based work. To that end, two multiple-item scales were developed and administered to the household managers in the sample who were also the home-based worker. In the total sample 482 household managers were also the home-based worker. In the rest of the sample, the person interviewed was the manager of a household in which home-based work occurred but he or she was not the home-based worker.

Measurements of family management behavior. Table 5.2 lists the specific questions asked of household managers to measure their family management processes; these questions are similar to those asked about home-based work management in Chapter 3. The family management questions were developed to represent the major concepts of the Deacon and Firebaugh (1988) depiction of family management. The labels used in Table 5.3 and Table 5.4 relate directly to these major concepts represented by the question asked. The leading question asked was "Which number (1 = not at all; 3 = somewhat; 5 = exactly) describes how much the statement is like you?" The management concepts represented by each of these questions are the same as those listed for management of the family work: goals (setting), standard setting, demand clarification, resource assessment, action sequencing, actuating, checking, adjusting, demand responses, and resource changes.

The nature of management of the home-based work has been discussed in Chapter 3 and elsewhere (Heck, Winter, & Stafford, 1992). Higher scores indicated behavior most closely aligned with what were assumed to be better management practices. It was assumed that the more extensive these specific management practices, the more effective the overall management style. Respondents had no difficulty answering the management questions, and a range of responses was obtained.

Level of management behavior of household managers. The responses to each set of the 10 management questions were added together to calculate a combined total score for each scale (Table 5.3). Mean scores for each question within each scale were also computed, and an overall mean total score was derived for each scale. Higher values of the resulting sum for each scale were assumed to be associated with the use of better management practices.

Comparing household managers who are and are not home-based workers. Household managers who were also the home-based worker scored higher on the management scale than did household managers who were not the home-

Table 5.2
Family Management Concepts Related to Questionnaire Items for Family Work Management

Management concept	Questionnaire item
Input	
Demands	
Goals (setting)	Each week you decide some way you can improve your life. [a]
Events	
Resources	
Throughput	
Planning	
Standard setting	Before starting a job, you have a firm idea about how to judge the outcome.
Demand clarification	When planning a job, you think the plan through so that your goal is clear before you actually begin doing the job.
Resource assessment	Before you begin a job, you figure out how much of your time, money, and energy you can devote to this particular task.
Action sequencing	You think about when to do a job, and not just how much time it will take.
Implementing	
Actuating	When there is a chore to be done at home, you wait until the last minute. [b]
Controlling	
Checking	As you work, you check whether things are going as you want them to.
Adjusting	When things are not going well, you figure out another way to do it.
Output	
Demand responses	When a job is done, you think about how well you like the results.
Resource changes	You are pleased if the work just gets done; you do not spend time thinking about how effectively it was done. [b]

Note: Management concepts refer to definitions used in *Family Resource Management: Principles and Applications*, 2nd ed., by R. E. Deacon and F. M. Firebaugh, 1988, Boston: Allyn and Bacon.

[a] Actual statements are listed. Each statement was posed to all respondents (i.e., household managers) *in reference to their family life with emphasis on unpaid family work.* In this chapter, all household managers, including those who were and were not the home-based workers, were included in the analysis and their responses to the family work management scale were compared. Leading question was "Which number (1 = not at all; 3 = somewhat; 5 = exactly) describes how much the statement is like you?" *Statements were not given in the order listed.* [b] This statement was reverse coded in descriptive statistics and the factor analysis results.

124

Table 5.3

Frequency of Responses to Family Work Management Scale by Managers Who Were or Were Not Home-Based Workers, N = 899

Management concept	Home-based worker, n = 482					Not home-based worker, n = 417				
	Not at all		Somewhat		Exactly	Not at all		Somewhat		Exactly
	1	2	3	4	5	1	2	3	4	5
Input										
Goals	18.1%	7.4%	31.4%	9.9%	32.6%	20.1%	9.1%	32.9%	11.2%	26.6%
Planning										
Standard setting	4.1	2.7	28.1	25.8	39.3	3.9	3.9	29.5	26.6	36.0
Demand clarification	4.8	4.1	23.8	18.4	48.8	6.3	4.7	29.5	22.2	37.3
Resource assessment	9.1	6.0	27.9	20.2	36.8	11.7	6.0	33.7	19.8	28.7
Action sequencing	13.2	4.5	36.2	12.6	33.5	9.4	5.2	42.6	13.6	29.2
Implementing										
Actuating	17.4	6.0	36.6	10.1	29.8	13.3	8.6	36.3	8.1	33.7
Checking	4.7	2.5	31.1	20.0	51.7	3.4	3.1	25.8	21.7	46.0
Adjusting	3.5	1.2	17.1	21.3	57.0	3.9	1.8	20.9	25.8	47.5
Output										
Demand responses	2.3	1.9	13.4	14.7	67.6	2.9	2.3	11.7	15.9	67.1
Resource changes	15.5	7.6	22.5	14.9	39.5	13.8	6.5	29.2	19.6	30.8
Total scale mean			38.04					37.38		

based worker (Table 5.4). The only management process identified as "exactly like me" by a greater percentage of household managers who were not the home-based worker was actuation. The difference in the percentage of household managers responding "exactly like me" was especially large for the management processes of demand clarification, resource assessment, adjusting, and monitoring resource changes.

For their own family work, home-based workers/managers also engaged in standard setting (i.e., demand clarification and resource assessment) and adjusting more often. This is reflected in their higher mean scores for these items (Table 5.4). Furthermore, as a group, they engaged in these management practices more consistently than their counterparts who were household managers but not home-based workers. The greater consistency of use is reflected in the smaller standard deviations for the two standard-setting items and adjusting. Finally, the overall score for the family work items was higher for the household managers who were also the home-based worker than for the household managers who were not the home-based worker. This statistically significant difference suggests that household managers may transfer the management skills used in their home-based employment to their family work tasks. On the other hand, more extensive family management may be necessary if a person is to perform the roles of both employee and family manager. Said another way, this finding may also indicate that work, whether home-based or family in nature, is work to these home-based workers/managers and that more work requires more extensive management.

In summary, one of the ways homeworking households and families make it work for them is managing. All household managers scored above the midpoint on the management scale. When the household manager also was a home-based worker, the score was higher on the management scale. When both household management and home-based work management are the responsibility of one person, management is practiced even more frequently than when the responsibilities are split. Not only do home-based workers/managers do more management, but they also do it differently. They practice more standard setting and adjusting.

LINKING FAMILY FUNCTIONING TYPES AND MANAGEMENT STYLES

The functioning style of families is also a precursor and indicator of the way that a family manages its household or family tasks. Deacon and Firebaugh (1988) talk of family systems having subsystems that are managerial (i.e., instrumental) and personal (i.e., affective), respectively. The family manages its everyday activities in a way that is well defined and articulated in the managerial subsystem. But this sphere of activity takes its cues for what is important from the personal subsystem. Importance stems from family values

Table 5.4
Means, Standard Deviations, *t*-values, and *p*-values for Family Work Management Scale, *N* = 899

Management concept	Home-based worker, *n* = 482		Not home-based worker, *n* = 417		*t*-test for differences	
	Mean	Standard deviation	Mean	Standard deviation	*t*-value	*p*-value
Input						
Goals	3.3	1.4	3.2	1.5	1.5	0.13
Planning						
Standard setting	4.0	1.0	3.9	1.1	0.9	0.36
Demand clarification	4.0	1.1	3.8	1.3	2.9	0.004*
Resource assessment	3.6	1.2	3.5	1.3	2.5	0.01*
Action sequencing	3.4	1.3	3.5	1.3	0.1	0.93
Implementing						
Actuating	3.2	1.4	3.4	1.4	1.2	0.23
Checking	4.1	1.1	4.0	1.1	1.1	0.28
Adjusting	4.3	0.9	4.1	1.1	2.3	0.02*
Output						
Demand responses	4.4	0.9	4.4	1.1	0.2	0.83
Resource changes	3.6	1.4	3.5	1.4	0.9	0.38
Total scale	38.0	5.5	37.4	6.4	2.2	0.03*

*Statistically significant at the .05 level or less.

and purposes. From this base, the family derives goals around which it organizes its managerial activity. How would we know what we wanted to be without the influences of family members? In what ways do we want to make a difference in the lives of those we care for? How do we know the ways our emotional needs for belonging and sharing get met without experience in loving and sharing? The personal subsystem provides the framework and impetus for activities to meet such needs; the managerial subsystem provides the framework for activities that secure the material and physical well-being of the family and its environs.

In addition to responses that yielded a family functioning score, this study of home-based working families examined management strategies for the family unit using two different methods. The first analysis used a multivariate research model to explore why managers manage as they do. Management scores, the dependent variable in the model, were examined using a set of determinants including education of the manager, variables describing family structure and functioning, and characteristics of the home-based work (Table 5.5).

The only two factors affecting the management score were autonomous family functioning and income from the home-based work. The more autonomously the family members functioned, as measured by the family functioning scale, the less the manager managed. This may indicate that when family members operate more independently, it becomes more difficult or meaningless

Table 5.5
Factors Related to Family Work Management, $N = 899$

Variable	Significant effects
Education of the manager	
Household size	
Number of members requiring care	
Autonomous functioning	
Manager owns a home-based business	
Net home-based work income	+
Home-based job is hectic	
Other employment	
Constant	
$F(8, 799) = 12.77$, significant at .001 level	
Adjusted $R^2 = .10$	
$N = 899$	

Note: Effects were statistically significant at the .05 level or less.

to implement family management behavior as assessed by the scale. For example, checking and adjusting as work or activities are completed may not occur as frequently if each family member operates in an individualistic fashion. The more income was derived from home-based work, the more the manager managed. Higher levels of income may simply require more intense efforts, including management activities, to achieve.

In the second analysis to delineate further the relationship between how the family functioned and how it managed, family management scores were matched to each defined family type and hybrid type. Closed families and the 149 families who scored closely on the time, space, and energy dimensions approximated the average for managing well, but other family types showed significant variation. The relatively random families managed less extensively while the open/closed family type scored much higher than the average for all families. This is consistent with the first model, which found that the more autonomously family members function, the less management is practiced. This assumes members of random families operate more autonomously than do members of other identified functioning types. Figure 5.2 shows the deviation from the mean management scores of the family management scale by family types.

In summary, one of the ways homeworking households and families make it work for them is managing. All household managers scored above the midpoint on the management scale. When the household manager also was a home-based worker, his or her score was higher on the management scale. When both family work management and home-based work management are the responsibility of one person, management is practiced even more frequently than when the responsibilities are split. Not only do home-based workers/managers do more management, but they do it differently. They practice more standard setting and adjusting. The more income generated by the home-based work, the more management is practiced. However, the more autonomously the family members function, the less family management is practiced.

ADJUSTMENT STRATEGIES IN HOMEWORKING HOUSEHOLDS

Many authors[9] have suggested that home-based work provides an effective way to balance the demands of paid employment and family responsibilities, particularly for women. The family has the potential to reduce the pressures from home-based work by assuming a lighter work load when important family activities are planned, or to modify their standards for household production during times of pressure in the home-based work. If it can be assumed that income-producing activities take precedence over household work and/or leisure, then the question of time management becomes a question of the choice of strategies for increasing the time devoted to home-based work.

Figure 5.2
Deviation from the Mean Family Work Management Score by Family Type,
n = 823

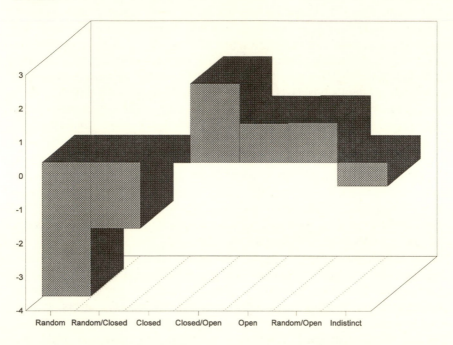

Previous Research on Adjustment Strategies for Competing Work and Family Demands

Very little research has been completed that indicates the mechanisms by which competing work and family demands are met. That a shifting takes place between the demands of home-based work and those of the family has been shown by Ahrentzen (1990), Beach (1987), and Christensen (1988b). Through observation of 15 homeworkers and their families, Beach (1987) noted that the "work time" reported in daily logs by the respondents was, in fact, not uninterrupted work time. Rather, it was often interrupted by children, household chores, and telephone calls. Ahrentzen (1990) found a considerable amount of role overlap between home-based work, household responsibilities, and leisure in her study of 104 homeworkers. The strategies used to minimize conflicts among these competing activities were a strict scheduling of work activities (setting times when people could call, for instance); maintaining a separate work space; restricting access to the work space; and establishing boundaries between work activities and family activities by starting, eliminating, or relocating activities outside the home (entertaining and socializing away from the home, for example).

Insights into the strategies that might be used by homeworking families can be found in research on approaches used to accomplish household responsibilities when both husband and wife work outside the home. In one of the first studies to focus on time-management strategies, Berry (1979) suggested that a "time-buying" consumer would use time-saving meals and time-saving shopping. Examples included buying food in quantity, patronizing less-crowded stores, shopping by catalog, using convenience stores, and purchasing prepackaged food items. Sharpe (1988) focused on two strategies: (a) substituting the labor of others in the household for women's household labor and (b) substituting market goods for women's household labor. She found that women used a market substitute, meals purchased in a restaurant, to replace their own time in meal preparation and cleanup. Furthermore, married women were able to substitute their husbands' labor for their own labor in household tasks. They also had more opportunity to substitute the paid services of others or the services of household durables for their own labor in the home.

Strober and Weinberg (1980) have asserted that several potential strategies or combinations of strategies could be used by women working outside the home to economize on time: (a) substituting capital equipment (i.e., household durables such as dishwashers) for nonmarket labor, (b) substituting the labor of others (e.g., paid help, husband, or children) for women's nonmarket labor, (c) reducing the quality or quantity of household labor or working more intensively or efficiently when doing such work, (d) decreasing the time allocated to volunteer and community work, and (e) decreasing the time allocated to leisure or sleep. Nickols and Fox (1983) replicated and extended the work done by Strober and Weinberg by comparing the strategies used by employed wives with those used by nonemployed wives. They concluded that employed wives did not substitute capital equipment for their nonmarket labor, nor was the labor of other family members substituted for that of the wife. The families of employed women were more likely to use strategies such as purchasing meals away from home or using disposable diapers. Employed women did not spend less time in volunteer and community activities, sleeping, or other personal care, but they did spend less time in leisure.

Research Results on Adjustments Made by Homeworking Households

In the special case of homeworking households, a broader range of strategies should be available than two-earner households enjoy. In particular, the allocation of time among paid work, household labor, leisure, and personal maintenance could be changed more readily because of their spatial proximity.

The purchase of human resources through hiring help, either for the home-based work or for household chores, was a strategy used by only a quarter of the homeworking households in the nine-state sample (Winter, Puspitawati, Heck, & Stafford, 1993). Almost half (47.4%) of the sample, however, had family and friends help out, individuals who were probably less likely to be paid. More than half of the sample also reported using one of five other strategies. Reducing housecleaning time was the most popular strategy, followed by reducing sleeping time, cutting down on social activities, reducing time spent with the family, and eating out or bringing food in.

Theoretically, time-management strategies used in households in which the household manager was also the home-based worker could be expected to differ from those used in households in which the household manager was not the home-based worker. Preliminary analyses revealed that this was true. Household managers who were also the home-based worker had higher levels of education, were less likely to be married, more likely to be male, more likely to report full-time rather than part-time employment, and had lower household incomes and smaller household sizes. This group also was more likely to report reallocating personal time and less likely to report obtaining additional help than household managers who were not also home-based workers. In both groups, respondents from households with higher incomes who reported that demands of the home-based work were greater at some times than others were more likely to report reallocation of personal time as a strategy than those from households with lower incomes or in which the demands of home-based work were relatively constant throughout the year.

Although reallocation of personal time is used more often as a time-management strategy among households with home-based work than obtaining additional help is, the choice of strategy varied according to whether the household manager was also the home-based worker. Individuals who fill both roles are more likely to report the reallocation of personal time, usually their *own* time, than are individuals who manage only the household. Conversely, household managers who are not the home-based worker are more likely to report using a different strategy, obtaining additional help, to meet unusual demands from home-based work.

Total household income, all or part of which was derived from the home-based work, was also a significant factor in using a variety of time-management strategies to meet the demands of the work. When more income will be gained from meeting the deadlines of the home-based work, individuals employed full-time are more likely than individuals employed part-time to obtain additional help.

A final conclusion is that even though being more dependent on home-based work for income means that the household will endeavor to meet its demands, experience, as measured by age, helps ease the pressure. Reallocating personal time becomes less necessary as the household gains more experience in handling the demands of the work.

SUMMARY AND CONCLUSIONS

Family Composition

The households and families surveyed in this study of home-based work emerge as a stable population dominated by married couples with children or adult-only families. A majority of the home-based workers were married men living in full-nest families. They were business owners who had lived in their present community for nearly 2 decades.

Having children 18 years or younger in the home depressed the number of hours spent in paid work, and having children under the age of 6 affected paid work hours even more. Many home-based workers did not purchase outside child care. Thus it could be assumed that home-based employment was used as a coping strategy to ease child care needs. However, it is also clear that some households engaged in home-based work do use child care. Male home-based workers experienced fewer negative effects on their work hours than female home-based workers.

Having children also affected the size and type of home-based work. Families with children were less likely to have large-scale businesses, to own their own business, or to be involved in seasonal work.

Family Management and Family Functioning

One of the ways that homeworking families and households make it all work for them is by managing. All the household managers interviewed in this study scored above the midpoint on a family management scale. When the household manager was also a home-based worker, scores on the management scale were even higher. Home-based workers/managers engage in more standard setting and adjusting than do household managers who are not home-based workers. The more autonomously family members function, as measured by a family functioning scale, however, the less management is practiced. Comparing respondents' scores on the family management scale with scores on the business management scale showed that managerial strategies employed in business life are different from those practiced in family life.

Adjustment Strategies

Because the nature of home-based work varies, so does the amount it intrudes into family life. For example, clients coming into the home can be potentially disruptive to family activities and to the home-based work itself. Also, hectic times for the business elicit a variety of responses to alleviate the pressure. There are also better matches between certain family functioning styles and different types of home-based work. Families who value new experiences would be expected to enjoy a business that brings them into contact with new persons or new situations and to be less bothered with intrusion into family life. Families who value their privacy would rather limit their contact with clients.

In the special case of homeworking households, a broader range of strategies to deal with intrusiveness should be available than two-employee households enjoy. In particular, the allocation of time among paid work, household labor, leisure, and personal maintenance could be changed more readily because of their spatial proximity.

A final conclusion is that working at home may not be amenable to every type of family structure and composition. Home-based workers and their families may be just as stressed at the end of a workday as workers in other types of employment. The inherent nature of home-based work is diverse, and the type of work may be a more important determinant of its fit with the family than whether the paid work is based in the home or elsewhere.

NOTES

1. Life stage is a shorthand designation for an individual's or family's position in the life span as determined by age and normative or nonnormative life events such as entering the work world, marrying, becoming a parent, divorcing, being a single parent, remarrying, being married with responsibility for the care of elderly parents, or being widowed.

2. For further explanation of this trend, see Diebold Automated Office Program (1981); and McLaughlin (1981).

3. Paid work hours for men and women and family work roles are discussed more fully in Ericksen, Yancey, and Ericksen (1979); Farkas (1976); Gordon and Kammeyer (1980); and Marsh (1981).

4. See Gramm (1975); and Hill and Stafford (1985).

5. All multivariate research models in this book refer to regression procedures, either as ordinary least squares (OLS) regression or as a logistic regression depending on the nature of the dependent variable in the model. The OLS regression was used in the case of a continuous dependent variable such as income. If the dependent variable was binary in nature, meaning it had a value of either 0 or 1, a logistic regression procedure was used. For further discussion of either procedure, see standard statistical references such as Kmenta (1986).

6. Further insight into the managerial concepts underpinning this study can be obtained from Bubolz, Eicher, and Sontag (1979); early editions of Deacon and Firebaugh (1975, 1981); Edwards (1970); the two editions of Gross, Crandall, and Knoll (1973, 1980); Knoll (1963); Maloch and Deacon (1966); Nickell, Rice, and Tucker (1976); and Paolucci, Hall, and Axinn (1977).

7. Other family time-use research has been conducted by Key (1990); Morgan, Sirageldin, and Baerwaldt (1966); Robinson (1977); and Sanik (1981).

8. Further references to family managerial studies are listed in Berger (1984).

9. For examples, see Horvath (1986) and Voydanoff (1987).

Chapter 6

The Community Connection

Suzanne Loker, Alma J. Owen, and Kathryn Stafford with the assistance of Ramona K. Z. Heck, Barbara R. Rowe, and Elizabeth Scannell

INTRODUCTION

Home-based work is usually framed as a benefit to the family that does this work for income. Without income, however, families are a net deficit to a local economy. Services are provided by local communities, but there would soon be no services or local economy without residents who own homes, pay taxes, and spend money at local stores. Home-based work is an example of the closest connection between income generation, traditionally performed outside the home, and families. In spite of the relationship between community service needs and community service funding, almost nothing has been written on the role of home-based businesses and wage workers in individual and community economic well-being and development.

Changes in local economies—fewer industrial jobs, a larger service sector, and increasing numbers of working mothers and two-earner families, as well as lower net incomes from agricultural production in rural areas—have implications at family, community, regional, and national levels. Families and individuals who have lost income or jobs because of one or more of these economic changes often look for other ways to replace income with minimal disruption to other parts of their lives. They want to continue to live in a community where they have established their homes with familiar neighbors, services, and other surroundings. Often another family member is employed nearby. Perhaps they are well on the way to paying for the house they have made home.

This chapter looks at the connection of home-based work and the community with emphases on differences in populations. For workers living near metropolitan areas, employment disruption may be remedied by finding another job. For those with less access to labor markets, income alternatives are more difficult to find. Each type of worker has different needs and objectives in engaging in home-based work. Flexibility and convenience of the workers and their families are paramount in home-based work situations in or near urban environments. These communities may be less supportive of home-based work than ones where work is imported to home-based employees and/or home-based businesses provide otherwise absent goods and services to the local population. These two perspectives are displayed in the literature about home-based work and community development.

This chapter begins with a brief review of the economic development literature. Because home-based work and self-employment have been more deeply explored as a rural development strategy and because many of our findings support rural/urban differences from a community perspective, rural economic development and self employment are explored in some detail. The larger interface between the community and home-based work is explored in four areas: (a) sustaining both home-based work and a residential climate, (b) developing home-based work as an economic incentive for local communities, including the support it provides to local businesses, (c) describing the economic contributions of home-based work to the larger political and economic domain, and (d) explicating the context of the nine-state study's respondents in their communities and in the United States.

Home and work spheres overlap generously in all types of work (Staines & Pleck, 1983; Voydanoff, 1987). For 58.9% of U.S. workers, employment takes place in the counties in which they live (U.S. Bureau of the Census [BOC], 1991a). For these workers, the community and the workplace are, by definition, domains that have a great deal in common. Air, water, roads, parks, museums, and shopping districts are but a few of the physical aspects of this shared environment. Intangibles such as legal constraints, neighborliness of residents, and safety also influence the environment in positive or negative ways. All these are shaped by geography and by the persons and institutions that make decisions in a community.

Home-based workers balance an even more intimate environment—the competing demands of work and life. For them, the workplace is subsumed by the residential component of the community, with all the benefits and constraints one strives for in a home environment. This leads to unique issues of legality, zoning, space use, conflict, and opportunity.

In the context of community concerns about home-based work, the popular press, educational materials, and public policy focus on taxes and zoning. Legal entities that implement local decisions about taxes and zoning may be counties, townships, or subdivision covenants, thereby increasing the complexity of legal issues for home-based workers.

State-level attention includes taxes and zoning but extends to concerns about regulation (e.g., licensing, pollution control, and worker protection). Efforts at the state level also include oversight for production and distribution within and outside the state.

Because large metropolitan areas have their own economic development offices and strategies, branches of state government have initiated economic development efforts to focus on portions of their states that do not have such organized efforts to enhance the relative income of the state. These units seek to create jobs, retain and expand existing businesses, assist counties in supporting their infrastructure, and improve the economic welfare of families in their areas without the need to move into urban areas and tax already strained social services. Many states and some industries view home-based work as a way to secure economic advantage while keeping costs both to institutions and to individuals low in the early stages of development.

Previous Research on Economic Development

In recent years, it has become commonplace to promote small-business development and self-employment as a component of economic development equal in importance to industrial recruitment. Because 74.6% of the sample for the nine-state study were businesses, a brief review of the literature on economic development follows. Because the role of home-based businesses and wage workers in community welfare and economic development has not been addressed specifically in the economic development literature, the emphasis will be on the role of small business and self-employment in economic development, especially in rural areas.

Small business and self-employment. Economic development literature has generally addressed the relationship between the large- and small-business bases and the level of economic well-being of the country in terms of population, jobs, and income (Birch, 1987; Brock & Evans, 1986; Brown, Hamilton, & Medoff, 1990; Solomon, 1986; Steinmetz & Wright, 1989). The start and continuation of industrial firms and the large number of urban areas have played a major role in the economic development of the country (Amos, 1987; Hansen, 1972, 1988; Mayo & Flynn, 1989).

Major themes in the economic development literature are public policy formation and consequences (Bartik, 1991; Bruno & Tyebjee, 1982; Fox & Murray, 1991; Mokry, 1988) and issues such as tax incentives for businesses (Steinnes, 1984). Some have specifically developed a public policy framework for small-business development within communities (Aram & Coomes, 1985; Berney & Owens, 1985).

Rural areas, small business, and self-employment. Traditional economic development policy and research have not yet fully addressed the complex nature and dynamics of rural economies; therefore, it is still difficult to design and implement effective strategies in rural areas that promote small-business development and entrepreneurship (Amos, 1987; Aram & Coomes, 1985; Bartik, 1991; Berney & Owens, 1985; Bruno & Tyebjee, 1982; Hansen, 1972, 1988; Kent, 1982; Steinnes, 1984). Researchers are now rapidly expanding the frontier of rural economic development research and policy (Barkley & Hinschberger, 1992; Fox & Murray, 1991; Fuguitt, Brown, & Beale, 1989; Hansen, 1988; Miller, 1985, 1989, 1990, 1991; O'Malley, 1994).

Mokry (1988) has suggested that more attention be paid to indigenous business enterprises in rural areas and to examining how to remove the barriers to such business and self-employment activities by building a supportive environment. Henry, Drabenstott, and Gibson (1987) have also argued that the uniqueness of rural areas demands specific research and policy attention. O'Malley (1994) has reported the preliminary findings of a new demographic study by Kenneth M. Johnson of Loyola University of Chicago and Calvin Beale of the U.S. Department of Agriculture. These demographers have uncovered a major "rural rebound" or an economic rebirth of certain rural areas; businesses are playing an important role in this demographic and economic trend (O'Malley, 1994).

Although there are regional and state differences, small business and self-employment fare well in rural areas both in the incidence of new starts and the survival rate for the time period from 1978 to 1986 (Lin, Buss, & Popovich, 1990; Miller, 1985, 1990, 1991; Whatmore, Lowe, & Marsden, 1991). Rural areas are competitive with urban areas in fostering new business starts. Miller (1991) has shown that in rural areas small businesses grow faster and survive better than large corporations. Yet the surviving small businesses in rural areas expand employment opportunities at about half the rate of such businesses in urban areas. Flora and Johnson (1991) have concluded that small firms are the fastest-growing segment of business enterprises in most sectors of metro and nonmetro areas. In addition, small businesses often play a major and vital role in the economic activities of rural communities. Rural new businesses contribute substantially to employment opportunities and diversification (Lin et al., 1990).

Aronson (1991) and others (e.g., Casson, 1991) have begun to conceptualize the self-employment experience manifested as labor market behavior; however, little attention has yet to be paid to possible rural and urban differences. Moreover, there is a paucity of empirical work that specifically incorporates rural dimensions in analyzing individuals and their self-employment experiences. No attention has been paid to specific groups such as immigrants, minorities, women, or the disadvantaged within rural areas.

Previous Research on Home-Based Work and the Local Environment

Butler (1988) investigated the effects of local zoning on home-based work. Her specific analyses will be shared in topical sequence. In general, she has suggested that legal challenges of home-based work may develop as home-based work grows in popularity. Lozano (1989) has noted that home-based workers can be thought of as an "invisible work force" and has examined the effects of home-based work on the traditional organizational structure of the businesses and their ongoing operations.

A few researchers contributing to this book have used rural/urban variables in other analyses of home-based work. Heck (1992) found that higher work hours in home-based work, lower total family income, and more seasonal work occurred in towns of less than 2,500 population, rural areas, and farms than in urban areas. Furry (1993) compared home-based workers and their work by rural and urban residence. Home-based workers in rural areas were older, less educated, and more likely to be single, had fewer children, had lived longer in their communities, and made lower incomes. These workers were more often doing seasonal work and had been engaged in the work for a shorter period of time than other urban workers. Rowe and Arbuthnot (1993) studied rural home businesses and reported that businesses with a product as opposed to a service had higher net business incomes; those with in-state sales had lower incomes.

SUSTAINING HOME-BASED WORK IN A RESIDENTIAL CLIMATE

Butler (1988) framed home-based work as a balancing act between personal property rights and community interests. She suggested that "the potential to interfere with the residential character of a neighborhood" (p. 197) was the real issue for the community. Securing and using income are activities of interaction for the family and the community in several ways. The community provides jobs for workers, consumers for products and services, and outlets for consumers to purchase the goods they need for their everyday existence. A family uses employment as a means to an end: to secure a quality of life for its members.

Characteristics of the Family and Community Interface

Previous chapters have included information about the business, employment, and family situations of the respondents in the nine-state study. Some of that information and other characteristics of the home-based workers and their families are also important in the context of the community in which home-based workers reside.

Family employment characteristics. Respondents to the survey reflect the family characteristics expected of home-based workers. Eighty-five percent (84.7%) of the workers were married; 87.0% of their spouses worked full-time, 7.3% worked part-time, and the rest were not currently employed. About 26.1% of the home-based workers also held jobs outside the home, and an additional 60.6% had worked outside the home prior to the year of the nine-state study.

Years of residency. Overall, higher years of residency may reflect some differences in the investment home-based workers and their households made in the community. Thirty-eight percent (37.9%) of the home-based workers had lived in their communities for more than 20 years, the largest proportion of the sample. About one-quarter of the households (25.4%) had resided in the community for 11 to 20 years, 16.6% for 6 to 10 years, and 20.1% for 5 years or less. Clearly, home-based workers are longtime community members and thus share many of the concerns of their neighbors.

Eighty-seven percent (87.3%) owned their own homes. The commitment of the family to the community is reflected in its ownership, employment, and duration of tenancy. In addition, three-fourths (74.8%) of the home-based workers had lived in their communities longer than they had been in home-based work. All these results indicate that this sample represents a population wherein place of residence and lifestyle were strong influences in the choice of home-based work as a means of income generation.

Community size. Another salient characteristic of these households is the size of the community in which they reside. Even though most respondents listing farming as a sole occupation were eliminated from the response pool, 7.0% of the sample resided on working farms where they may have done value-added production or retail sales or some nonfarm home-based work. In addition, U.S. Bureau of the Census (BOC) data indicate that 70.3% of the sample reside in counties that are part of a metropolitan statistical area,[1] yet only 53.9% say that they live in communities of more than 2,500 residents. This indicates that home-based workers reside in the less populous areas of their counties, stimulating an argument that the distance needed to travel for services or goods spurs certain home-based work. This can happen in two ways. First, a long commute may keep employment from being cost effective for the jobs available. Second, certain market niches may be available for persons to fill in goods or, especially, services that customers would use more or pay a premium for if they were located closer to their homes.

Occupational classifications reflect both the market needs and the skills of workers. The preponderance of rural dwellers in the nine-state sample, after weighting of the sample and above the numbers indicated by the types of counties sampled, indicated that these persons were seeking to maintain a lifestyle for which income-producing alternatives were minimal. This conclusion was also supported by the fact that 22.9% of the sample households had more than one home-based job, and some did as many as six different types of work.

Data presented in Chapter 3 indicated that 75.0% of the total sample did some work at sites other than home, although this varied significantly by occupation. Cross-tabular analysis of occupations and work site location indicated that workers in marketing and sales and in contracting overwhelmingly used away-from-home work sites (88.0% and 95.6%, respectively). In contrast, service workers were much more likely to use their homes as their sole work site (63.9% worked at home only). Clerical and administrative agricultural workers were evenly split. The other occupational categories displayed approximately the split of the overall sample (75.0% away from home; 25.0% solely at home) with respect to the location of their work sites.

Figure 6.1 displays the length of time the business-owning respondents had home-based businesses. Although during the period from 1976 to 1988 only 29.1% of all firms survived 8 years or longer (U.S. Small Business Administration, 1992), the businesses in this sample (i.e., not including the home-based wage workers) had been in existence an average of 9.5 years. Furthermore, over half (53.6%) had been operating for 6 years or longer and 28.2% for over 10 years (Figure 6.1). In comparison, the wage workers had worked at or from home for less time, an average of 8.2 years. Changing community zoning regulations may have allowed these older businesses or employment options to be grandfathered into housing covenants so that long-term workers can remain in home-based occupations that immigrants to the neighborhood cannot initiate.

Zoning Issues

Zoning has ancient roots, but it became more pervasive during industrialization for sound reasons. Essentially, zoning ordinances are designed to protect the character, integrity, property values, and ambiance of residential districts.

Figure 6.1
Duration of Home-Based Business Ownership, *n* = 670

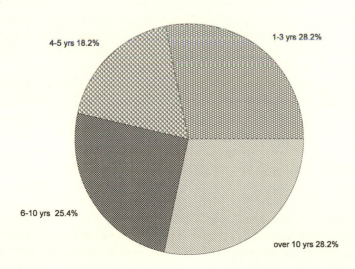

4-5 yrs 18.2%

1-3 yrs 28.2%

6-10 yrs 25.4%

over 10 yrs 28.2%

Traditionally, communities have used geographic perimeters to define residential, industrial, commercial, and agricultural zoning. For home-based workers, these definitions are considered vague, obsolete, or difficult to apply consistently (Butler, 1988). Similarly, the ordinances that implement these concepts lack insight into and accommodation to the changing nature of work.

Agricultural zoning. Agricultural production conveys images of pig or dairy farms, with their accompanying aromas, or crop production, with its potential for water contamination from fertilizer and pesticide use. Traditional agricultural production was deleted from the definition of home-based work for the nine-state study unless products were sold directly to consumers or another form of significant value-added processing was done to the product. Thus farmers remaining in the study were those who grew and sold flowers or organic produce as well as marketers of specialty livestock for breeding.

In most cases the nature of the production (e.g., animals versus flowers or fruits and vegetables) would dictate the acreage and distance from neighbors that would be appropriate for the pollution potential of the agricultural production. Zoning would impede direct marketers of food items from being convenient to their customers.

Industrial zoning. This type of zoning addressed the concern that large manufacturing sites might locate to the disadvantage of residential areas. These zones consist of work sites that contribute to pollution of air, water, and/or sound. Such manufacturing is necessary to the overall level of goods consumption in our society, but society has made a conscious decision to place it away from areas where constant exposure might jeopardize the health and safety of citizens. This sample contains a mix of manufacturing enterprises that are different from the industries that led to the initial industrial zoning prototypes. Though classified as manufacturing, writing computer software, embroidering sweatshirts, and attaching handles to ski ropes do not justify the same environmental controls as paper processing or fuel oil storage and delivery.

Commercial or retail zoning. This zoning is the one most likely to share space with residential areas but under restrictions. Small grocery or "mom and pop" convenience stores often exist in residential neighborhoods of older cities or in small towns. In contrast, suburban neighborhoods usually eliminate even this intrusion of the public economy into the home environs. Rather, shopping is done in a separate area often far removed from home, thereby increasing the time and effort of household and family maintenance.

This pattern is to be expected in the portions of the sample that live in suburbs. Much of the nine-state sample, however, was from smaller communities or rural areas. Although home-based workers in marketing and sales were likely to work at sites other than their homes, 63.9% of the service providers worked at home versus only 25.0% of the total sample of home-base workers. Examination of the actual job descriptions that make up these occupational codes indicates that commercial zoning is not affecting these persons. Yet it is impossible to predict how many persons are constrained in what they would like to sell from their homes if zoning restrictions were eased.

Residential restrictions and variances. Almost every ordinance prohibits the employment of people outside the family and specifies the percentage of floor space that may be allocated to a business. Again, these limitations are relevant only when the home-based business might "change the character of a neighborhood" (Tepper & Tepper, 1980). Professionals who are hired as unrelated employees may be an exception. No zoning ordinance is violated if a homeowner in a nonbusiness situation hires employees outside the family as maids or gardeners on a daily basis. Such inconsistencies in most zoning ordinances might be considered as unequal treatment because they allow upper classes to hire work done but forbid the more common practice of lower classes—hiring employees to work either in the employer's or the employee's home.

Traffic. All of these alternative uses of land in residential areas share one good reason for restricting all businesses or wage working in the home: the potential for increased traffic that contributes to pollution, compromises safety, and may tax the road system. Increased traffic can come from clients seeking services or home sales of goods. Pickup and dispatch of supplies and products by employers or delivery trucks affect traffic and roads even if home-based workers do not deal with the public directly.

The issue of traffic may be one that keeps the level of home-based work, especially businesses, small-scaled. One home-based business owner stated that her neighbors did not mind the candle making in her garage and kitchen until tractor trailer trucks started unloading pallets of candle wax onto the cul-de-sac where neighborhood children played. Such a business owner will have to balance the savings and convenience she derives from working at home with the increased income that more production could yield to her family. This is but one example in which monetary and intangible values have to be reconciled with each other and with neighbors to allow home-based workers to meet the multiple objectives of home and workplace.

The Impact of Zoning Restrictions

The distinction of work and home is even more blurred in the current information age. According to Edwards and Edwards (1994a), "zoning ordinances have not kept pace with the dramatically changing nature of work. Archaic laws treat non-polluting, unobtrusive businesses like someone typing on a personal computer as if they were Wal-Marts or factories" (p.7). They have further estimated that 10% of all localities effectively prohibit people from working in their homes through these unreasonable zoning provisions (Edwards & Edwards, 1994a). For example, in the cities of Chicago and Los Angeles, home businesses are currently prohibited by local zoning laws (Edwards & Edwards, 1994a); these laws may be rationalized relative to the management and use of public utilities or the amount of traffic on neighborhood streets. Zoning laws continue to be unnecessarily restrictive, and they can become obstacles to almost every home business owner or wage worker.

These cautions made researchers expect that a sizable home-based working population would express legal conflicts over their work. Therefore, it was surprising that only 11.9% of the respondents in the nine-state study cited any laws or regulations that created a problem for their home-based work. The three areas that did raise concerns for them were proper waste disposal, state and federal taxes, and government regulations related to licensure and storage of hazardous materials. A few noted issues of insurability and hiring laws. Neither community size nor years of residence in the community were significant in determining whether home-based workers must contend with legal issues. This finding could suggest that there is no basis for concern that excessive regulation is squelching the home-based entrepreneurial impulse. Perhaps workers in this sample have overcome these issues. Alternately, workers who would have been affected by zoning may have been deleted from the homeworker pool either by never starting or by getting out in the early years of business. They also could be operating outside the law, without the proper licenses, tax numbers, and records.

Occupations and the law. Caution must be exercised in analysis of the effect of zoning on occupations because so few home-based workers expressed concerns. However, the occupation-related issues are instructional. In the nine-state study, only 15.9% of the home-based workers were pursuing occupations considered to have potential pollution issues that may be affected by related zoning ordinances. These were in the mechanical and transportation trades (11.6%) and agricultural work (2.7%). An additional 14.9% of the home-based workers were contractors in plumbing, excavation, welding, and so forth. Though focused on persons whose work site is the home, the nine-state study included workers if they had no other permanent work site and did some of their work at home. For example, plumbers do their work away from home but schedule appointments and do their billing and other paperwork at the home site. Both the mechanical and transportation and contracting categories included workers for whom the "dirty" part of their jobs was at the work site, not in the residential area where they lived.

Of the occupations expected to have legal disputes, only one cited legal issues at a significant level above the overall average of 11.9% of the home-based workers. Although the number was small ($n = 27$), mechanical and transportation workers were twice as likely to have legal issues with which to contend. Nearly half cited storage and waste disposal as the legal problem for their work. The nine-state study lacked further specificity to determine the exact nature of the difficulties.

In service occupations, only 12.6% (12.5% of 109 or $n = 14$) had legal issues; traffic and noise pollution were cited. This finding is because these home-based workers saw clients in their homes. The service occupations in the nine-state study were predominantly high-traffic occupations or those that had peak traffic times. Beauticians and dog keepers predominated in those who cited legal concerns although peak traffic is a classic concern of day care providers for children or elder care facilities. Service workers also cited waste disposal as an issue of concern, which can be explained by the janitorial and other cleaning services in this occupational category. Only clerical work seems relatively free of legal restrictions.

Community issues. Zoning ordinances are usually more stringent in areas of higher population density. Thus residents of larger communities were expected to have more zoning and other regulatory problems. There was no pattern that was based on population density of their residential neighborhoods (i.e., as measured by farm, rural, or town size) for whether or not home-based workers had legal concerns, although the 11.9% who did cite legal issues were most likely to be in counties that are part of metropolitan statistical areas. They also resided in the more populous parts of those counties (i.e., in towns of more than 2,500 persons).

Again, these results could indicate that persons have already self-selected out of homework that violates zoning restrictions in their areas. It could also indicate that longevity of residence, responsible, considerate local citizenship, and the positive role these businesses and employment serve in the neighborhood have alleviated potential conflict. Over 89.6% of the home-based workers citing legal issues ($n = 107$) were home-based businesses, indicating that businesses have more concerns than wage workers. In this case, the relatively modest size of the businesses in the sample may partly explain the lack of community conflict. The customers may be neighbors. The roads may not be blocked by cars at peak hours. These are issues of responsible citizenship in small communities and rural areas, not business zoning.

The Impact of Home-Based Work on Community Ambiance

Underlying zoning restrictions is a desire to sustain the residential character of the neighborhoods in which people live. Promotional signs, traffic created by customers and delivery services, and the use of home space for work can alter the peaceful character of a neighborhood.

Traffic issues. For home-based workers, traffic issues were evaluated by client visits to the home and by delivery service use. Almost two-thirds (64.2%) of the sample saw clients at home. Nearly half (48.6%) of the home-based workers seeing clients at home saw them at least two to three times per week. Home-based workers living in small towns were most likely (70.5%) and those in cities with a population over 2,500 least likely (59.9%) to see clients at home. These results reflect expected differences of these respective environments and reinforce the theme that home-based workers are woven into the fabric of community life in jobs and places where interaction at home is expected and acceptable. Other residential categories (i.e., rural farms and nonfarms) were between the small-town and large-city dwellers. For these home-based workers, both the distances between residences and type of work may dictate less contact by clients at home.

In the total sample, those in clerical and administrative support and in management occupations were much less likely to see clients at home (36.9% and 39.7%, respectively, versus 64.2% for the entire sample). But of those who did, 67.8% and 62.2%, respectively, saw clients at home at least two or three times a week. In contrast, 77.2% of persons in professional and technical occupations saw clients at home, although only 26.8% of these saw clients at home more often than once a week. Thus, although home-based professional and technical workers are dominated by persons who see clients, they are less likely to face frequent disruption from client visits.

When occupations represented in the nine-state study were examined for likelihood of rural residents seeing clients at home versus urban ones,[2] service workers and contractors were more likely to see clients in their homes (i.e., 94.8% versus 77.5% for service workers, and 73.7% versus 51.5% for contractors, in rural versus urban areas). Examination of the actual work descriptions in the two occupational groups indicated that there is little difference between the rural- and urban-dwelling contractors. The types of jobs were similar in the service occupations except the rural group had a preponderance of beauticians, and urban service workers included more child care providers.

Space. Chapter 3 addressed many of the issues of intrusion by work on the space used for home and family activities, essentially a family concern rather than a community one. This section considers the impact of work space usage by the home-based worker in relation to neighbors and the neighborhoods in the community.

All home-based workers did some work at home, but the extent to which household space was used differed in several ways. Fifty-six percent (55.9%) of the home-based workers had space devoted exclusively to their home-based work. Of the rooms used exclusively for work, an office, workroom, or study was most often cited as the space set aside for home-based work. Another example of exclusive space was a garage or an detached building.

Forty-four percent (44.1%) shared work space with some family activities. Although an approximately equal percentage of men and women reported that they did home-based work in shared space, women were more likely to share the room with family activities "always or often" when they worked. Male workers reported that they "seldom" or "sometimes" shared work space.

To some extent, home-based work space within homes affects how visitors or neighbors coming by are handled and determines whether activities performed with visitors or neighbors present are carried out in close proximity to the ongoing home-based work activities. Overall, 51.0% of the home-based workers used only one room of their house for work, 28.0% used two rooms, and 21.0% used three or more. The picture that emerges from this profile is of home-based work that is performed adjacent to, rather than integrated with, family living. This contrasts with Beach's (1989) findings of an integrated work-family space and may reflect both the larger sample size of the nine-state study and the nature of the work. Beach primarily studied home manufacturing, whereas in the nine-state study there was a more diversified set of home-based employment and the dominant occupations were those that often required more intellectual absorption than work performed by hand did.

The extent of integration versus proximity varied by gender and occupation of the worker. Higher family expectations (leading to fewer hours worked) of female home-based workers is a corollary assumption. Female home-based workers may well be expected to maintain neighborhood responsibilities. This expectation leads to the disadvantage often cited by home-based workers that neighbors feel free to drop by at any time. Neighbors often call on home-based workers to interrupt work schedules to watch for United Postal Service deliveries, let a repairman in, or do the day duty for the neighborhood watch. With the steady increase of single-parent households and of families in which both spouses are employed, home-based workers fulfill familial and household functions for themselves and their neighbors who work away from home. Having someone at home in the neighborhood enhances the safety and security of all residents. Thus home-based workers allow many sectors of the economy to continue to pretend that all families have a member at home during the workday so that repair and delivery industries need not extend service hours.

HOME-BASED WORK AS ECONOMIC DEVELOPMENT FOR LOCAL COMMUNITIES

Community infrastructure and availability of community services to support both home and work requirements often influence residential and home-based work choices. Community infrastructure includes the permanent physical and legal groundwork on which living and working in a community are based. Physical variables include water, electricity, sewage capacity, and roads. Communities generally balance zoning, tax revenue, and infrastructure issues in making policy decisions about land use. Infrastructure issues were beyond the scope of the nine-state study, but future research should explore direct and indirect relationships between infrastructure and home-based work characteristics and profitability.

Services Use by Home-Based Workers

One way to examine the extent to which home-based workers contribute to their community's economy is to look at their use of local services. Table 6.1 displays the percentage of home-based workers who used banking, accounting,

Table 6.1
Usage and Distance Traveled (in Minutes) to Use Services by Residency of All Home-Based Workers, $N = 899$

| | Residency | | | | | | | |
| Service | Town of 2,500 or more | | Town under 2,500 | | Rural nonfarm | | Farm | |
	Percent Used	Mean distance	Percent Used	Mean distance	Percent Used	Mean distance	Percent Used	Mean distance
Banking	83.9	9	82.2	9	87.6	13	92.1	14
Accounting	47.2	23	40.2	21	48.6	23	50.8	22
Legal	31.5	23	20.7	18	28.8	25	38.1	19
Supply	85.6	18	85.1	30	91.0	27	90.5	21
Copying	60.4	9	36.8	12	57.1	14	54.0	13
Post office	100.0	8	100.0	6	100.0	9	100.0	9
Grocery store	100.0	7	100.0	10	100.0	13	100.0	15
Medical care	100.0	12	100.0	15	100.0	18	100.0	18
$n =$	485		174		177		63	

Note: Distance was expressed in minutes for *only* those who traveled to obtain the service; those who did not travel to use the services were excluded from the distance analyses.

legal, supply, and copying services classified by the location of their residence: city, small town, rural nonfarm, or farm. Banking and supply services were most often used; they were necessary for nearly all business owners and most wage earners, although usage varied slightly by residential location. Residents of small towns used all services less than other home-based workers did. Because businesses were the more likely users of services, Table 6.2 displays the types of services and the frequency with which they were used. Table 6.2 also displays the mean travel time to services. Because it was assumed that all households would require access to food stores, routine medical care, and postal services, respondents were asked for the time needed to get from their homes to these services. As expected, the average distance and time needed to access these necessary personal services were lower than for business services.

Aggregate Financial Contributions of Home-Based Business

Another way to gauge the financial contribution of home-based work to businesses and local governments (through taxes) is to examine the expenditures they make to run their businesses. In the nine-state study, respondents were asked both the gross and net business income declared on their income tax forms. In every state, over 60.2% of income from home-based businesses went for expenses (Table 6.3). In three of the states, expenses exceeded 74.0% of business income. In the nine states studied, home-based businesses contributed $31 billion to their communities in the form of business-related expendi-

Table 6.2
Usage and Distance Traveled (in Minutes) to Use Services by Home-Based Business Owners, *n* = 670

Service	Percent used	Percent who traveled for use[a]	Mean distance
Banking	90.3	90.0	10
Accounting	53.3	42.5	22
Legal	31.6	27.2	19
Supply	93.1	78.9	24
Copying	49.7	49.1	11
Post office	100.0	100.0	8
Grocery store	100.0	100.0	9
Medical care	100.0	100.0	14

Note: Distance was expressed in minutes for only those who traveled to obtain the service; those who did not travel to use the services were excluded from the distance analyses.

[a]Reflects percent of businesses, *n* = 670, and not a percent of those who used the service.

Table 6.3
Home-Based Business Expenditures by State and Urban/Rural Areas, $n = 670$

State	State aggregate	Urban (top) and rural aggregate	Urban (top) and rural per business
Hawaii	$716,847,867	$619,997,102	$44,163
		96,850,765	33,340
Utah	863,682,680	569,154,483	25,520
		294,528,197	29,855
Iowa	984,523,916	540,064,415	18,095
		444,459,501	14,209
Missouri	3,026,545,164	1,506,766,999	34,250
		1,519,778,165	37,852
Michigan	3,158,648,303	2,108,974,519	38,012
		1,049,673,783	29,260
Ohio	7,491,637,339	5,617,337,052	49,475
		1,874,300,286	28,191
Pennsylvania	2,730,405,612	1,423,940,274	13,932
		1,306,465,338	22,496
New York	11,120,524,559	10,513,745,457	77,545
		606,779,101	13,282
Vermont	920,321,911	161,577,340	41,722
		758,744,572	50,486
Total	31,013,137,349	23,061,557,641	—
		7,951,579,708	—
Average per business	—	—	44,305
		—	26,073

Note: States are listed in geographic order from west to east. Aggregate figures were extra polated from per business mean expenditures in last column.

tures.[3] As suggested earlier, public policy and specifically tax policy are important themes of the economic literature (Bartik, 1991; Bruno & Tyebjee, 1982; Mokry, 1988; Steinnes, 1984). Special tax treatment may be viewed as a vehicle for attracting businesses to a particular area.

Four of the states in the study were more urbanized than the other five. In the more urbanized states of Michigan, Ohio, Pennsylvania, and New York, aggregate business expenses were larger for the urban areas than for the rural areas. The urban impact was greater in these states not only because there were more urban households, but also because expenses for each business were greater in the urban areas. The only exception was Pennsylvania, in which the rural businesses had greater expenses.

In the more rural states of Hawaii, Utah, Iowa, Missouri, and Vermont, the impact of business expenses on the economy also was greater in the urban areas because of the greater number of households in these areas. In three of these five states, average per business expenses were greater for rural businesses than for urban businesses. In all of these states except Hawaii, the rural businesses spent a greater proportion of their gross income on business expenses than did the urban businesses.

Economic Impact of Home-Based Work

Taxes paid for the home and home-based work are obvious financial benefits that home-based work contributes to a community. Almost 9 out of 10 (87.9%) home-based workers owned their own homes and, therefore, paid local and state property taxes. Compared to the national population (see Chapter 3), homeownership rates among home-based workers were considerably higher. Although only 20.5% of the home business owners ($n = 670$) borrowed money or found others to invest in their business, the process added or kept investment funds in communities that would otherwise be dispatched to financial centers for investment elsewhere.

Another way to look at the impact of home-based work on local communities is to explore the manner in which goods, services, and job creation are provided to the community by the home-based work. Data for these contributions come from the home-based businesses in the sample, not the wage workers. Eighty-eight percent (88.1%) of the home-based business owners in the sample sold most of their products or services within their state or within one hour's drive of their homes. In addition, 86.9% of the business owners bought supplies for their businesses within their state.

These persons contribute to the local economy in two ways. Revenues for local governments are provided from the sales tax collected for goods and, in some cases, services sold in the small towns and rural areas that compose nearly half the sample. Perhaps as important, these businesses provide goods and services to a population that would otherwise have to travel farther for them.

On the other side of the counter, these businesses are also consumers of other local businesses' goods and services. As Table 6.2 indicates, the percentage of businesses that used the services of other businesses varied from 31.6% for legal to 90.3% for banking services. Home-based business owners traveled to their banks rather than performing all their banking functions by mail or phone, and they banked as well as made photocopies at businesses relatively close to their own. In contrast, 15% of the home business owners who required supplies had them delivered, probably because they had specialty needs not well filled by local vendors.

Procurement of supplies took the greatest mean travel time for those who did not have them delivered; travel to accountants was a close second. Both these types of services enjoyed rather large usage by home business owners. Accounting services may be a market niche that is not saturated in communities with significant numbers of home businesses. The potential for supplying home-based businesses is more difficult if the supplies are industry specific. This is an area that warrants further study to discover if coordination at local levels, including adding product lines or extending business hours, could bring more of these sales closer to the site of the home businesses if there is enough of a market.

Filling Market Niches

Home-based workers, especially those who own and run businesses, can be vital to their community in ways beyond the income they bring into the family and spend in the community. Many businesses were instituted to fill market niches not well met in established trade areas. In some areas, the client base was too small to support a separate outlet. Especially in rural areas, travel to a larger outlet was not cost effective for either producers or consumers. To the extent that occupational choices shore up a community's economic diversity, they influence the extent to which laws, ancillary services, and infrastructure impinge upon and are affected by home-based work.

The range of occupations revealed by the nine-state study indicates that home-based workers fill a range of market niches within local economies. For some, this was a preplanned, deliberate occupational strategy. Others were driven by instability within their local economies. The 1980s and 1990s have been marked by widespread early retirement options, departure incentives, and forced layoffs as both large and small companies have been forced to adjust to global economic changes. In rural areas, the farm economic crisis of the 1980s and the continuing reevaluation of agricultural profitability have also driven many to alternative work options. In labor markets where employment is scarce, low-paying, or insensitive to the simultaneous demands of work and family, home-based work can be pursued when other work runs out, as a supplement to away-from-home income and as a full-time, long-term option.

Home-Based Work as Supplemental or Alternative Income

Over the life course, home-based workers combine away-from-home employment with home-based work as necessary. For the great majority of the sample households, home-based work provided supplemental rather than primary income. For 61.0% of the households, home-based work provided less than 50% of the household's income. On average, home-based work provided 39.7% of household income. As for the home-based workers themselves, in only 61.0% of the survey households had the home-based worker ever been employed away from home before 1988, the year before the survey was conducted. Over one-quarter (26.1%) of the home-based workers were moonlighting currently, working away from home while also pursuing home-based work. For 11.4% of the sample, home-based work provided at least 90.0% of the household income.

The multiplier effect of economics says that a community benefits the more times money is turned over in the local economy. The centralization of jobs and shopping areas to encompass a larger geographical area, however, has had a minimizing effect on some communities' ability to sustain themselves. By filling market niches, undertaking unusual jobs that do not need the support of surrounding major market and industrial areas, home-based businesses can make a positive difference in the livelihood of a community.

A community's infrastructure, including other in-place businesses and the skilled labor pool, influences the attraction of new businesses to the community. The use of local services by home-based workers raises the gross sales of such businesses and increases the likelihood of these services being available locally. Availability of these services, in turn, attracts complementary or dependent businesses and services to the community.

HOME-BASED WORK AND LARGER POLITICAL AND ECONOMIC DOMAINS

It would seem that most political issues that relate to home-based work would impinge upon and be regulated by community, town, or city legislation. In some instances, however, home-based work has gained the attention of legal or economic entities in larger political bodies.

Though applying only to businesses, the recent U.S. Supreme Court decision that interpreted the tax deduction granted home office use in a more restrictive manner than in the past will probably affect the economic advantages of part-time home-based work in the future (*Commissioner v. Soliman*, 1993). The case involved an anesthesiologist who saw patients at three different Maryland and Virginia hospitals but was denied tax deductions on his home office, even though he was not provided office space in any of the three hospitals. The Court ruled that his home office, where he did all his billing, did not meet the criteria for "principal place of business." They argued that a comparison of the "relative importance of the activities performed at each business location and the time spent at each place" (p. 646) established the hospitals rather than the home office as his principal work location, thus creating a new standard for deductibility of home office expenses.

Fewer home-based work spaces for business activities will qualify for tax breaks under this legal interpretation. For example, the contractors in the sample who work at sites other than the home but have no office other than their homes may not be able to earn tax advantages for their home offices. In contrast, the wage worker who works at home on a computer terminal and connects electronically with a main office would qualify for the deduction. This new ruling may influence the feasibility and profitability of a home location for certain home business owners and wage workers.

Home-based work sometimes has an economic advantage to home and community in taxation issues and displays a significant interaction with state as well as federal governments. For example, in Hawaii, a 4% excise tax is imposed on goods at each stage of the production process. Thus the tax imposed on each succeeding stage of manufacture includes the amount of the previous 4% tax as a portion of the basis for taxation at the current stage. This compounding of tax adds an extra 1% to the cost of a product in just five turnovers of goods, that is, the number of times goods are sold to another person as part of getting them from the raw stage to the consumer. If home-based workers sell goods they have taken from raw product to retail, they do all the value-added production. When factory-produced goods and home-produced goods are sold at the same price in the market, the sales of the home-produced goods make more money available to the family and for use in local economies because less of the sales price goes to the state government as value-added taxes.

The Macroeconomic Effects of Home-Based Work

Home-based work is not peripheral to the income stream of the U.S. economy. Using the narrower definition of home-based work from the nine-state study (i.e., at least 312 hours per year and no other office), 6,077,578 households had a member engaged in home-based work. If each of these more than six million households earned $17,835, home-based work contributed $108.4 billion dollars in net personal income in the U.S. economy. The mean net income from home-based work was $20,119 in urban areas versus $13,673 in rural areas.

Using the prevalence rate—based on the survey response that someone in the household was engaged in home-based work—to impute a national figure, 9,017,224 households in the United States have at least one adult engaged in home-based work; the corresponding impact on the economy would be 48.4% higher than the amount obtained using the narrower definition of home-based work.

Given a mean of $34,017 in household income in 1988 for the national population, home-based work contributed 3.4% of total personal income on a national basis. By comparison, nonfarm sole proprietorships contributed 3.9% of household income, and farming contributed 1.8% of household income (BOC, 1993).

In addition to its contribution to household income, the contribution of home-based work to the economy can also be gauged by comparing the gross and net income of home-based businesses with comparable figures reported on federal income tax returns by various types of businesses. At the prevalence rate of the nine-state sample, there were projected to be 4,529,452 home-based businesses in the United States in 1989. As reported on their tax returns for 1988, these home-based businesses pumped an estimated $247 billion of gross income directly into the economy, 36.8% as much as nonfarm sole proprietorships, 53.2% as much as partnerships, and 2.5% as much as all corporations (BOC, 1993).

In the nine-state study, home-based businesses' average net income from the business reported on their tax returns for 1988 was $15,628. At that level of net income, home-based businesses contributed $70.8 billion to the economy in 1988. By comparison, nonfarm sole proprietorships reported $126 billion in net income, partnerships reported $15 billion, and corporations reported $413 billion on their tax returns for 1988 (BOC, 1993). In other words, home-based businesses reported 56.3% as much net income as all nonfarm sole proprietorships, 473.3% as much as partnerships, and 17.2% as much as all corporations.

Miller (1990), among others, has shown the importance of small businesses to the rural economy. In the nine-state study, the rural home-based business grossed a mean of $38,229 and netted a mean of $11,925 for the household. Using the nine-state study's sampling frame, the projected impact of the home-based businesses on the economies of nonmetropolitan counties in the United States was $64 billion in 1988 gross income. Their contribution to household income in these nonmetropolitan counties was $20 billion in net income in 1988. Finally, the wage workers generated a mean net income of $26,324 in urban areas compared to a mean of $19,787 in rural areas. Their economic impacts on the local and national economies were considerably less than those of the home-based businesses because of their relatively low prevalence rate.

Family Financial Impacts of Home-Based Work

It is one thing to discuss the impact of home-based work on communities and nations; family financial impact offers another dimension to the benefits this form of employment provides. The conclusion reached after analyzing income data from the nine-state study is that home-based work has a substantial impact on the household's financial well-being and, therefore, its level of living. In the households in which at least one adult was involved in home-based work, net income from that work provided nearly 39.7% of the family's income. Because over 46.1% of the sample lived in small towns and rural areas, locales that often suffer from chronically low family incomes, this 39.7% can mean the difference between security and deprivation in a family budget.

Another way to gauge the positive contribution of home-based work to family financial welfare is to look at its magnitude relative to the poverty threshold, a measure of the minimum temporary income needed to sustain a family in the United States. This measure is used to determine eligibility for various transfer payments and in-kind support from state and federal levels and to assess the financial well-being of geographic areas. In 1989, the poverty threshold was $12,091 for a family of four (BOC, 1990b). Although the average household size in the sample was somewhat less than four (3.4), the average net income just from home-based employment was $17,835, making these households, from their home-based work alone, almost half again better off financially than those at the poverty threshold (Figures 6.2 and 6.3). Median income from home-based work, although not as high, nearly equaled the poverty threshold at $11,188.

Median income statistically adjusts for any unusually high incomes from home-based work, but the statistical calculations cannot adjust for nonnumerical issues such as a home business being in an expansion year that resulted in nominal losses for only the current year. They cannot accommodate the goals and strategies of families who plan for home-based work to account for only a portion of the family's income. This may be done to maintain time for family activities or to maintain employment with a firm that offers health benefits necessary for the welfare of the entire family.

Implicit Income Values

The income figures are consistent with the usual practice of two earners or one earner with two jobs in many families in the United States today. This is only part of the income picture. So far, the impact of home-based work on the economy has been discussed in terms of monetary income. Home-based work also affects household finances in the implicit income garnered either through saving money otherwise necessarily spent on employment or through being able to do tasks related to home and family work while meeting income production demands.

Popular literature cites some advantages of home-based work: saving money through not eating lunch out as often, saving money on workplace clothing, and cutting down or eliminating travel time and costs associated with traveling to another work site. Of the home-based workers in the nine-state study who were also the household managers, only 9.7% cited savings as a primary advantage of choosing this form of work. Another 5.5% cited cost cutting and low overhead as a primary advantage.

Pratt (1984) and others have found that a major motivation for women to be employed at home was to be able to care for their children while making some money. Chapter 5 discussed the extent to which the nine-state study indicates that home-based work does not always allow for the simultaneous care of children. Some workers, however, have combined child and elder care with business, by watching their own children while getting paid to care for others, for example, or by running an elder care home that includes aged relatives, as one respondent did. These unique situations obviously dovetail family responsibilities with income, and savings from not purchasing such services with income generated.

Fan (1993) analyzed data from the nine-state study to ascertain the implicit income, or money that would otherwise have to be spent, that results from being

Figure 6.2
Financial Contribution of Home-Based Work to Households in Urban Areas, *n* **= 527**

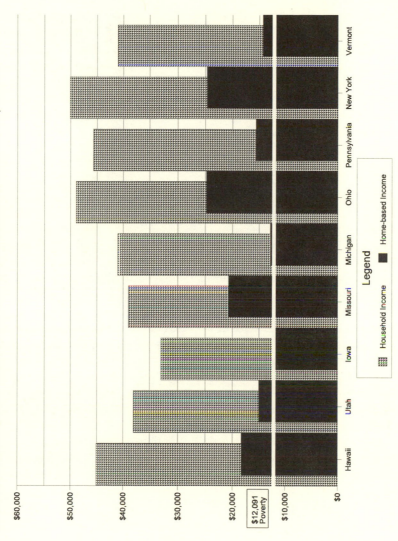

Figure 6.3
Financial Contribution of Home-Based Work to Households in Rural Areas, *n* = 372

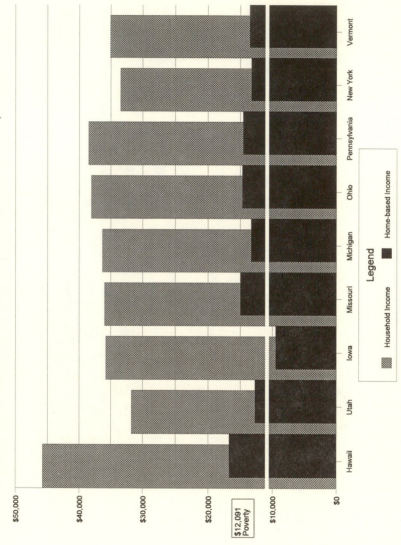

able to care for children while engaged in home-based work. For families that indicated they had youngsters who required care and none was obtained outside the home, the estimated implicit income ranged from $2,564 to $1,652, further adding to the money available to the household for the purchase of other goods and services.

THE COMMUNITY CONTEXT: MICRO TO MACRO ANALYSIS

A look at the communities in which home-based workers resided can provide information about the role the local environment can play in the choice and success of home-based work. Information about the counties in which the nine-state sample of homeworking households resided was compared with all counties in the United States using FIPS codes data.[4] This section of the chapter summarizes the meaningful comparisons among the homeworker sample from the nine-state study, the resident counties, and the general population in the United States. Table 6.4 compares general characteristics and demographic information from these three data sources. Note that 58.9% of the population within the resident counties worked in that same county; clearly, many are following centralized jobs, and the meaning of mobility in the work sphere of their lives is different than for their nonwork time. In other words, job mobility is not the same as residential mobility or migration (Coontz, 1992).

Female Employment Patterns

Although in the nine-state study the percentage of the labor force that was female was close to the national percentage (41.9% and 45.2%, respectively), the sample resided in counties with an unusually high percentage (53.2%) of females in the labor force. It was unexpected that the female percentage of home-based workers would be this low, given that so much of the popular literature on home-based work has focused on female workers. Article after article on home-based work has stressed the advantage of home-based work to women, the normative caregivers in most families, allowing them to meld their family responsibilities with income generation. Heck, Saltford, Rowe, and Owen (1992) found that both men and women used care providers for children, indicating that home-based work is not the unparalleled advantage touted in the literature.

Another potential reason for the lower employment rate than expected for women may be that some of the businesses in the sample were reported as being the work of the male householder but were, in fact, two-person businesses. Even in businesses like long-haul trucking and contracting work, where the husband was usually the one going out on the job, other family members may have been responsible for the home base, taking calls, scheduling work, picking up parts, and/or keeping books. Women may or may not report themselves as joint

Table 6.4

Comparisons of Characteristics from the Nine-State Sample of Home-Based Workers, Resident Counties, and U.S. Population, 1989

Characteristic	Nine-state sample	Counties where sample resided	U.S. population
Percent who worked in county of residence	100.0	58.9	na
Percent of labor force that is female	41.9	53.2	45.2
Median age (all household members)	30.5	33.6	32.6
Median years of education	14.0[a]	12.5[b]	12.6[b]
Mean family size	3.6	3.1	2.6
Percent single-parent households	3.3	na	14.8
Female	2.0	6.3	11.7
Male	1.3	na	3.1
Median family gross income	$38,872[c]	$35,356	$32,191[c]
Median household gross income	$38,000[c]	na	$27,225[c]
Mean per capita income	$15,318[c]	$16,227[c]	$16,630[c]
Median net home-based income			
All workers	$11,000[c]	na	na
Wage workers	$20,000[c]	na	na
Business owners	$10,000[c]	na	na
Mean net self-employed income[d]	$15,628[c,e]	$18,618	$15,241[c]
Percent self-employed[d]	74.6[c,e]	11.8	10.3[c]
Percent home-based self-employed[d]	74.6[c,e]	na	74.7[f]

Source: Data from nine-state study and from *1990 Census of Population and Housing* (1991a), *1990 County Statistics*, and *Statistical Abstract of the United States* (1991d & 1993) by U.S. Bureau of the Census, Washington, DC: U.S. Government Printing Office.

[a]Home-based worker only. [b]Adults over age 25. [c]Denotes that figure was for 1988 and not 1989. [d]Nonfarm. [e]Based on interview questions, business ownership was equivalent to self-employment in the nine-state sample. [f]Work at home and compensated for work at point of May 1991 U.S. Bureau of the Census Survey.

partners in the business because the legal structure was that of a sole proprietorship. Yet the demands of the business did absorb the time and energy of the wives who helped out. These businesses may have been profitable because of this unpaid labor pool at home.

Age of Family Members

The home-based workers in the sample were drawn from counties with a median age of 33.6, which is higher than the median age of 32.6 for the general

U.S. population. This is probably because the research was conducted in states that have, on average, older populations. For example, the Sunbelt states were not represented in the nine-state study. There is an overrepresentation of farming states that have been losing younger populations to the Sunbelt, notably Iowa, Missouri, and Ohio. New York and Pennsylvania, though represented, were not sampled in their areas of highest population concentration (i.e., New York City and Philadelphia). These metropolitan areas are statistically younger in age than the more rural areas of these states, which, like their midwestern rural counterparts, are losing their younger residents to urban and/or warmer climates where job markets are more promising.

The median age of the family members of households that included home-based workers was younger than the median for the counties (30.5 years versus 33.6 years, respectively). This is explained in part by the relatively larger size households—they contained more younger members thereby lowering the median age.

Educational Level of the Home-Based Worker

With respect to education, the counties from which the home-based worker sample was drawn are similar to the U.S. population as a whole. Counties containing home-based workers had a median completed education level of 12.5 years compared to 12.6 years for the U.S. population. The sample of home-based workers had completed about 1.5 years of education more than the U.S. median education level and more than others in their communities. Thus home-based workers in this sample were more educated than their immediate neighbors and than the national average. This is consistent with findings that self-employed persons are better educated than the general population (Aronson, 1991; Evans & Leighton, 1989; Fredland & Little, 1981).

Family Size

Besides consisting of younger members on average, families with home-based workers were also larger than the average U.S. family or the families in the counties of the respondents. This is consistent with one of the reasons often cited for engaging in home-based work: to be available to care for younger family members. Some households had businesses that allowed them to mesh work and family responsibilities more intimately by providing such services for others as well as for their own family members. Although child care is often thought to be synonymous with preschool, this is not always the case. Home-based workers can combine after-school care of their children with many different kinds of work.

Finally, one of the most striking demographic characteristics of this population is that many had adult parents and children at home. This is an increasing trend in the United States but may be exaggerated in this sample, where many businesses used other household members as part of their labor force.

Single-Parent Households

This family type constituted a very small portion of the sample. Although available county and national census data are not directly analogous to the nine-state study's sample, they are comparable in an instructive manner.

Single-parent households composed only 3.3% of the home-based worker sample, and one-third of the single parents were males. For the counties in which the sample resided, 6.3% of the households were headed by single-parent women, compared to the national average of 11.7% female household heads. Single-parent males head only 3.1% of households in the United States. Clearly, single-parent homeworking households are extremely rare.

This finding has important policy implications for welfare reform policies that encourage self-employment or home-based work for low-income and single-parent populations. The findings from the nine-state study cast doubt on the feasibility of this option, especially for female heads of single-parent households. Although home-based work is thought to assist in making time use more flexible for the worker, it does so within definite constraints. Time use may be flexible in that activities can be scheduled to be more convenient to the worker than is the case with structured 8-to-5 employment. Nevertheless, home-based work remains a time-intensive way to make money. There may be certain times of the day, week, or year that are inflexible for certain industries, times that are also inflexible in the schedule of parents caring for children.

Income

Five measures of income are reported in Table 6.4: The first three income measures, median family gross income, median household gross income, and mean per capita income, related to the income families and individuals use to fulfill their needs and wants. The fourth measure, median net home-based work income, was compared with the fifth measure, net self-employment income, to draw the most analogous comparison available from census sources.

The median family and median household gross incomes for the sample were higher than those available to their countywide neighbors or the nation as a whole, but median per capita income (total median family income divided by the average number of persons per family) was lower than the other measures. The home-based working families had families that were larger than those of their counterparts in their counties and much larger than the national average. This demographic characteristic partially explains the low per capita income, because it decreases as each family member is added into the calculation.

Thus the counties represented in the sample have populations doing better economically than the national average for families but not as well by individual measures. Again, this may be a Sunbelt effect for income (i.e., the sample did not include these states). The loss of incomes for city residents of New York, Detroit, and Philadelphia, all of which were not included in the nine-state study, may have no net effect because both lower and higher incomes in these areas persist.

The income medians for home-based work were disaggregated into those for wage workers and businesses to compare business income to self-employment income for the resident counties and the United States. Although the median net income from all home-based work was $11,000, it was less for home-based businesses ($10,000) and more for wage workers ($20,000). The mean net self-employed income in the nine-state study was $15,628 in 1988. For the counties in which the home-based businesses were located, mean net income from nonfarm self-employment was $18,618 (in 1989 dollars), somewhat more than for the home-based businesses in the nine-state study. The mean net 1988 income from nonfarm self-employment within the U.S. population was very similar to that in the nine-state study. At 74.6%, the percentage of self-employment (i.e., business owners who were all self-employed) in the nine-state study was around seven times higher than in the resident counties or the general population. Because the home-based businesses must maintain economic viability in the same markets as these self-employed persons, it can be concluded that running their businesses from home allows them to stay in business with a lower profit margin, lending weight to the argument about the cost savings of doing business at home.

SUMMARY AND CONCLUSIONS

This chapter contained information on the interface of home-based workers with their community. Clearly, there are issues that need to be addressed at the point where home-based work intersects the community that surrounds it. Although most home-based workers in the nine-state study did not cite legal or regulatory issues that impinged on their home-based work environment, traditional separations of work and residential life do not necessarily conform either to the needs or to the demands of home-based workers.

Community Interface

The majority of home-based workers have long histories of both working and living in their local community. Indeed, we have argued that the desire to sustain an economic livelihood in the community of residence is, for some home-based workers, a driving force in establishing and sustaining home-based work. The by-products of their work may burden the local infrastructure in certain ways, for example, by causing more traffic and air, noise, or water pollution. On the positive side, they enhance safety and convenience by being present in their neighborhoods when others are at their places of employment.

Using space in the home for work is in the limelight because of the recent Supreme Court decision establishing both "the relative importance of the activities performed at each business location and the time spent at each place" as criteria for tax deductions of home-based business space. This decision will continue to influence the manner in which both the Internal Revenue Service and individuals who want to work from home view the benefits of home-based work.

Community Development

Home-based work can be considered a form of community development for its potential as an alternative or supplemental income source for residents and for its economic multiplier effect on a community and region. Availability of particular services (i.e., due to occupation of the home-based worker) and use of services of other retailers were benefits of having home-based workers located in the community. Additional research on the direct and indirect relationships between infrastructure and home-based work characteristics must necessarily be explored at the level of the community in order to understand the full range of assets and liabilities that home-based work offers. This study offers guidelines on what issues to explore.

Implications for Neighbors and Nations

Comparison of the sample respondents with census data from the county in which they resided and the United States in general reveals that these are not strikingly unusual persons. They are a little older, in larger households, and somewhat more educated. They have higher family incomes but lower per capita incomes than residents in either their surrounding county or in the United States as a whole. Home-based work seems to serve as an alternative form of income generation that allows families to be larger and, in some cases, to take care of extended family members.

These results point to an even stronger need to respect the family issues in home-based work. The home-based workers involved are entrenched in communities with large families and their attendant responsibilities and are contributing to the economic livelihood not only of themselves but also of other businesses in their communities. The work they do provides needed services and further humanizes the face of business and workers in the United States today.

NOTES

1. The BOC designates metropolitan statistical areas as those counties that contain or are contiguous to a city with a population of 50,000 or more. This population level of the county in which the home-based worker resided was used in this measure of population density (BOC, 1990a).

2. A nonurban area was based on the size of community variable. It included the farm and rural nonfarm residents as well as those who lived in villages with less than 2,500 in population.

3. Aggregate contributions of home-based work to the economies were calculated from the statistical prevalence rate of the businesses for each state and stratum of the sample multiplied by the average expenditure for each business in that state/stratum. See Table 6.3 for the state-by-state totals.

4. The Federal Information Population Statistics (FIPS) are codes that enable researchers to make the link between county location and county-level aggregate information from census data. Numbers (FIPS codes) are used to match other data sets to these data. Data from counties where each participant in the nine-state study resided were matched to the same variables in the U.S. population. The context in which community variables were evaluated was clarified with this comparison technique, providing information that distinguishes the communities in which home-based workers live from the general U.S. population.

Chapter 7

Three Years Later

*Suzanne Loker, Charles B. Hennon, and Ramona K. Z.
Heck with the assistance of Barbara R. Rowe, Mary
Winter, Margaret Fitzgerald, and George W. Haynes*

INTRODUCTION

Home-based work has shown growth and popularity in recent years, but what happens to individuals who participate in it over time? As families and individuals change, how is their continuation in home-based work affected? Does home-based work serve the needs of the individuals and families over successive years?

One way to examine the continuation of home-based work is to use job tenure statistics for the general labor force as a baseline. As of January 1991, median tenure for workers with the same employer was 4.5 years, and median tenure for workers in the same occupation with the same or different employers was 6.5 years (Maguire, 1993). The national statistics for job turnover are harder to produce, and no usable data source exists.[1]

The average job tenure of about 9 years for the home-based workers[2] in the nine-state study might lead to the conjecture that the tenure of a home-based worker is longer and the number of job changes fewer than for the general labor force. More likely, home-based work was chosen because it accommodated the life and family of the home-based worker.

Even though business continuations in any setting are difficult to measure, examining business failures is important because the majority of the sample were home business owners. The Small Business Administration defines business failure as a "closure of a business causing a loss to at least one creditor" (U.S. Small Business Administration [SBA], 1992, p. 437). A comparison of the number of closings during the calendar years 1989 and 1990 shows that the number of business failures was 20% higher in 1990 than in 1989 (SBA, 1991). The latest period of business failures reported is between 1990 and 1991 (counted for January through September of both years), and the number of failures more than doubled to 47.2% (SBA, 1992). The number of years that firms survive has been most recently studied over the time period of 1976 to 1988. During these 12 years, 76.1% of all firms survived 2 years or more and 47.9% survived 4 years or more (SBA, 1992).

This chapter briefly reviews existing literature on job tenure and turnover and the viability of businesses over time. Comparisons are then made between the original sample of 899 workers and a follow-up survey taken 3 years later. Reasons for exiting home-based work are explored, and those who were doing the same home-based work are compared with those who exited for positive reasons and those who exited for other reasons. Finally, factors associated with the continuation of home-based work are analyzed.

Previous Research about the Continuation of Work

Job continuation has been studied in two major areas. First, job tenure, particularly in relation to the worker's human capital development, has been studied by economists. Job tenure has been found to be a function of the size of the rents (i.e., wages for the worker) and the characteristics of the workers. Second, the personnel literature has addressed job turnover both as a staffing concern at the institutional level and as an individual behavioral phenomenon for the workers. This body of literature has examined the rate of job turnover and factors related to turnover behavior.

Job tenure. Maguire (1993) has suggested that job tenure is related to (a) age of the worker, with older workers having longer job tenure, (b) employment trends, with rapidly growing employment translating into low job tenure, (c) education and training, with higher levels of education attainment being related to longer job tenure, and (d) compensation and benefits, with greater compensation being related to longer job tenure. Job tenure is also related to other worker demographics, including gender, race, and ethnicity, with gender effects being related to age and the effects of race and ethnicity varying by gender. In addition, job tenure is related to self-employment status, with the self-employed experiencing much longer job tenure than other workers.

Job tenure with the same employer has been shown to be related to occupation stability, with women changing occupations more rapidly than men (Sehgal, 1984). Involuntary occupational change has been found to be related to younger ages of the workers, higher levels of education, and lower incomes after the change (Markey & Parks, 1989). For 1 in 8 workers, such change was the result of the loss of a previous job. Voluntary occupational change is more common. More than one-half of the workers switching occupations were motivated by better pay, working conditions, or advancement opportunities.

Brown and Light (1992) studied the variability of job tenure measures using data from the Panel Study of Income Dynamics (PSID) and suggested using imputed measures for job tenure that are internally consistent. Also using PSID data, Topel (1991) found that after 10 years of current job seniority, the typical male worker in the United States has a wage 25% greater than the average.

Eriksson (1991) integrated traditional human capital theory with a theory of permanent job switches and developed a model that simultaneously determines capital investments, wages, and labor mobility. This model has shown that predictions of an individual's self-investment and wage growth through the life cycle were consistent with those suggested by traditional human capital theory. Furthermore, the probability of job changes, with and without job tenure, declines at a decreasing rate as age increases, and this probability is negatively correlated with current wages, both with and without holding age constant (Eriksson, 1991).

Job turnover. Igbaria and Siegel's (1992) study of information systems personnel examined the effects of individual characteristics, job type, role stressors, boundary-spanning activities, career outcomes, and job characteristics on turnover propensity. Their results indicated that age, organizational level, organizational tenure, job tenure, and number of years in the computer field were all negatively correlated with the intention to leave the organization. Job involvement, career plateau, promotability, salary, organizational commitment, job satisfaction, and satisfaction with progress, promotion, pay, status, and projects were also negatively related to turnover intentions while education and career opportunity were found to be positively correlated.

Both Steers and Mowday (1981) and Baysinger and Mobley (1983) have offered extensive reviews of previous research on job turnover and have criticized this research for a lack of comprehensive modeling. Baysinger and Mobley, in particular, have noted that little research recognized that job turnover is both an individual behavior and an aggregate or institutional phenomenon. Baysinger and Mobley's review of previous research yielded seven interrelated factors that are associated with job turnover: (a) attraction of the present job, (b) future attraction of the present role, (c) external alternatives, (d) investments such as vested benefits and loss of seniority, (e) nonjob factors, (f) integrative constructs, namely, intention to stay or leave and/or commitment, and (g) other variables such as job performance and generalized training. In their conceptualizations, these factors have been combined under various assumptions about their relationship to one another, and the dynamics of the turnover process are facilitated by feedback loops.

Consequently, both sets of authors developed new models for further empirical testing; only the individual-level model of turnover or exit behavior will be briefly summarized here. Steers and Mowday's (1981) model concentrated on the causes of individual turnover behavior. Their model assumed that workers perceive three basic categories of causal agents, namely, characteristics of the individual employee, environmental factors, including the job and its external environment, and the circumstances under which the behavior occurred. These causal agents are all part of a psychological and behavioral process used by the individual worker to evaluate a turnover decision, including accommodation processes following the decision.

Baysinger and Mobley (1983) developed an employee turnover theory with an organizational perspective. Within this broader view, they explored the individual's propensity to exit. They identified the following costs: (a) cost of exiting or staying, (b) opportunity cost of staying or exiting, and (c) transaction costs of exiting. Each cost is related to three dimensions, including individual factors such as age, organizational factors such as technologies, and environmental factors such as job vacancies in the geographical area.

Continuation of home-based employment. No previous studies have explored new start-ups, exits, job tenure, or general turnover rate phenomena over time within the arena of home-based work. Thus all that is known is that the number of home-based workers has likely been growing since the 1980s. It is not known to what extent newer home-based workers may be replacing more experienced home-based workers.

In February 1993, LINK Resources, after conducting a national survey, reported that 39 million or 31.4% of adults in the United States worked either part-time or full-time at home (Sloane, 1993). This number included after-hours homeworkers. Using the 1991 Current Population Survey, Deming (1994) estimated that approximately 20 million nonfarm employees were engaged in some at-home work as part of their primary job, accounting for 18.3% of those employed. Only 40% or 8 million of these were being compensated for their work at home. Of those who were paid or were self-employed, only about half or 4 million worked at home for 8 hours or more per week. Based on these data, Deming (1994) suggested that the incidence of home-based work is on the increase.

Based on the count of 94,312,000 households in the United States in 1990 (U.S. Bureau of the Census [BOC], 1991b), the estimated prevalence rates from the nine-state study can be used to extrapolate the number of home-based workers for the entire country. Using the more restrictive criteria of the nine-state study,[3] the resulting number for 1989 was 6,077,578 households in which at least one family member engaged in home-based work. More detail on the nine-state prevalence rate is discussed in Chapter 3.

Previous Research on the Continuation of Businesses

Previous literature on business continuity is relevant to any discussion of home-based job tenure because home-based businesses constitute 74.6% of the original sample of homeworkers and 73.7% of the follow-up sample. Direct comparisons with the general business failure literature are inappropriate, however, because the selection criteria for the home businesses in the nine-state study specified that the business had to be in existence 1 year before the original 1989 survey. Therefore, failures of start-ups or newer enterprises cannot be explored using these data.

Business continuation is likely tied to financial success, growth, and viability over time, but none of these measures were included in the follow-up data reported here. All that is known is whether the home-based worker in the original 1989 sampled household was still doing the same, other, or no home-based work, either as a home business owner or wage worker.

General business viability over time. Only a minority of new businesses last more than a few years, and what constitutes or promotes success or effectiveness in a small firm remains elusive. The literature on family-owned businesses and other literature on the viability of businesses are relevant for comparisons.

Some researchers have concentrated on family firms (Donnelley, 1964; Hollander & Elman, 1988; Keough & Forbes, 1991; Nelson, 1991; Pratt & Davis, 1986). A home-based business is a special case of family-owned business. In troubled economic times, family businesses often survive when other businesses fail. They survive not because of "good business" but because of the family and its values and economic needs (Keough & Forbes, 1991). Even though family firms may be more likely to survive than other businesses, they do face the problems of succession between generations. Only about 30% of family-owned businesses survive into the second generation of owners (Hershon, 1975; Lansberg, 1988).

Other researchers of business viability have focused on the characteristics of the business owner or entrepreneur for all businesses in general. Studies by Cooper, Dunkelberg, and Woo (1988) and Bates (1989) found that age and education of the business owner were positively correlated with viability of the business. Male entrepreneurs who were nonminorities were more likely to stay in business than were female and minority entrepreneurs (Buss & Popovich, 1988; Cooper et al., 1988; Loscocco & Robinson, 1991; Loscocco, Robinson, Hall, & Allen, 1991). Surprisingly, researchers found that entrepreneurs with greater experience in an industry were no more likely to survive than those with less experience (Buss & Popovich, 1988; Cooper et al., 1988; Kalleberg & Leicht, 1991). Being simultaneously involved in a business other than the one studied was a significant negative predictor of business viability (Cooper et al., 1988; Kalleberg & Leicht, 1991).

Features of the business itself, which reflect organizational context and structure, can predict longevity; these include the industry or product market in which a business is located and the size and age of the firm (Aldrich & Weiss, 1981; Kalleberg & Berg, 1987; Lieberson & O'Connor, 1972). Kalleberg and Leicht (1991) examined small businesses in the midwest to ascertain the relationship between survival and success of the business based on industry differences, organizational structures, and attributes of the owner-operator.

Their findings indicated that older companies were more likely to survive over time, regardless of the gender of the owner-operator or the size of the business. Bates (1989) also found that age of the company was positively related to viability.

Other studies of small business firms have also found that the age and size of the firm are important in determining success and longevity. Jovanovic (1982) concluded that small firms tend to fail at a higher rate than large firms of the same age, and that younger firms tend to fail at a higher rate than older firms of the same size. Studies by Bates (1991) and Dunne, Roberts, and Samuelson (1987) support Jovanovic's claim that the size and age of a firm are important determinants of its financial success.

The literature on economies of scale shows that smaller firms have a higher probability of being excluded from financial credit markets than larger firms because lenders have inadequate information about these borrowers and their products (Stiglitz & Weiss, 1981). Smaller firms are also charged higher prices by lenders for the loans they do get because the administrative costs of processing their loans are high in relation to the size of the loan (Constand, Osteryoung, & Nast, 1991; Gaston, 1989; Krinsky & Roteberg, 1991; Murphy, 1983; Rhyne, 1988; Stoll, 1981; Stoll & Whaley, 1981). Literature on defaults of small businesses indicates that when small firms do obtain loans, they have a higher probability of failing and defaulting on them (Bates, 1991; Jovanovic, 1982).

Edwards (1965) and Scott (1977) have shown that smaller firms also pay higher interest rates in markets where the lender has some degree of price-setting (i.e., market) power. Because 91% of the small businesses recently surveyed by the Federal Reserve Board use commercial banks for some financial services, higher interest rate charges and other financial service fees imposed on small businesses are of importance for public policy (Elliehausen & Wolken, 1990).

Home-based business experience over time. Research on home-based businesses is just developing, and one area that is especially in need of study is the viability of home-based businesses over time. Because home-based businesses are a special case of family businesses and they tend to be classified as small businesses, the longevity research on family and small businesses lays the base for home-based businesses. But the unique nature of home-based businesses may affect their long-term viability in special ways.

A few researchers involved in the nine-state study have examined home-based business experience over time in other analyses. Winter and Fitzgerald (1993) used data from the nine-state study to examine home businesses in which the owner was the respondent. Factors associated with the continuation of the home business included age and education of the business owner, the number of years in business, positive feelings about the work, and expectations about changing attitudes toward the business. Neither income nor attitudes about income from the home-based work were significant predictors of the owner having the same home business 3 years later.

Although their study was not longitudinal, Rowe and Arbuthnot (1993) examined 414 rural households who owned home-based businesses to explore factors that might be related to continuation. Male owners made approximately twice as much money as female owners. Higher levels of education were also correlated with higher incomes. Hours in paid work had a positive effect on net income, and business management practices, as measured by the business management scale from the nine-state study, had a negative effect. Rural home-based businesses were more likely to be in lower-earning service-oriented fields than in higher-income product-related fields, netting business incomes of $11,987 versus $17,430, respectively. Finally, hiring help was related to higher net business income, as was out-of-state sales.

THE UNIQUENESS OF THE FOLLOW-UP DATA OF THE NINE-STATE STUDY

Description of Follow-Up Data

In the spring of 1992, approximately 3 years after the original nine-state study, a 5-minute follow-up telephone interview was conducted by the Statistical Laboratory at Iowa State University. Data obtained from every household that could be located for the follow-up interview were merged with those obtained in the 1989 interview to form a two-wave panel. The purpose of the follow-up interview was to ascertain whether the home-based worker was still engaged in the same or other home-based work and to gather selected other information such as possible reasons for exiting.

The original 1989 sample data were weighted by their relative proportion of the nine-state population and the rural/urban areas of those states. Weights for the 1989 sample were further adjusted for the two-wave panel to reflect the attrition of households within the nine states and their rural/urban stratum. This additional adjustment ensured that households in the follow-up data from each state and stratum represented the same proportions as in the original sample of 899. The follow-up data reported here were weighted,[4] meaning that they were representative of households with a home-based worker in the nine states originally studied.

Of the original sample of 899 homeworking households, 730 (81.2%) were located, contacted, and reinterviewed. In 93.2% ($n = 680$) of the cases, the household manager[5] who was originally interviewed was the respondent in the follow-up, as were 6.8% ($n = 50$) of the home-based workers. One hundred seventy of the 1989 households were not reinterviewed.

The follow-up questionnaire consisted of 11 questions that addressed issues such as:

(a) What proportion of home-based workers continued working at home after 3 years?

(b) What reasons did the reinterviewed households who had ceased working at home since the first interview give for the change?

(c) What characteristics best describe individuals who remain home-based workers compared to those who no longer work at home?

(d) In what ways does information gathered about home-based workers and their families assist in better understanding who is likely to drop out of home-based work? Is it possible to predict who will drop out or continue home-based work?

Following Home-Based Workers over Time

Of the 730 households reinterviewed in 1992, 549 had owned a home-based business in 1989; 181 were wage workers or earners in 1989. By 1992, 520 households had a home-based worker who was still doing the same home-based employment as in 1989. Two hundred ten households were not engaged in the same home-based employment (see Figure 7.1). Of these 210 households, 25 (11.9%) had a worker who was still working at home but at something else.

A majority ($n = 383$ or 73.7%) of the 520 households in which a worker was still doing the same home-based employment at the follow-up were home businesses; 137 (26.3%) were wage workers. These percentages were similar to those in the original sample. Of the 210 households that had discontinued the same home-based employment, 166 (79.0%) were originally home business owners in 1989; 44 (21.0%) were earners. These proportions are close to the original distribution because 74.6% of the workers in the 1989 study were business owners. The continuity of owners over time appeared to be slightly lower than that of wage workers, although the difference was very small.

Representativeness of the Follow-Up Sample

Several comparisons were made between the follow-up sample ($n = 730$ or 81.2%) and the 170 (18.9%) households from the original sample that were not reinterviewed. Citing responses from the original 1989 study, Table 7.1 shows that the home-based workers in the follow-up survey differed in several statistically significant ways from those who were not reinterviewed. Respondents in the follow-up study were older, lived in larger households, had lived in their communities longer, were more likely to be living in rural areas, had worked more hours in home-based work in 1989, had been involved in home-based work for more years, and were less likely to be engaged in seasonal work than those home-based workers who were unavailable for the reinterview. On the other hand, those interviewed in the follow-up ($n = 730$) did not differ

Figure 7.1
Distribution of the 1989 and 1992 Samples, Weighted Data, *N* = 899

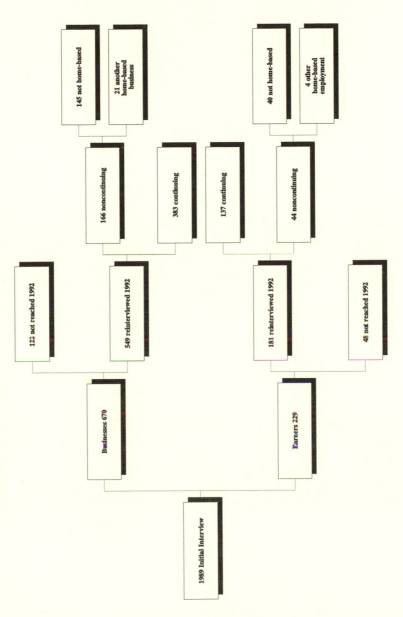

Table 7.1

Comparisons of 1989 Nine-State Data for Follow-Up Households and Those Not Reinterviewed, *N* = 899

Variable	Follow-up households *n* = 730	Not reinterviewed *n* = 170	*t*-value *N* = 899
Worker characteristic			
Male[a]	57.9%	58.5%	.16
Mean age	44.2	40.7	-3.54*
Median age	42	38	—
Mean education	13.9	14.0	.71
Median education	13.0	14.0	—
Mean household size	3.4	3.1	-2.83*
Mean years in community	21.4	13.8	-6.14*
Rural/urban residence[b]	3.1	3.4	3.18*
Work characteristic			
Business owner[c]	75.3%	71.1%	-1.17
Mean gross household income[d]	$42,705	$40,120	-1.14
Mean net home-based work income[d]	$18,132	$16,522	-.70
Total home-based work hours[e]	1,895	1,506	3.82*
Median home-based work hours	2,000	1,092	—
Duration	9.6	7.8	-2.53*
Median duration	6.0	5.0	—
Seasonality[c]	11.2%	23.4%	4.42*

Note: 1989 weighted data. Two-tail test of probability. Estimates based on pooled variance. This procedure is appropriate when variances within the two groups are similar.

[a] ANOVA calculated on means with female = 0 and male = 1. [b] Farm = 1; nonfarm = 2; small town = 3; town of over 2,500 population = 4. [c] *t*-test calculated on means with no = 0 and yes = 1. [d] *t*-values and probabilities reported for log values of income. [e] Number of hours worked in last 12 months.

*Statistically significant at the .05 level or less.

from the rest of the original sample in terms of gender or education of the home-based worker, gross or net 1988 household income, or the percentage who owned their businesses.

These results reflect important differences between the reinterviewed households and those who could not be recontacted. Some of the results reinforce conclusions derived from the cross-sectional analyses; that is, reinterviewed home-based workers had been living in their communities and doing work at home longer. Others illuminate new areas of interest. Over time, the home-based work force may confront negative forces similar to those affecting the centralized work force; for example, both types of work may be unstable or intermittent if the work is seasonal and carried on over annual cycles.

Conclusions drawn from these results have to be considered in the context that, even with appropriate weighting procedures, the reinterviewed sample was composed primarily of older home-based workers in larger, less mobile, more rural households who had a greater commitment to nonseasonal home-based work. All of these characteristics probably made these households easier to contact and more willing to complete the follow-up telephone survey. Any conclusions drawn from the results should take these factors into consideration.

Limitations

There are a few limitations to the follow-up aspects of this study. Although a member of a large proportion of the households that had been interviewed in 1989 was reached about 3 years later, there were still about 18.9% who could not be reinterviewed, and they differed in some ways from those who were interviewed. It is unclear whether these differences reflected characteristics related to unwillingness to continue participation in the study, geographic mobility and difficulty in relocating the participants, other transitions such as marital disruptions or economic difficulties, or exiting from home-based work for other reasons.

The data-gathering technique is also a limitation. Telephone interviews facilitate contacting and reinterviewing a large number of people in a relatively economical fashion. But a short (i.e., approximately 5 minutes) interview is not conducive to gathering in-depth information. Although providing valuable information concerning the number of people still in home-based work, the methodology also did not allow for insightful interpretation of the home-based work situation experienced by the participants. The hopes, fears, dreams, and other subjective thoughts and feelings that people brought to their situations and the pleasures and meanings home-based work held for them remain untapped. Likewise, the fine shadings of meanings contained within or behind answers (e.g., why the person was or was not still in home-based work) were missed.

Another limitation might be the somewhat arbitrary nature of the categories used to order the data. Providing a number to the rate of staying in or dropping out of home-based work was somewhat complex. First, a time base needed to be established. In this case, it was the approximately 3-year period between the two interviews. Second, not all of the original households could be reinterviewed. Thus a decision had to be made concerning how to count these people to calculate retention rates. A conservative answer, and one ultimately used, was to consider that they were no longer engaged in the same home-based work. Another possibility would have been to assign them the same average of continuity or discontinuity in home-based work as found among the various other segments of the follow-up respondents. Ignoring them was another possibility and was also employed in some instances.

Third, decisions had to be made about how to count continuity or discontinuity among the 730 people who were recontacted. Did selling the business, expanding the business out of the home base, retiring, or dying constitute equal reasons for considering the person to be no longer engaged in home-based work? Were those still engaged in home-based work, but in different work than they had been doing when first interviewed, dropouts or survivors?

A decision was made to create different categories of reasons for discontinuing the 1989 home-based work; some were classified as "positive" reasons and the rest as "other" reasons. Positive reasons included those who exited because they outgrew the home-based work, sold the home-based business, moved to another location, or took on a different kind of home-based work. Those who exited for these positive reasons were grouped separately from all other exits. These two categories for exiting home-based work, positive and other, were also used for data-analysis purposes. Although this conceptualization proved useful here, it might be expanded upon or changed in other analyses of these or similar data.

CONTINUITY OF HOME-BASED WORK OVER TIME

Home-Based Work Retention Rates

After 3 years, 520 people or 71.2% of the households reinterviewed in the follow-up were continuing in the same home-based work, providing one retention rate for home-based workers. Some others, however, had outgrown home-based work in a business sense, while others had perhaps outgrown home-based work in a personal (i.e., human capital or need) sense. Thus an additional 3.0% ($n = 22$) had exited their 1989 home-based work for reasons that might be considered to indicate success. This conceptualization assumed that outgrowing the same home-based work, selling the home-based business, or moving to another location defined success. Additionally, some workers ($n = 9$, 1.2%) who were no longer doing the same work as in 1989 took on a different home-based work, another possible indicator of success. Given these considerations, a second retention rate was established by combining positive exits (i.e., those who left for success reasons, including those who exited to take on different home-based work) with those still involved in the same work. Using this calculation, 75.5% could be defined as successful in home-based work.

A third rate was also established. Only respondents who indicated that the worker was no longer doing the same home-based work as in 1989 were asked specifically if this worker was doing any other home-based work. This third rate was based on those who were continuing in the same home-based work (n

= 520, 71.2% of 730) plus those who indicated that they were no longer doing their 1989 work but were still involved in other home-based work ($n = 25, 3.4\%$ of 730).[6] Therefore, this retention rate based on those working in any home-based situation in 1992, either the same work as three years earlier or another endeavor, was 74.7% ($n = 545$ of 730). This retention rate represented people who were actively engaged in any home-based work in 1992.

It appears that a retention rate of 71.2% to 75.5% (continuing, successful, and/or actively engaged) can be reported for home-based workers. Caution must be observed, however, when using any of these terms. For example, the assumption was made that selling the home-based business indicated success or that staying in the same or taking on other home-based work indicated continuation or active engagement. Yet some of the home-based workers had relatively low incomes and some worked extraordinarily long hours. Can this really be defined as success? Information on the conditions of the sale of the businesses was not gathered; perhaps a business was sold because a person could not make a living from it. Perhaps those who changed their home-based work were not that similar to continuing workers. Maybe these home-based workers were not actively engaged but were opportunistic or victims of other circumstances.

A noncontinuing or nonretention rate might be more meaningful. For example, one could ask, "How many people drop out of home-based work over a 2- or 3-year time period?" or "Is home-based work a viable option?" If the focus is only on those no longer in their 1989 home-based work, then a noncontinuing rate of 28.8% can be reported ($n = 210$). If only those who are no longer in *any* home-based work ($n = 185$) are considered, then a nonretention rate of 25.3% is appropriate.

It would appear, based upon the behavior of this sample, that home-based work is at least feasible for the vast majority of those who enter it. In sum, after about 3 years, and considering only those respondents who were reinterviewed and were continuing in home-based work, 71.2% were continuing in the same home-based work; 75.5% were either continuing in the same home-based work, had expanded out of their home-based work, had sold their businesses, or had moved; and 74.7% were still actively engaged in some home-based work, either the same or new endeavors.

Assuming that the 170 respondents from the original study who were not available at the follow-up were also no longer in home-based work, 576 of the original home-based workers were still working at home or had sold or expanded the homework, representing a 3-year continuity rate of 64.1% (576 of 899). This can be seen as the most conservative estimate of the proportion of this sample of home-based workers still actively involved in home-based work 3 years later.

For most occupational categories, between 67.9% and 73.1% of the workers were still doing the same home-based work at the time of the reinterview. A

larger proportion of continuers were managers (85.0%) and clerical and administrative support workers (82.3%), whereas only 59.5% of people working in
services were doing the same work approximately 3 years later.

These results indicate that people working in services were the most likely
(40.5%) to have exited home-based work over the 3-year period. Managers
were the least likely, with only 15.0% exiting during the interval between the
surveys.

Reasons for Exiting or Leaving Home-Based Work

One of the questions asked of the respondents to the follow-up survey was
whether the home-based worker was still doing the same work. In response,
28.8% indicated no. The reasons for exiting the home-based work done in 1989
were given in response to the open-ended question "Why did (the home-based
worker) stop doing (type of work) from home?" These results are shown in the
first column of Table 7.2. A small proportion (4.2% of 730) exited for what
might be considered positive reasons, including growing out of the home-based
work, finding different home-based work, selling their business, and moving
their workplace. Almost 15% (14.8% of 210) of those who were no longer doing
the same home-based work fell into this category of positive reasons.

The other reasons given for terminating were divided into two subcate-
gories: (a) health/family reasons or other life course transitions and (b)
market/employment conditions. Of those no longer in the same home-based
work (24.2% of 210), respondents indicated that they were no longer doing
this work because of marriage or other personal/family transitions, retirement, illness, time limitations resulting from family obligations, or death.
Steers and Mowday (1981) might have included these reasons as circumstances of job turnover; Baysinger and Mobley (1983) might have classified
them as nonjob factors.

In the second category of other reasons, 57.2% of the 210 respondents were
no longer in the same home-based work because of market/employment conditions, including, in descending order of frequency, (a) finding outside employment, (b) irregular or not enough income, (c) tiring of the work, (d) lack
of work, (e) conflict with another job, (f) layoff or contract expiration, (g)
conflict with employer, and (h) lack of product to sell. It is notable that the most
frequently given reason for exiting the original home-based work was outside
employment, a response given by 25.7%. These workers may have originally
chosen home-based work because they could not find employment that was not
home-based. Aronson (1991) suggested that the self-employed may be motivated to work for themselves because of the lack of other employment. Thus
when employment that is not home-based becomes available, home-based
workers move into it. In their models, Steers and Mowday (1981) might have
treated this reason for exiting as an environmental factor; Baysinger and Mobley

Table 7.2

Reasons for Exiting Home-Based Work Among Follow-Up Households, $n = 210$

Reason	Total 100% (1)	Owner 79.1% (2)	Earner 20.9% (3)	Women 48.6% (4)	Men 51.4% (5)	Other 11.9% (6)	None 88.1% (7)
Positive reason							
Grew out of home-based work	4.8%	6.0%	2.3%	1.0%	8.3%	4.0%	4.9%
Found different home-based work	4.3	4.8	2.3	4.9	3.7	36.0	0.0
Sold home-based business	3.3	4.2	0.0	1.0	5.6	0.0	3.8
Moved to new location	2.4	3.0	0.0	3.9	0.9	0.0	2.7
Subtotal	14.8	18.0	4.6	10.8	18.5	40.0	11.4
Health/family reason or other life course transition							
Marriage or other personal/family transitions	9.0	10.2	6.8	17.6	0.9	8.0	9.7
Retirement	7.1	5.4	13.6	3.9	11.1	0.0	8.1
Illness	5.7	7.2	0.0	1.0	10.2	0.0	6.5
No time, family obligations	1.9	2.4	0.0	1.0	2.8	0.0	2.2
Death	0.5	0.0	2.3	0.0	0.9	0.0	0.5
Subtotal	24.2	25.2	22.7	23.5	25.9	8.0	27.0
Market/employment condition							
Found outside employment	25.7	21.1	43.2	32.4	19.4	0.0	29.2
Irregular or not enough income	14.3	15.1	11.4	16.7	12.0	16.0	14.1
Became tired of work	7.6	9.6	2.3	6.9	8.3	20.0	5.9
Lack of work	4.8	5.4	2.3	2.0	7.4	4.0	4.9
Conflict with another job	1.9	1.8	2.3	0.0	3.7	0.0	2.2
Laid off or contract expired	1.4	0.6	6.8	2.0	1.9	0.0	1.6
Conflict with employer	1.0	0.6	2.3	0.0	1.9	8.0	0.0
No product to sell	0.5	0.6	0.0	1.0	0.0	0.0	0.5
Subtotal	57.2	54.8	70.6	61.0	54.6	48.0	58.4
Don't know why/no response	2.4	2.4	2.3	3.9	0.9	4.0	2.2

Note: $n = 210$ for total; 166 for business owners; 44 for wage workers; 102 for women; 108 for men; 25 for other home-based work; 185 for no home-based work.

(1983) also have identified external alternatives representing other job opportunities.

Because only the first response was coded and in-depth interviews were not conducted, it was impossible to know how much overlap there may be in some of these response categories. For example, it was not clear whether outside employment represented new or better opportunities, fringe benefits such as health insurance, or steadier, more reliable, or increased income. Likewise, it was not known whether the respondents were just "tired of it," had family situations demanding different working conditions, or, in the case of earners, had sensed that they might be laid off from their home-based work.

Despite these limitations, it was still possible to locate patterns in the accounts given and to compare categories of responses to explain why people left home-based work. The prevalence of the three categories of reasons was, in descending order, conditions related to the marketplace or employment (57.2%), transitions in health or one's personal situation (24.2%), and the positive reasons (14.8%) listed above.

Differences in the reasons given for exiting home-based work were compared using various subgroups of the sample. These results are shown in Table 7.2.

Business owners versus earners. Columns 2 and 3 of Table 7.2 show the reasons given for exiting by business owners and wage workers, respectively. A notable difference was that business owners were more likely to exit for positive reasons (18.0%) than were wage earners (4.6%). In contrast, 70.6% of the earners compared to 54.8% of the owners exited because of market/employment conditions. A larger percentage of wage workers (43.2%) than owners (21.1%) left because they found centralized employment. Both business owners and wage workers, however, were reported to have left more often because they found outside employment than for any other single reason. The second most common reason given for wage workers was retirement (13.6%), whereas owners cited irregular or not enough income (15.1%).

The same general pattern prevailed for both subgroups. Within the 3 broad categories, market/employment conditions were the most common reasons, followed in descending order by health/family transitions and positive reasons. The percentage of wage workers who exited for market/employment reasons was about 13.4% higher than that for the total follow-up sample (i.e., 70.6% minus 57.2%), although finding outside employment was specifically mentioned by 43.2% of wage workers, compared to 25.7% for the total subsample of exits in the follow-up. Wage workers made up about 20.9% of the total subsample of exits.

Women versus men. The results of comparisons by gender are shown in columns 4 and 5 of Table 7.2. Both women and men most frequently reported that market/employment conditions were the reasons they had exited home-based work. Health/family transitions and positive reasons followed in frequency. The most notable difference was the percentage of women

(32.4%) who exited to take outside employment, compared to men (19.4%). The next most common (17.6%) reason given for women exiting was marriage or other personal/family transitions; this reason pertained to only 0.9% of the men. The second most frequent reason given for men was irregular or not enough income (12.0%), a reason cited by 16.7% of the women. Retirement and illness were reasons cited by more than 10% of the men but infrequently by women.

Doing other home-based work versus no home-based work. Not all people who stopped doing their 1989 home-based work left home-based work entirely. These results are reported in columns 6 and 7 of Table 7.2. Some respondents (11.9%, $n = 25$) were still doing home-based work 3 years later, but of another kind than that originally reported. Only seven reasons for exiting were given by those taking on other home-based work. Compared to those who were not working at home at all in 1992, these people more often (36.0% versus 0%) reported having exited because they found other home-based work and less often (0% versus 29.2%) because they found outside employment. Twenty percent (20.0%) of those doing other home-based work, versus 5.9% of those doing no home-based work 3 years later, had exited because they became tired of the work they were doing in 1989. Other than those reasons already mentioned, irregular or not enough income was given as the reason for exiting by 16.0% of this subgroup. For those doing no other home-based work, irregular or not enough income was the second most frequently given reason (14.1%).

The typical pattern of exit reasons for those doing no home-based work at the follow-up was in this order: market/employment conditions (58.4%), health/family transitions (27.0%), and positive reasons (11.4%). A different pattern of specific reasons was observed for those doing other home-based work at the follow-up. They most often reported having left their 1989 homework to do other home-based work (36.0%). The market/employment conditions labeled as tiring of the work (20.0%)and irregular or not enough income (16.0%), were second and third in frequency. Marriage or other family transitions (8.0%) and conflict with one's employer (8.0%) tied for fourth.

Comparisons of Continuing Home-Based Workers with Those Who Did Not

The 730 workers identified in the 1992 follow-up were classified into three groups: those continuing with their same home-based work, those who had left for positive reasons, and those who had left the home-based work reported in 1989 for other reasons, including health/family transitions or market/employment conditions.

For these three groups, selected 1989 characteristics, group means, and other summary statistics are reported in Table 7.3, as are the results of analysis of variance procedures. Multiple comparison procedures were used to locate

Table 7.3

Comparisons of Continuation Status for Follow-Up Households Based on 1989 Sample Characteristics, $n = 730$

Variable	Continuation status of follow-up households			
	Continuing same home-based work	*Exit, positive reasons*	*Exit, other reasons*	*F-score*
Worker characteristic				
Male[a]	60.6%$_a$	61.2%$_{ab}$	50.3%$_b$	2.89*
Mean age	44.7	42.5	43.2	1.35
Mean education of worker	14.0$_a$	14.6$_a$	13.2$_b$	10.47*
Mean household size	3.3$_a$	3.3$_{ab}$	3.7$_b$	4.87*
Homeownership[b]	88.6%	94.6%	93.5%	2.18
Mean years in community	21.0$_{ab}$	15.8$_a$	23.4$_b$	3.45*
Urban residence[c]	51.1%	38.2%	54.1%	1.36
Work characteristic				
Mean gross household income[d]	$44,380$_a$	$49,373$_b$	$36,623$_c$	9.27*
Mean net home-based work income[d]	$20,486$_a$	$17,016$_{ab}$	$11,616$_b$	9.84*
Mean home-based work hours[e]	1,981$_a$	1,623$_{ab}$	1,710$_b$	3.64*
Mean duration	10.3$_a$	6.5$_{ab}$	8.1$_b$	5.39*
Seasonality[f]	8.4%$_a$	9.4%$_{ab}$	19.5%$_b$	8.33*
Respondents (% follow-up sample)	71.2%	4.2%	23.8%	—

Note: Percentages and means were based on 725 valid cases; there were 5 missing cases. Two-tail test of probability was used. If the *F*-score was significant, means with different subscripts differ from each other. Even though the number of households who exited for positive reasons was small ($n = 31$), differences were found.

[a] ANOVA calculated on means with female = 0 and male = 1. [b] ANOVA calculated on means with no = 0 and yes = 1. [c] ANOVA calculated on means with rural (i.e., farm, rural nonfarm, and small town) = 1 and urban (i.e., town of over 2,500 population) = 2. [d] *F*-values and probabilities reported for log values of annual income. [e] Number of hours worked in last 12 months. [f] ANOVA calculated on means with no = 0 and yes = 1.

*Statistically significant at the .05 level or less.

group means that significantly differed from others. These procedures resulted in identifying some characteristics that distinguished the three groups.

Those who were continuing in the same home-based work approximately 3 years later tended, in some ways, to be different from those who had left home-based work for reasons other than positive ones. Compared to those still doing the same home-based work, those who were no longer in the same home-based work for "other reasons" were proportionately more likely to be female, less educated, living in larger households, with lower gross household and net work incomes in 1988, working fewer hours,[7] in home-based work for fewer years, and seasonally employed. A significantly higher percentage of men continued in the same home-based work than left for other reasons. Looking at this another way, proportionately more women exited for other reasons than had continued with the same home-based work.

Interestingly, the multiple comparison procedures indicated a lack of statistically significant differences between the group that left for other reasons and the positive exit group for gender, household size, net home-based work income, home-based work hours, years in home-based work, and the proportion engaged in seasonal work. Age, homeownership, urban residence were not significantly different among the three groups.

The group that exited for positive reasons also did not differ from those continuing in the same home-based work on most variables studied. The only variable that distinguished among the three groups was average gross 1988 household income. The average number of years in the community also distinguished positive exits from those who left for other reasons. Thus positive exits differed from other exits in that they had lived in their communities for fewer years (15.8 versus 23.4) and had higher average gross household incomes ($49,373 versus $36,623) in 1988. These results concerning net home-based incomes were similar to the findings of Maguire (1993), who found that compensation was positively related to longer job tenure, and Eriksson (1991), who found that wages were negatively related to job change. Igbaria and Siegel (1992) found salary negatively related to turnover intention.

PREDICTING THE CONTINUATION OF HOME-BASED WORK

Multivariate Research Model of Continuing Home-Based Workers

The factors related to continuation or job tenure for all home-based workers were investigated using a multivariate research model.[8] The probability of doing the same home-based work in 1992 as in 1989 was examined using two models that used 1989 data for the explanatory variables but included different variables in the model. The first model consisted only of basic worker characteristics, including age, education, and household size, and work characteristics, including business ownership, whether the respondent was the home-based worker, net home-based income, duration of the home-based work, and distance from essential services. This model was estimated for the entire follow-up sample of 730 households using a binary dependent variable that was equal to 1 if the household continued to do the same home-based work in 1992 as in 1989 and 0 otherwise.

The choice of variables in the two models was supported by previous research findings. Maguire (1993) found age and education to be related to job tenure.

Eriksson (1991) also found that the probability of job changes decreased as the worker became older. Igbaria and Siegel (1992) found that older workers, more experience, higher salaries, and greater job satisfaction were negatively related to job turnover while more education was positively related. Compensation was found to be positively related to job tenure (Eriksson, 1991; Maguire, 1993).

A second research model included all these characteristics except that whether the respondent was the home-based worker was omitted and four attitude variables were added to the model. These attitude variables applied only to the home-based worker and included attitude toward the work, expected attitude toward the work, adequacy of income from the work, and expected income from the work. Each variable was placed on a 4-point scale with the value of 4 meaning the most positive answer.[9] This second model was estimated for a subsample of 376 follow-up households in which the home-based worker was the respondent in the original 1989 survey. Again, a binary dependent variable was used and was equal to 1 if the household continued to do the same home-based work in 1992 as in 1989 and 0 otherwise.

The results of the multivariate models showed that education of the home-based worker and number of years spent in home-based work were positively related to the continuation of home-based work in both models (Table 7.4). Higher levels of education and experience appear to support the home-based worker and allow continuation of the work. This finding was similar to those in previous literature, which suggested that education was positively related to longer job tenure (Maguire, 1993). Igbaria and Siegel (1992), however, found that education was positively related to higher job turnover. In contrast, household size had a negative effect in both models. Having a larger household may have impaired the ability of the worker to manage not only the existence but the continuation of home-based work.

Although net home-based income and distance from essential services increased the likelihood of continuing the home-based work in the model without the attitude variables, these two variables were not significant in the model that included the four attitude variables. This finding was in contrast to previous findings of a positive relationship between compensation and longer job tenure (Maguire, 1993) and lower job turnover (Igbaria & Siegel, 1992).

Both the attitude toward the work and the expected attitude toward the work were positively related to continuation. Not only did these two variables become significant, but neither the net home-based income nor the distance from essential services remained significant in the second model. The attitude variables related to adequacy of current income and expectations about future income were also not significant.

The model including the attitude variables performed better in the sense of producing a higher chi-square value, meaning that this model did a better job of predicting the continuation of home-based work. This model performance and the relative importance of one's feelings about his or her work compared to evaluations

Table 7.4
Odds of the Worker Being Engaged in the Same Home-Based Work Three Years Later, *n* = 730

Variable	Significant effects of model without attitudes	Significant effects of model with attitudes
Worker characteristic		
Age		
Education	+	+
Household size	-	-
Work characteristic		
Business owner		-
Respondent was home-based worker		omitted
Net home-based work income	+	
Duration	+	+
Distance from essential services	+	
Attitude		
Attitude toward the work	omitted	+
Expected attitude toward the work	omitted	+
Adequacy of income from the work	omitted	
Expected income from the work	omitted	
Constant		-
Chi-square =	52.02	100.99
	significant at .001 level	significant at .001 level
n =	730	376

Note: Effects were statistically significant at .10 or less.

of income adequacy and future income suggests that neither income nor attitudes about income were important in predicting continuation. How one feels about the work, that is, how much he or she likes doing it, is the more important dimension.

Multivariate Research Model of Coninuing Home-Based Businesses

The researchers were interested in differentiating between models that would predict continuation for the whole group (*n* = 730) versus the business owners (*n* = 521). Therefore, factors related to continuation for home business owners were investigated using two similar multivariate research models. Again, the model with the attitude variables (*n* = 268) performed better (i.e., had a higher chi-square value) in predicting business continuation (see Table 7.5).

The results of these analyses showed that education and the number of years spent in home-based work again had a positive significant effect in both models. Age was positively related to business continuation in the model that included attitude variables. These findings are supported by previous research. Cooper

Table 7.5
Odds of the Owner Being Engaged in the Same Home-Based Business Three Years Later, *n* = 521

Variables	Significant effects of model without attitudes	Significant effects of model with attitudes
Worker characteristic		
Age		+
Education	+	+
Household size		
Work characteristic		
Net home-based work income	+	
Duration	+	+
Distance from essential services		
Attitude		
Attitude toward the work	omitted	+
Expected attitude toward the work	omitted	+
Adequacy of income from the work	omitted	
Expected income from the work	omitted	
Constant		-
Chi-square =	34.55	81.21
	significant at .001 level	significant at .001 level
n =	521	268

Note: Effects were statistically significant at .10 or less.

et al. (1988) and Bates (1989) both found that age and education of the business owner positively correlated with business viability. Both the attitude toward the work and the expected attitude toward the work were positively related to continuation.

These findings suggest that business owners are like other workers in the first two models. Liking their work was again more important than either actual income or expectations about future income. Also, the significance of age denotes a possible connection between business continuation and being an older home-based worker.

SUMMARY AND CONCLUSIONS

Both the original survey and the follow-up interviews were limited by their method of gathering data—the telephone survey. Therefore, one way to categorize home-based work is to examine those who are continuing in the same home-based work that they have been doing for some specified time. In this study, these are the people who were still doing the same home-based work in 1992 that they were doing in 1989, about 71.2% of the sample. Using a second definition of retention, 75.5% were successful home-based workers in that they either were continuing in the same home-based work, had expanded out of their home-based work, had sold their businesses, or had moved. In addition, there are those who exited their 1989 home-based work but were engaged in other home-based work in 1992. When they are combined with the continuing group, they constitute about 74.7% of the sample. Even if we consider all those not responding to the follow-up as exits, 64.1% of the original home-based workers are still engaged in some home-based work.

Only a minority of the sample indicated that the worker had taken on new home-based work, and the reasons why a number have left such work have been pinpointed. Most likely to continue in the same home-based work are managers and clerical and administrative support staff. Most likely to no longer be in the same home-based work are service-sector workers.

Regardless of the retention rate used, some characteristics of the households and workers engaged in sustained home-based work and the reasons why a minority have left such work have been identified. Most workers (i.e., 7 of every 10, or 71.2%) are still doing the same home-based work 3 years later. Some exits are because of market or employment conditions, or because of health, family, or other transitions. Some respondents reported that the worker exited for positive reasons, such as outgrowing the business, doing different home-based work, selling the business, or expanding to a nonhome site.

Home-based wage workers are more likely to exit for market/employment reasons and less likely to exit for positive reasons than are home-based business owners. Both former home business owners and wage workers included in the sample are more likely to exit because they found centralized employment than for any other single reason. The results of this study also show that a larger proportion of women than men are likely to leave home-based work because of taking outside (i.e., outside the home) employment. Both, however, are more likely to exit for this reason than for any other, although leaving because of irregular or low income is also an important factor. More women than men left for marriage or other personal/family transitions, while more men than women left because of retirement or illness. Thus the three most frequent reasons for exiting by women are outside employment, irregular or low income, and marriage or personal/family transitions. These reasons are given by two-thirds of the women who left home-based work, while about one-half of the men exit home-based work for outside employment, irregular or low income, retirement, and illness.

Some people who exit home-based work do not take up any other home-based work. The results indicate that about 7 out of every 10 of these people left because of outside employment, irregular or low income, marriage or other personal/family transitions, retirement, illness, or because they grew tired of the home-based work. Interestingly, some individuals who grow tired of their home-based work exit and rather quickly take on different home-based work. People who exit and then take other home-based work also do so because of irregular or low income and because they find other, presumably more remunerative, home-based work. A majority of workers (72.0%) who continued with other home-based work do so for these three reasons.

In general, those continuing in home-based work versus those no longer doing the same home-based work are more likely to be men, to be better educated, to live in smaller households, to have higher gross household and net home-based incomes, to have worked more hours in the home-based work during the past year, to have been engaged in the home-based work longer, and to work nonseasonally. Those exiting for positive reasons are more likely to have lived in their communities fewer years and to have higher household incomes than those who left for other reasons. A higher gross household income also distinguishes the positive exits from those continuing in the same home-based work.

Multivariate analysis shows that continuation of home-based work is related to higher levels of education and experience of the home-based worker. Neither income nor expectations about income are important in predicting the likelihood that a home-based worker would continue doing the same work 3 years later. The continuation of home businesses is also related to higher levels of education and experience of the home-based worker. Comparing business owners to all workers, attitudes about their work are more important than their actual incomes or their attitudes about income. The significance of age denotes a possible connection between the continuation of a home business and being an older home-based worker.

These results have identified areas deserving further qualitative research. In-depth interviews eliciting the attitudes of home-based workers and others (i.e., those considering this work option, those having stopped being home-based workers, and significant others such as family members, employers, and employees), observational studies, and careful case studies of more successful and less successful home-based work experiences can yield important information. Cross-society and subculture research is also needed to build better theory. More informed decision making allowing for choice among alternative wage or self-employment options can result from the dissemination of such information.

Determining insiders' worldviews, how they interpret their actions to themselves and others, the options they see, and their assessed alternatives to home-based work would begin to clarify the decision-making processes followed by people getting into, getting out of, or switching home-based work. Evaluating certain segments of home-based workers, such as business owners, women, isolated rural households, and particular occupational types, may identify factors relevant to the success of these special home-based worker groups. Studying the coexistence of home-based work with other household members' employment and personal and/or family obligations and desires can provide valuable insights to the work-family interface in general and to the home-based work environment in particular.

It is hoped that the conceptualizations and data presented here will prove beneficial to researchers and practitioners, and especially to home-based workers. Much has been learned by reinterviewing home-based workers 3 years later, but much remains to be understood.

NOTES

1. A pilot study of selected industries showed that about 37.3% of jobs were open for more than a 4-week period during the 6-month study period; caution was made not to generalize these results (Devens, 1992).

2. One of the eligibility requirements for inclusion in the sample for the nine-state study was that the home-based worker had to have been engaged in the work covered by the interview for at least the previous 12 months. This eligibility requirement likely excluded several newer home-based workers and thus skewed the sample to workers who had been engaged in home-based work longer. It may have also affected the job duration for these workers and therefore the probability of continuation.

3. In the nine-state study home-based work was defined as paid work activities performed *in* the home or *from* the home. The sampling frame was based on a two-stage process in which households were screened for specific additional criteria, including (a) a minimum of 312 hours of home-based work per year by at least one person in the household, (b) participation in home-based work for the year prior to the survey, and (c) home-based work that was not production agriculture.

4. The sum of 730 and 170 is equal to 900 instead of 899 due to rounding error in the weights being used for this analysis. The actual number of contacts made was 729; adjustments in weights produced cumulative rounding errors resulting in weighted cases of 730. Throughout this chapter, the *n*'s reported are weighted.

5. In the original study, the home manager (who could also be the person engaged in home-based work) was interviewed. For the follow-up, either the manager or the home-based worker was interviewed. See Stafford, Winter, Duncan, and Genalo (1992) for more information concerning the original study.

6. The 1989 interview revealed that 208 households had more than one home-based worker, some doing up to six different home-based jobs. Therefore, it was not surprising that 25 households (3.4% of 730) were still doing other home-based work even though they had exited the work covered in the 1989 interview. There was an overlapping group of 10 households who left the original 1989 home-based work for positive reasons and who also said that they were still involved in other home-based work. If these two groups are considered together, these overlapping households must be subtracted from these additional 25 people who were doing any other home-based work to avoid double counting.

7. Averages per week were determined by dividing the mean figures shown in Table 7.3 by 52. Total weeks worked were calculated by taking the figures in Table 7.3 and dividing by 40. These figures were 49.5, 40.6, and 42.8 weeks for those continuing, those exiting for positive reasons, and those exiting for other reasons, respectively.

8. All multivariate research models in this book refer to regression procedures, either as ordinary least squares (OLS) regression or a logistic regression, depending on the nature of the dependent variable in the model. OLS regression was used in the case of a continuous dependent variable such as income. If the dependent variable was binary in nature, meaning it had a value of either 0 or 1, a logistic regression procedure was used. For further discussion of either procedure, see standard statistical references such as Kmenta (1986).

Agricultural products and sales was the category used consistently in all multivariate research models or regressions as the occupation group to which the other eight occupation categories were compared if the effect was significant. Although one category in any series of groupings used as independent variables must be omitted from any regression procedure for statistical reasons, the choice of which category to omit is often arbitrary. In the case of the research models in this book, agricultural products and sales was chosen because it had the fewest home-based workers.

9. The four attitude questions were answered only by the home-based worker and included attitude toward the work, expected attitude toward the work, adequacy of income from the work, and expected income from the work. Attitude toward the work was a variable represented by the following question: "Overall, would you say you like this work 1 = not at all, 2 = a little, 3 = some, or 4 = a lot." Expected attitude toward the work was based on the following question: "Do you think the way you feel about the work will 1 = get worse, 2 = stay the same, or 3 = get better." Adequacy of income from the work was measured using the following question: "Thinking of the home-based work and how much money you make, you 1 = lost money last year, 2 = just meet expenses, 3 = make adequate money for the time, or 4 = make good money for the time you put in." Finally, the expected income variable was based on answers to the following question: "In the next 3 years, do you expect the money you make from this work to 1 = decrease, 2 = remain the same, 3 = increase, or 4 = you will be getting out of the business or quitting."

Chapter 8

What We Know and Do Not Know about the "Home" and the "Work" and the Implications of Both

Ramona K. Z. Heck, Barbara R. Rowe, and Alma J. Owen

INTRODUCTION

No one study can provide all the answers, particularly for such a complex entity as home-based work. There is still much we do not know about working at home and the people who do it. Yet the glimpse into homeworking that we now have enables us to design and implement better-informed surveys and to make some generalizations about what we do know. This chapter attempts to draw out some implications of the findings from the nine-state survey, address the gaps in our knowledge (i.e., the questions we wished we had asked), and translate this information for educators, practitioners, decision makers, and families. The first section of this chapter addresses the research implications of the following areas: characteristics of the worker and the work, comparisons between owners and earners, the homeworking family, the community connection, and continuation of home-based work. The next section addresses the implications for educators and practitioners in the same thematic order, followed by implications for policy makers and implications for people. The last section summarizes suggestions for the future: future research, future educational/practitioner issues, future policy, and, most important, the future for people considering going home to work or continuing, expanding, or terminating their home-based work.

RESEARCH SUMMARY AND RESEARCH IMPLICATIONS OF FINDINGS FROM THE NINE-STATE STUDY

The Worker and the Work

Characteristics of the worker. The typical home-based worker as profiled in popular press descriptions is an apple-cheeked homemaker doing crafts at home, her children quietly playing nearby while a pot of stew gently simmers on the stove. The real typical home-based worker is male, older, and has an above average education. He is married with children, owns his own home, and has lived in the same community for some time.

National statistics for female workers show that the same percentage participate in home-based work as participate in work that is not home-based. Given the opportunity of mixing work and home responsibilities, it is surprising that the rate of participation by women in home-based work is no higher than in other forms of employment.

The ethnicity and race of the sample in the nine-state study are unknown, although census data show that Caucasians are much more likely to be engaged in home-based work than either African-Americans or Hispanics. Further study should be done of women and minorities to ascertain potential reasons for their level of participation in the arena of home-based work.

Clearly, older and more educated people are most likely to engage in home-based work. These characteristics may denote a worker who has more employment options and may be tired of commuting and the hassles of a centralized work site. The older worker may be someone "downsized" or given a "golden parachute" out of the traditional labor force, who as a result sought home-based work as an alternative. As constructed, the nine-state sample does not permit such comparisons, but it would be important to compare these profile characteristics with a sample of workers including both home-based and not home-based.

The average home-based worker and his family are long-standing members of their communities. Because the highest rates of participation occurred in small towns and rural communities, it may be that workers who live in such communities are attracted to home-based work to enable them to stay where they are and support their families at the same time. Similarly, such employment may make them less susceptible to fluctuations in the traditional labor market. Further analyses are needed to study the motivations behind the home-based work choice although major advantages and disadvantages are known.

Home-based workers cite the major advantages of such work as flexibility, ability to care for family, and saving time and hassles. They report the major disadvantages as being unable to get away from the work and always feeling as though the work is there waiting for them, a lack of privacy when the family interrupts work, and work that limits time spent with their families.

Health insurance. Almost two-thirds of home-based workers are covered by insurance policies provided through other jobs they or other family members hold or by privately held insurance. Indeed, the provision of health insurance elsewhere appears to enhance the possibility of engaging in home-based work. Information from the nine-state study did not indicate the level or amount of health insurance coverage; therefore, it is not known if the coverage of home-based workers is less adequate than that of workers in the centralized workplace. What is clear is that usually someone in the household does remain in the traditional labor force in order to ensure health care coverage for the family. It is speculated that if health insurance coverage were to become universal and portable, the numbers of people engaging in home-based work would increase dramatically.

Nature of home-based work. The types of work were investigated and examined independent of the worker. The majority of the sample consists of self-employed business owners. The rate of self-employment among home-based workers is about seven times that of the national population. This may reflect the past resistance of employers to permit work away from a centralized work site; this trend may be reversing with the recent downsizing of corporations. It is cheaper to move workers out of the centralized work site. Also, disasters such as the 1994 Los Angeles earthquake forced some employers to experiment with allowing employees to work at home with some success.

Home-based work is a viable financial alternative for many households in the sample. Home-based wage workers, on average, do better than their working peers in the centralized workplace. Home-based business owners do worse, making about half the average income of self-employed workers who are not home-based. On average, home-based income augments total household income by about 40% and in most states helps to keep the household above the poverty level. Although overall the net income from home-based work is competitive with that from other work choices, it is important to make a proper estimate of its financial meaning for the household at the time when a decision to select such work is made. It is also important to follow the income flow over time so that the rate of return from this work alternative can be properly evaluated. For example, the returns to education have not been investigated for the home-based worker. These workers are better educated than the general population, yet business owners in the nine-state study earned less than their labor force counterparts. In addition to the implications for returns to education, this finding surely indicates that other than strictly monetary factors must play a greater role in motivating such work.

One such motivator may be fewer work hours. Almost all home-based workers, including business owners, put in a little more than 36 hours per week, which is the cut between full-time and part-time employment used in national statistics. Thus it appears that some home-based workers are working fewer hours than other workers yet still earning sufficient income for their needs.

Because many centralized, on-site jobs tie the worker to the job for 40 hours or more, home-based work may allow flexibility in work effort. This would be particularly true in the case of the disabled or elderly home-based worker. On the other hand, home-based work may be a second job for the worker, a supplemental work effort, or a deliberate work choice for those workers desirous of more time for their families. About one-quarter of the sample engage in other employment outside the home. An additional one-quarter of the sample is designated as multiple homeworking households (i.e., more than one household member engages in home-based work); some households engage in as many as six different home-based jobs. Unfortunately, data from the nine-state study did not permit a more detailed examination of hourly wage rates and other financial returns to home-based work by owner status or occupation. Future research needs to explore these aspects.

The nine-state sample includes a wide spectrum of occupations; the four most common occupations are marketing and sales, contracting, mechanical and transportation work, and professional and technical jobs. Clearly, some occupations are more adaptable than others to home-based work. Actual job titles are diverse, and telecommuting is noticeably absent from the nine-state sample. Seasonal work is the choice of about 1 out of 10 home-based workers.

Comparisons of home-based workers to other workers who are not home-based relative to occupation and seasonality are not possible for the nine-state sample; such comparisons would reveal whether certain occupations or types of work lend themselves more readily to being home-based.

Those engaged in home-based work have been at it about twice as long as the average job tenure in the centralized workplace. This fact might suggest that home-based work is most likely chosen because it accommodates the lives and families of the workers.

Home work space, intrusiveness, and management. Most workers perform their home-based work in a separate work space, for example, an office or detached building, basement, or recreation room. Work space choices within and around the home appear to reflect the desire on the part of the workers to keep their work world separate from their household or family activities. About one-half use a work site kept exclusively for the home-based work, and about one-half use more than one work site within or around the home. Unfortunately, data from the study do not reveal anything about the frequency of use of the chosen work space or spaces. Furthermore, it is not known how the work is spaced throughout the workday in different work sites. Because the nature of home-based work allows flexibility and interaction between work and home, much more research is needed to determine the specific interactions between work activities and home activities relative to intensity of effort, sequencing, duration of work segments, and other details about the nature of the work and its attendant tasks.

The intrusiveness of work was examined relative to four measures: telephone calls, client visits, location of work activities, and use of family vehicle. Well over half of the sample receive telephone calls daily. About one-half of the workers see one person about once a month in relation to their home-based work. Over one-half of the sample use an exclusive work space so that the work is never in family activity space for long. In most cases the family vehicle is used for both work and family needs with no resulting conflict.

Intrusiveness is experienced more by female workers, workers in larger households, and workers with lower incomes. Their responses to intrusions to their work vary. This may be related to the specific worker's ability to fend off intrusions or the tenacity of family members in their demands on the home-based worker (i.e., adults versus children). Again, more study is needed to understand better the dynamics of work and family interaction.

With the exception of goal setting, most home-based workers engage in common management practices relative to their home-based work, although specific conceptual segments of accepted managerial models were not identifiable. More investigation of specific management practices such as planning and other work management practices innovated by the home-based worker is needed. Like other employed persons, the home-based worker is faced with complex work and family responsibilities. But little is known about how disparate demands are handled throughout the workday or over longer periods of time.

Owners versus Earners

Data from the nine-state study are ideal for studying the differences among major groups of home-based workers, such as how business owners differ from wage workers.

Worker differences. Male workers dominate both owner and earner groups, making up more than 60% of each. Among business owners, in general, the rate of self-employment for women is half that of males. Female home-based workers compared to workers in general participate in business ownership more on a par with males, although not equally. Possibly, home-based work settings present fewer barriers to entry for females, or perhaps more females seek home-based work as a partial solution to their family demands. Larger samples of both home-based workers and workers who are not home-based are needed to explore comparisons within major groups of workers such as females, minorities, and low-income households. The isolated nature of the home-based work may allow enough flexibility for workers and tolerance and inclusion of certain worker groups that have historically had difficulty meeting the demands of the centralized workplace.

Work differences. Home-based wage workers make $8,000 more than home-based business owners, but business owners work about 3 hours less per week. Multivariate analysis reveals that the probability of business ownership is affected by higher incomes, being a professional or technical worker, being a clerical or administrative worker, being involved in seasonal work, and having other employment. It may be that for earners home-based work is their main job but for owners it is not. The net income from home-based work as a proportion of total household income is also less for business owners than earners—35.7% and 51.4%, respectively. These figures may be skewed by the number of part-time, female-owned businesses in the sample. It may also be that business owners are involved in other work or income-earning activities that detract from the amount of time they can devote to home-based work. Data from the nine-state study are limited relative to this detailed information. Previous research has alluded to distraction for business owners and its effect on the viability of the business. More research is needed concerning this more intricate look at the overall work activities of earners and owners.

Health insurance. Owners are more than twice as likely as earners to obtain their health insurance through other jobs held by themselves or other family members or through a privately held insurance policy. Privately held policies are owned by three times more owners than earners even though owners are more likely to have no health insurance than earners are. Only one out of every five wage workers has health insurance provided and paid for by their employers.

Clearly, some of the risks of business ownership are ameliorated by the provision of health insurance from other jobs. The downside of this advantage is that those jobs pursued and held mainly for the health insurance provision may detract from the viability of the home business over time. There is a need for better health insurance availability for all home-based workers, especially business owners. Affordable health insurance provided through professional home business organizations would alleviate some of these concerns.

Differences between owners and earners relative to the level and amount of health insurance coverage are not known. Further study of this issue is necessary. Indeed, the prevalence of home-based work, and in particular the formation of home businesses, may be crucially tied to such job features as health insurance, forcing employment choice to be based on access to health and disability benefits.

Home work space. Nearly two-thirds of the earners but only about one-third of the owners had a separate work space, such as an office, workroom, or study, attached cottage, shop, studio, or office in an attached business, as the main site for their work activities. Owners were just as likely to use a basement area or recreation room in their homes for their separate work space. Exclusive work space is used by over one-half of the owner and earner groups, but earners seem to isolate their work space more than owners. This may be owing to the nature of the wage work. Owners may be less involved with the paperwork of the business and may be traveling more to deal with business matters or even selling on the road. Because the work effort of these owners is less relative to income and time spent, separate office space may not be rational for all. The work space needs of home-based owners and earners are understudied. Popular press reports to the contrary, little is known about the size, arrangement, or amenities needed for the home office, and such information cannot be ascertained from these data.

The gender factor related to owner status, income, hours, and job duration. Some of the gender effects common to the centralized workplace exist among home-based earners and owners. In this study, home-based male earners make the most income, followed by male owners; female earners make more than female owners. Male earners also work the most hours, followed again by male owners. Although female owners make less, they work slightly more hours than female earners. Female owners spend 85% of their work time at home. Male earners work the least number of hours at home—39%—probably because of the large number who are employed in sales. Both male earners and owners have been engaged in home-based work longer than either female owners or earners. In fact, male earners have been working twice as long as female earners.

A multivariate analysis of gender differences for income reveals that home-based work is similar to other income-generating activities—men make more money. Having a child under 6 years has a negative effect on the income of females but a positive effect for men.

Just as in the general labor force, males have jobs that yield more income. Although the rate of home-based business ownership for women is close to that of males, female rates of business ownership in the work world that is not home-based are about one-half those of men. Yet female owners work more hours and make less income even than female earners.

Clearly, the female business owners in the nine-state study are working hard and making very little money. They may be choosing to work at home so they can dovetail employment and family responsibilities, but the result appears to be detrimental to income production. It may be that they are forced into or self-select low-paying businesses because of their inexperience in the business world or their inability to attract financing or sales. Further research is needed about businesses, in general, that are owned and operated by women.

Relative to home-based businesses, much is unknown about the female owners. Why do they continue to work at such low-paying ventures? What are the nonpecuniary attributes of such businesses that have not been measured? How and why do women choose the type of business to own and how do they go about setting up and operating the business? Finally, it appears that women are moving into home-based work at different rates than men. More needs to be discovered about home-based workers over time relative to the gender of the worker.

Gender and occupation. The data show the usual gender segregation by occupation. One exception is that there were as many female earners in marketing and sales as males. Interestingly, male business owners are in craft and artisan occupations at about one-half the female rate. Although management and retail agriculture are less common occupations for the sample as a whole, about half of the people in these categories are women. Even though craft and artisan and service occupations are dominated by women, it appears that home-based work permits women greater occupational choice than do many segments of the centralized labor force. Again, more research is needed from the perspective of women.

Operating, financial, and marketing strategies. Most home-based businesses are organized as sole proprietorships. Only about one in every five owners borrowed capital to start or run a business. Well over half have separate bank accounts for their businesses. Nearly all rely on word-of-mouth or referrals as a marketing strategy. Newspapers, yellow pages, and direct mail are commonly used approaches to marketing; all these methods are used by about one-fifth or less of the businesses. In addition, most restrict sales of their products or services to their home states, although those who do not, make more money. Most of the businesses are service related. A little under one-third of the businesses are in crafts and artisans and marketing and sales. All of these measures reflect the degree of professionalism displayed by business owners and, possibly, their profit margin.

Owners' employees and helpers. Home-based businesses traditionally rely on a work force of paid workers, contracting workers, and unpaid helpers. These categories may be broken down into family, related (i.e., other relatives), and unrelated. Not all of these workers and helpers make optimal contributions to business outcomes. Although contracting family workers, unpaid family helpers, and paid and contracting unrelated workers all have positive effects on net business income, unpaid related helpers have a negative effect. Related and unrelated contract workers increase the work hours of the business owner and do not appear to substitute for the hours put in by owners themselves.

Subjective outcomes. Multivariate analyses on quality of life, income adequacy, and degree of control reveal that the likelihood of feeling positive about the quality of life and about income adequacy is higher for owners in adult-only families than for those in other family types. Rural owners are less likely to feel good about their quality of life than city owners. Very little is known about the subjective outcomes related to work, especially home-based work. Why do rural owners feel less positive about their quality of life than city owners? Is it difficult to run a business in a rural area, even in the new electronic age? The data for the nine-state study were collected at a time when the farm crisis of the 1980s may have forced some families into home-based work to hang on to their land. In other words, the decision to engage in home-based work was not a freely made choice. Although farm prices have rebounded somewhat since the height of the farm crisis, farming in general continues to decline as a percentage of all adult employment, and the rural economic structure is in transition with hope of new inbound migration and renewal. Rural residents also have fewer vocational opportunities and access to services than urban dwellers do. These quality of life effects may disappear as more information-age workers abandon life in large cities and their positions in the 8-to-5 work world to move back to small-town America or to an adjacent area. Clearly, more research is needed into the details of business ownership and its effect on the worker and the family.

Inside the Homeworking Family

Family structure and composition. The home-based work force is dominated by married couples with children and by adult-only families. Moreover, the majority of home-based workers are married men living in full-nest families. Families appear to provide a support structure for the home-based worker as well as a possible incentive for productive and financially rewarding work. The low number of single-parent households speaks further to this point. Single parents experience a shortage of many resources, most especially time. How actual family members interact to support or hinder the home-based worker is not known, nor is it known how well family activities mesh with home-based work. More research is needed to reveal a potentially different division of labor within the family relative to the unpaid household work such as cleaning the house, preparing meals, and doing the laundry. Is the division of unpaid household labor different in homeworking families? Do the amount of and responsibility for the unpaid household work, as well as the income-generating home-based work, change among family members and over time?

Effects of children and use of child care services. Having a child 18 or younger reduces the number of hours spent in paid work regardless of gender; having a child under 6 years depresses the work effort even more. Families with children are less likely to have large-scale businesses, to own their own business, or to be involved in seasonal work.

About 4 out of every 10 home-based workers with at least one child age 18 or under who was designated as needing care use child care services. Usage of child care services is not related to the gender of the home-based worker—child care services are often needed and used regardless of whether the father or mother is the home-based worker.

Children and home-based work do not mix as readily as some popular press reports would lead one to think. This is particularly true of home-based business owners. Some researchers have suggested that working at home may meet the simultaneous needs of income and child care. The results from the nine-state study suggest the opposite. On average, about two-thirds of the homeworker's time is spent at home; for the remainder of the time, the worker is working *from* the home. Such circumstances and the nature of the home-based work would affect the child care arrangements. Although home-based workers may have more flexibility in meeting short-term or emergency child care needs such as the case of a sick child, these workers still need uninterrupted periods of time for their income-generating work. It is true, however, that home-based workers may be better able to intermix work and the supervision of their children during parts of the workday. For example, working at home may allow parents to arrange their work time during periods when children are at school or asleep. They may also be able to interrupt their work throughout the workday or workweek. Much more research is needed to reveal the specific interplay between income-generating work and family responsibilities. To uncover the sequencing of work and family activities would necessitate the collection of time-use data through open-ended time diaries. Such research is expensive but necessary to capture the complex and detailed nature of home-based work and family work and leisure activities.

The effects of parents' home-based work on children have not been addressed. Parents who are preoccupied with the general well-being of their preschool children are seldom as productive at work; good day care may be the answer. Are the children of home-based working parents who do not use child care better off under their care or supervision while these same parents engage in income-generating work? What are the psychological effects on children when parents simultaneously try to work and care for them? Constantly trying to "shush" them and expecting them not to interrupt would be a losing battle. Children may feel that their personal space has been invaded and that family activities have taken a back seat to the work. The phone and family car may become battlefields.

On the other hand, these children could be better off. Most children don't have the faintest idea what their parents really do "at work." When parents work at home, children become involved just by being around when the phone rings, when clients call, and when deadlines have to be met. There is anecdotal evidence that children in homeworking families gain independence, learn responsibility and respect for work, and gain an intimate understanding of the economic system. No one really knows about this aspect of home-based work, and much further research is needed.

Family functioning, family management, and adjustment strategies. Three types of family functioning have been identified in previous literature, namely, open, closed, and random families. These three basic functioning types yield six major functioning categories among homeworking families, in descending order of frequency: closed/open, open, random/closed, random, open/random, and closed. Furthermore, members of more autonomously functioning families practiced less management. All household managers from the homeworking households scored above the midpoint on the family management scale. When the household manager is also the home-based worker, scores on the family management scale are even higher. In particular, home-based workers/managers engage in more standard-setting and adjusting behaviors than do household managers who are not home-based workers.

As a time-management adjustment strategy, home-based workers reallocate their personal time more often than they hire help. Hired help are used by about one-quarter of the home-based workers; however, almost half the sample have family and friends who help out. Other adjustment strategies used by more than half the sample are, listed in descending order, reducing housecleaning time, reducing sleeping time, cutting down on social activities, reducing time spent with the family, and eating out or bringing food in.

Clearly, home-based work affects family life as well as the reverse. It appears that certain types of families may be better able to adapt to home-based work than others. Random families usually consist of very independent and different individuals who may have difficulty accommodating to the structure of home-based work, whereas open families or some variation thereof may thrive when the home-based work flourishes. More research is needed to understand which combinations of family functioning and home-based occupations are optimal.

It also appears that families of all types react to home-based work via their management practices and adjustment strategies. Common adjustment strategies seem to be related to what the home-based workers/manager can control and seem not to depend upon others in the family or outside the family, such as hired help. Household managers scored high on the management scales with the exception of goal setting. The management models tested in the nine-state study warrant further empirical validation, particularly related to possible gender differences. Furthermore, management styles relative to family life appear to be somewhat different than those used to organize the home-based work. Researchers involved in the nine-state study suspect that management behavior within family life has not yet been properly identified and that a more realistic conceptualization of this aspect of family life is needed.

The Community Connection

The prevalence of home-based work has much to do with the receptiveness shown by the community within which the household lives and works. Community factors both motivate and hinder the home-based work enterprise.

Local community. Most workers in the sample did not cite legal or regulatory issues such as zoning as barriers to home-based work. The incidence of zoning problems may be low, however, because zoning regulations automatically exclude the existence of home-based work or because such workers go "underground" to operate their home business or perform wage work.

Issues of community ambiance, traffic and pollution, and internal residential work space are not pressing concerns to the home-based workers in the nine-state study. Nonetheless, traditional separations of work and residential life do not necessarily conform either to the needs or to the demands of the home-based worker. For example, almost two-thirds see clients at home, and about one-third see them at least two to three times per week. Such interactions between clients and home-based workers do not appear to conflict with residential community life. Many home-based workers may likely keep a low profile to preserve the residential character of their neighborhoods. They may use small or no signage outside their homes, travel to collect supplies rather than having them delivered, and use other strategies to keep good neighbor relations.

Future research samples need to include both home-based workers and workers who are not home-based so that comparisons between the two groups can be made. With such comparisons, the barriers to home-based work could be explored further. It is certainly possible that more centralized workers would have been or would become home-based if local community factors such as zoning were made less restrictive.

Local community and the economic impact of home-based work. Of all the services used by home-based workers, banking and supply services are used most often. Residents of small towns use all services less frequently than others, including those living in towns with a population larger than 2,500, rural nonfarm residents, and retail farmers. About one-third of the businesses use legal services; 9 out of every 10 businesses use banking services.

The importance of the income generated by home-based work varies among the households in the study. For nearly two-thirds of the households, home-based work provides less than 50% of the household's income, although on average home-based work provides nearly 40% of household income. In about one-eighth of the households, home-based work provides 90% of the household income.

Overall, the economic impacts of home-based work on the family and community are significant. Not only are families helped financially, but community income streams are bolstered by the labor of home-based workers. Sixty percent of the income generated from home-based work goes for business-related expenses. In dollar terms, that is an input of $31 billion to communities in the nine states studied. The local economic development literature appears oblivious to the monetary contribution of home-based work and in particular home-based businesses. Additional research is needed to document in detail the economic impact of home-based businesses on communities; even without such detailed research, the impact appears to be substantial.

Larger macro community and the economic impact of home-based work. Based on the prevalence of home-based work in the nine states studied, over six million households are estimated to be engaged in home-based work, with average annual earnings of $17,835 from this work. This translates to $108.4 billion in personal income in the U.S. economy. On a national level, home-based work contributes 3.4% of household income, compared to 3.9% by nonfarm sole proprietorships and 1.8% from farming. That's not all. Home-based businesses pump an estimated $247 billion of gross income directly into the economy, over one-third as much as nonfarm proprietorships do. Net business income amounts to $126 billion, which is over one-half as much net income as that from all nonfarm proprietorships.

The economic well-being of homeworking families is well above such national statistics as the poverty threshold. Net income from home-based work provides nearly 40% of household income in the sample households. The average net income in rural areas is about two-thirds that of homeworkers in urban areas. This average proportion varies by state, but in nearly all states net home-based income is greater than the poverty threshold and therefore makes the difference in putting a household well above the poverty level. One exception is Iowa—in rural areas within this state, net income from home-based work is below the poverty threshold even though the average homeworking household in rural Iowa is well above the poverty threshold; still, total household income is considered.

The economic impacts of home-based work on the larger economy are also significant. Both gross and net income streams associated with home-based work make sizable contributions to the macro economy. In particular, net income from home-based business is over half as much as that for all nonfarm proprietorships. Future research also needs to document these economic impacts further and in more detail. With a larger sample of businesses, including both home-based and on Main Street, the contributions by type of business could be studied further.

Description of communities where home-based workers reside. Data from the U.S. Bureau of the Census yield characteristics of the communities within which households from the nine-state survey reside. Well over one-half of the population in the resident counties (i.e., those counties from which the nine-state sample was selected) work in their county of residence. Demographically, it appears that homeworking households differ somewhat from other households in their communities and in the nation. An unusually high percentage of females in the resident counties are in the labor force. In the nine-state sample, females are employed at the same rate as in the U.S. population. In comparison to the U.S. population, the median age of family members in homeworking families is younger, while median education is about 1.5 years more than in either the resident county profile or the United States. Homeworking families have more members than the average families in their county of residence and in the country in general. Moreover, there are far fewer single-parent homeworking households.

The median family income of the nine-state sample is about $6,000 greater than that of the U.S. population as a whole and about $3,000 more than that of their resident counties. The mean net self-employment wages are somewhat less than self-employment wages for their resident counties and similar to those of the general population. On the other hand, the rate of self-employment is about seven times higher than that of either the resident counties or the general population. Finally, the rate of self-employment among workers who work at home for pay was nearly identical between the nine-state sample and the U.S. population.

The community profile suggests that certain types of workers and their families choose home-based work for their livelihood. Larger intact families struggle to stay where they are, even at a lower financial gain. The tradeoffs between monetary and nonmonetary motivators of home-based work remain understudied. Even though home-based work is an economically viable alternative, some home-based workers work many hours with very little financial payoff. To do otherwise, however, they might have to move their residence, enjoy less family time because of commuting, and incur additional costs associated with employment in a centralized workplace. Future research needs to explore in detail the costs and benefits of various employment alternatives available to the home-based worker.

Continuation of Home-Based Work

Characteristics of the reinterviewed households. At the time of the original survey, respondents reported that they had spent an average of 9.1 years working at home. About 3 years later, 71.2% of the sample were still doing the same home-based work. At the point of exit, those who choose to discontinue their home-based work have been engaged in the work for shorter periods of time than those who choose not to exit. Using a multivariate research model, the likelihood of staying in home-based work increases with the number of years already spent working at home.

Retention rates. Retention rates calculated 3 years after the original survey are high: 71.2% are still doing the same work, 75.5% are doing the same work or have moved the business out of the home, and 74.7% are still in home-based work although not necessarily the same homework as that done at the time of the original survey. It appears that large numbers of those doing home-based work continue to do so over relatively extended periods of time or are successful in expanding their work to nonhome sites or selling their businesses. But caution should be exercised when making inferences concerning how well home-based work functions. Other ways of conceptualizing retention rates provide a rate as low as 56%. Future research needs to address more specifics about to what degree workers are satisfied, how this type of work meshes with family life, what human capital gains are made through this type of employment, or if alternative employment was sought or was available.

Reasons for exiting home-based work. The five most common reasons for leaving home-based work are, in order of frequency, a switch to outside employment, irregular or not enough income, marriage or other personal/family transitions, a feeling of being tired of the work, and retirement. All the specific reasons revealed in this follow-up interview should be used to provide a foundation for further research to help current and prospective home-based workers. Likewise, conditions related to business growth, family and health issues, market conditions, and the attractions of or barriers to outside employment can be examined to provide important insights into the continuity and success of home-based work.

Further investigation should be undertaken about how starting, stopping, or changing home-based work is structured by gender and gendered issues such as opportunity structures and constraints on life course choices; subcultural values; geographic location (i.e., rural or urban and region of the country); perceived occupational opportunities (i.e., home-based and otherwise); human capital characteristics; and market conditions. Constraints on capital for entrepreneurship or expansion can also be investigated. For example, women, certain ethnic groups, and some sociodemographic classes may experience or perceive more barriers to acquiring or controlling capital.

Other issues to address in future research include how home-based work, either wage work or business ownership, is constrained or enhanced by family or life course situations. For example, a longitudinal study could help pinpoint when it may be best to begin, change, or terminate home-based work given various family or life course issues. Some of these issues would include transitions such as pending marriages, divorces, births or adoptions, and caring for dependent elderly family members. Then the advantages and disadvantages of home-based work as it relates to the family and the worker over time could be discovered.

Whether sustained home-based work is family friendly must also be considered. Home-based work and its fit with the enhancement of family life are more than an economic development issue. Likewise, the part home-based work plays in creating stereotypical gender, family, and economic roles is underinvestigated. The information gained from such a survey can be interpreted in ways that provide a foundation for both continuing research and education programs for home-based workers (or those anticipating such wage work or self-employment) so as to effect more informed decision making.

Factors related to continuation. Those who continue their home-based work are most likely to be males, to be more educated, to live in small households, to have lived in their communities for fewer years, to have higher gross household income and higher net income from home-based work, to work more hours, to have been a homeworker longer, and to be involved in nonseasonal work. Multivariate analysis of continuation rates reveals that higher levels of education and experience of the home-based worker positively affect continuation, although a larger household size lowers the probability of continuation. Neither income nor attitudes about income are important in predicting the likelihood of continuing the same work, but attitudes toward the work are positively related to continuation. For home business owners, being older is also positively related to continuation of the business. Clearly, more complete multivariate models and empirical testing could be performed with a larger sample followed longitudinally, making it possible to uncover more factors associated with continuation. This is especially true for the group of workers who were no longer in the same home-based work but had expanded and moved the business to a new location.

IMPLICATIONS FOR EDUCATORS AND PRACTITIONERS

Educators, as the term is used here, refers to a broad set of professionals. These professionals can include both the traditional educator within the public and private educational institutions in our country and an array of educators who function within nonclassroom settings such as the extension faculties present at most state land-grant universities throughout the nation.

Practitioners refers to a set of professionals who have, in part, an educational function within a nonclassroom setting, such as a one-on-one advising or therapeutic setting. Practitioners include advisers or consultants of all types, but in particular they include the family therapist, the business consultant, and legal advisers. The implications shared here are for all practitioners who assist in the delivery of information and knowledge to the public to enhance decision making and improve people's lives in general and, more specifically, their work lives.

Until recently, workers sold their time and labor to centralized employers. With the advent of the information age, the economy is shifting from traditional manufacturing industries, which produce goods, to service industries. Over half of all U.S. workers now hold information- and service-related jobs. Technology has assisted deindustrialization and made it possible to live and work anywhere and remain connected to the outside world via computer. All of these factors, coupled with the downsizing and delayering of corporations and restructured labor markets, have left many individuals out of work and confused. The continued reengineering of the workplace is one reason self-employment has increased in importance. Educators and practitioners need to be prepared to assist individuals and families of all kinds to make more informed employment choices.

The Worker and the Work

The profile of the average home-based worker suggests that older and more experienced workers may grow into home-based work as a forced or self-chosen move. But what about the choices of the rest of the workers in the labor force? Educators and practitioners could be able to assist new and reentering workers in making more informed employment choices and adjustments to change or the need to improve the viability of their current employment.

Educators and practitioners could be particularly helpful in assisting individuals and families in dealing with the realities of home-based work. For example, one of the salient attributes of home-based work is health insurance coverage. Currently, anyone choosing to work at home will need to arrange for health insurance through another job, the job of another family member, or a privately obtained and paid-for policy. Potential homeworkers need to allow for this additional expenditure or cost within their family circumstances. Business consultants could be especially helpful in planning for the insurance needs of the individual worker, his or her family, and employees.

Work space needs for home-based workers are certainly apparent from the nine-state study. The most prevalent arrangement is a separate space within the home or on the property devoted exclusively to the home-based work. Of course, not all home-based workers in the nine-state study achieved this arrangement, but many did. Clearly, home-based work does not necessarily mean spatial mixing of work and family activities. Home-based work takes space, and potential homeworkers and their families need to know this. The special services of physical designers or architects may be needed in making major space adjustments for the home business.

Not only will the home-based work need its own space, but it often intrudes on home and family activities. What are the practical and psychological effects on the family of telephone calls and client visits related to the home-based work? Potential homeworkers need to plan for these intrusions and make changes in the home environment to minimize them. For example, separate telephone lines and a separate entry into the work space may be necessary to minimize disruptions to the worker and family. Both of these changes would likely involve additional start-up costs and maintenance costs over time.

Owners versus Earners

As noted earlier, owning and operating a home business is the predominant form of home-based employment. Business consultants specializing in home-based work could provide information and advice on how to own and operate a business in the same area in which a family lives. Such businesses need to be viable over time to the individuals, families, and communities to which they are connected.

Although male home-based workers dominate the sample of the nine-state study, women choose home-based business ownership at a rate almost equal to that of men. Whether this is a result of constraints or discrimination in traditional labor markets or a partial solution to family demands is unknown. Women, minorities, and other special groups may need more complete information from practitioners and educators about the implications of starting a home-based business. These special groups may not have experience or education in marketing, producing in quantity, developing financing, or managing employees.

Gender effects are still common among earners and owners who are home-based, as they are in the centralized workplace. Among home business owners, males work more hours and make more money than females. Female owners work the greatest percentage of their hours at home, nearly 85% of their work time. They also work more hours but make less money than female earners. Traditional gender segregation by occupation is present in the home-based work world and affects the potential income to be realized by the venture. Even in occupations such as marketing and sales and retail agriculture, where women are present in relatively large numbers, they are selling cosmetics and cleaning products or raising African violets and goldfish. Is this a process of self-selection or the result of their inability to attract financing or generate sales? Educators and practitioners could be helpful in pointing out the limited income potential of such ventures in relation to the investment.

Women who enter or are currently in the home-based work arena need to know that it may be a real balancing act—an enmeshed world of both work and home filled with constant demands from both. The implications of dovetailing employment and family responsibilities need to be explored in detail by each woman considering such an employment choice. Without such prior exploration, engaging in home-based work might result in negative outcomes to both the businesses and the families. On the positive side, the home-based work world, especially home businesses, may pose fewer barriers to women as workers, and as a result their balancing behavior between work and home may be easier and more manageable than it is for women in the centralized workplace.

Educators and practitioners could be particularly important in offering advice and services to improve the day-to-day running of a home-based business. Potential or current home-based business owners need to know the difference among and the tax implications of various business structures, including sole proprietorships, partnerships, and corporations. Strategies and skills in formulating business plans to attract outside capital to start or run a business may be particularly difficult for homeworkers. Educators and consultants could also assist with advertising and marketing strategies, the analysis of business trends, advice on legal considerations, and computer training.

The involvement of family members and nonrelatives in the home-based business needs careful consideration by the home business owner. Not all workers produce positive business outcomes, and hiring skilled employees may be out of reach to the beginning home-based business owner. Learning how to attract and manage workers, set personnel policies, and manage human relations within the home-based business may be difficult; thus professional information and advice may be crucial to success.

Finally, educators and family therapists may be very helpful in assessing the subjective outcomes of a home business. Exploring attitudes and feelings toward a home business may create a potentially explosive situation for both the business owner and other family members. Involving professional mediators may be the only or the best way to solve potential problems or concerns about the quality of family life, income adequacy, and degree of control in their lives. In small family businesses the owner may believe that "what is good for the business is good for the family," but success and profitability may impinge negatively on the quality of family life over time.

Inside the Homeworking Family

The conceptualization of family functioning types originated, in part, from the practice of family therapists. These same professionals and educators can be instrumental in helping potential or current home-based workers explore the implications of their particular functioning style. Practitioners and educators may also be extremely helpful in sharing what is known about managerial behaviors and strategies within a homework environment. As identified by the research results, common adjustment strategies seem related to the home-based worker/manager and not to other members of the family. Educational materials and practitioners could help home-based workers identify and evaluate their current management behaviors and develop approaches that garner cooperation from other family members or outside sources of assistance.

The Community Connection

Business consultants and educators may be most critical in advising home business owners about the resources available to and regulation of home-based work in a community. They could provide a simple listing of resources available, tell how and where to apply for and receive special business licensing, and interpret local zoning ordinances, for example. Attorneys and accountants can provide invaluable assistance in understanding and following the tax laws for home businesses. The business consultant could help the home business owner in starting, promoting, maintaining, and expanding the business within the local business environment. Helping owners professionalize their business activity can help raise the reputation of home-based work within the local community and the broader business environment.

An important contribution that educators and practitioners might make is helping home-based workers understand the economic contribution of such work not only to their families but also to their local communities. Home-based work makes a considerable economic contribution that has not been given the recognition it deserves in the political arena.

Continuation of Home-Based Work

Finally, educators and practitioners could help home-based workers explore the possible changes in such work over time. The home-based work, the worker, and his or her family will change over time; planning for such changes can prevent unnecessarily painful and disruptive adjustments.

The nine-state study reveals characteristics associated with continuation and the common reasons for exiting home-based work. Finding outside employment and receiving irregular or inadequate income are important reasons why home-based workers exit. The main role of a business consultant is to improve the operations and rewards of the enterprise. Educators, too, might help the home-based worker investigate ways to expand or alter the home-based work to improve its bottom line.

Next to financial reasons for exiting home-based work, in order of their importance, are family- or worker-related events such as marriage or other personal/family transitions, becoming tired of the work, and retirement. Educators and other professionals, such as therapists, could help individuals and families become more aware of these longitudinal possibilities and assist in the planning of employment transitions over time.

IMPLICATIONS FOR POLICY MAKERS

Although many authors have implied policy concerns for home-based workers—in taxation, zoning, licensing, and environmental issues—research has not addressed the way that home-based workers feel about or affect these issues. Several areas of this study as well as recent congressional and court actions make policy a premier implication area for this nine-state study. Much of Chapter 6 was focused on research findings that have policy implications. This section is organized into implications at national, state and regional, and local levels.

National Policy Issues

Home-based work has received intermittent attention at the national level, particularly as it relates to taxation and labor issues. The tax advantages available to home-based businesses have been tightened. Self-employment taxation, tax deductions for home offices, reporting requirements for home-based laborers who are not self-employed, and requirements for diary-entry proof of computer use for home-based work are but a few of the areas in which increased record keeping and other restrictions have lessened the advantages of home-based work.

The worker and the work. The range of home-based occupations in this study indicates that this type of work is much more diverse than previously documented. Although many tax concerns have centered around making sure that persons do not convert expenses into phantom businesses for the purpose of shielding from taxation expenses that are truly hobby costs, the predominance of occupations like plumbing, fuel oil delivery, and long-distance trucking would mitigate against this view of home-based workers. In addition, the lucrative returns after taxes for such occupations as crafts and services would indicate that these are not predominantly hobbies posing as jobs. Tests such as percentage of income from work, work hour minimums (i.e., as used in this study), and the continuing profit necessary in a minimum number of years should weed out tax abuse.

On the other hand, the recent Supreme Court decision in the *Soliman* case to restrict the home office deduction (reported in Chapters 2 and 6) could have a debilitating effect on home-based workers, preventing them from producing benefits to themselves and their local and national economies while doing little to curb abuses. For example, contractors, salespeople, carpenters, and others could lose deductions for home offices, as could farmers who only farm land not adjacent to their dwelling. On the other hand, home-based workers with more financial sophistication and those in more populous areas can merely rent a neighbor's spare room or a readily available storefront, or even trade home offices with each other, and take full deductions for such rentals with little loss of convenience or income.

Although we do not know the status of employers of home-based wage earners or of the employees of home-based businesses in this study, there are federal labor issues that probably affect each. One is the status of employees as independent contractors or as regular employees.

Following on the heels of the revisions of the Fair Labor Standards Act, the Internal Revenue Service (IRS) set out to ensure that home-based employees and small businesses that hired only a few employees were each paying appropriate taxes. This concern was both for income tax purposes and for the self-employment tax that feeds into the Social Security pool. There is a legitimate concern that employees may be victimized by employers, being paid a lower wage than is necessary for them to receive a decent wage and pay the taxes necessary for the independent contractor designation. In addition to cost savings for the firm, independent contracting of services also lowers the cost of paperwork for such employers because the independent contractor bears the major burden of tax reporting.

Under current tax law, employers must withhold payroll taxes for their employees and pay half of the employees' Social Security taxes and all of their unemployment compensation tax. If an individual is an independent contractor, the business using his or her services need only file a 1099 form reporting how much it paid that person. The contractor pays his or her taxes directly to the IRS. In 1988, the IRS began challenging the independent contractor status and forcing businesses that hire independent contractors to reclassify them as employees. The U.S. Small Business Administration estimates that there are five million independent contractors nationwide and that roughly two-thirds of them will be reclassified as employees by the IRS's new standards, forcing them to abandon their independent status. It is a legitimate concern that they be appropriately compensated, taxed, and monitored, but it is not clear whether the burden ought to be on the wage earners, many of whom are home-based, or on the employing firms, which are likely to be small and may also be home-based. There is a need to see that home-based workers are well informed and assisted at state and local levels to comply with these federal mandates.

Besides potential tax abuses, there is another potential abuse of home-based wage earners. Sweatshop exploitation of home-working wage earners and the misuse of child labor in either wage or business work continue to be concerns to be addressed at the federal level. Deregulation for most of the textile-related and craft industries covered by the Fair Labor Standards Act made many home-based workers potentially subject to exploitation under state control, but this issue continues to be of concern to unions and other national labor organizations. Although this study indicated that 68.7% of wage earners thought they had a lot of control over the timing of their work, there is no comparable measure of control for business owners. Future research should address some of the self-exploitation that business owners do to themselves to sustain their work.

Collective legal issues. Although most of the home-based workers surveyed had health care coverage, the data lack detail about the extent or cost of such protection. Because so many of the home-based workers were covered by health insurance from another job or other family member's job, it is assumed that attachment to the centralized work force is a critical necessity to these workers in order for them to receive health care benefits. Thus the numbers of people engaged in home-based work are expected to rise if any of the currently debated national health care plans are implemented.

State and Regional Policy Issues

Many of the policy issues for these political bodies concentrate on licensing, some environmental protection, and the safety and security of labor force participants. It is of note that the legal issue or regulation of most concern to the participants in the nine-state study was environmental. Unfortunately, limitations to the data do not permit further exploration of this issue; therefore, it is not known whether disposition of solid or hazardous waste material, air emission standards for vehicles, water contamination, and any of a dozen other regulations are particularly troublesome to home-based operations.

For many regions, and increasingly for state departments of economic development, home-based work is part of an overall strategy to attract more jobs, maintain an educated work force, and increase the multiplier effect of income generated within their boundaries. But upgrading existing businesses and providing start-up assistance to home-based businesses often lag behind efforts to attract an outside employer. As many rural communities have sadly discovered, outside employers often bring their own managers with them, recruiting only low-paid service workers from the local population. Under-standing the tremendous economic impact of the home-based businesses already in their communities may help restore equity to this situation. For example, 88% of the home-based businesses in the nine-state sample sold most of their products or services in their own states. A similar percentage bought most of their supplies in-state. This does not mean that the same dollars are changing hands. These businesses contribute to their local economies at least three times, in the original purchases and sales as well as in the first item each of their vendors and each of their customers spend their money on. This multiplier effect is healthy for local economies. Finally, the total purchases of all the businesses in terms of their expenditures, which average 60% of gross income for each business, are a large benefit to the immediate community as well as to the state, to which sales and income taxes are paid.

The results of this study indicate that it is in the states' best interest to support home-based work as an economic development strategy. It not only provides jobs and income for the family and some immediate workers, but it also ripples out through the local economy in the purchase of other goods and services. The low percentage of persons indicating conflict with laws or regulations shows that these workers have found information that assists them in avoiding legal conflicts. State-level dissemination of information can greatly assist in alerting potential home-based workers to legal and regulatory issues, thereby reducing the barriers to entry for new businesses and reducing hassles for established home-based workers. For example, designating a business ombudsman with authority and access across bureaucratic levels and adding toll-free hot lines for business information would be helpful. Furthermore, registering these businesses as a specific class of workers can facilitate their continued positive effect on local and state economies.

One of the more significant findings in this study was that there were so few single-parent households among the respondents. This indicates that while flexible time use is often cited as an advantage of home-based work, the definition of this flexibility may need to be reconsidered. The time demands of home-based work are heavy. The flexibility is that workers can schedule work periods even though the total hours worked may be fixed. For single-parent families, the demands of family are not sufficiently flexible to allow the benefits of home-based work to come into play. This is extremely important information for state-level policy makers who have touted welfare reform programs to lower the number of persons on aid by training women and encouraging them to set up self-employment enterprises. These data indicate that, to the extent that the population receiving benefits consists of single parents, great caution must be exercised in using this solution. Home-based workers who are single parents need support systems similar to the informal network that families provide. These systems may include child and elder care collectives, neighborhood accountability for capital development, and a careful understanding of the work-family conflict faced by these families.

Local Communities

Local communities are perhaps the most important to consider when discussing the policy implications of home-based work. They are affected both positively and negatively by such work. The prevalence of home-based businesses in rural counties and in sparsely populated regions of urban counties indicates that they may fill much needed niches in these communities. They provide services and goods that would be more expensive or less convenient for their neighbors to acquire if they had to travel greater distances.

At an even more immediate level, the opportunity to have home-based workers in neighborhoods has two faces. On the one hand, certain types of businesses, especially services, may increase traffic, causing wear and tear on roads and increasing safety concerns. But the flight from neighborhoods, especially suburban ones where mom and dad go to work and the children are off to school, leaves a community vulnerable to crime, especially break-ins. Home-based workers, with their flexible time schedules, intermittent traffic, and general presence, help deter crime not just in their own homes but in their immediate neighborhoods.

In addition, in most families, the children return from school earlier than the parents return from work. A home-based worker on the block deters groupings of latchkey children who may otherwise get in trouble as well as provides immediate support for his or her own children.

Although home-based work may not be an unmitigated blessing to legal entities at any level, it provides a basis for legitimate support in building a collaboration between federal, state, and local institutions and families to provide stimulating and rewarding work environments. Often people may be unable to maintain work skills and make money while simultaneously providing for the day-to-day needs of their families. Therefore, home-based work deserves careful attention and appropriate support from governmental entities and neighbors.

IMPLICATIONS FOR PEOPLE

The Worker and the Work

When researchers involved in the nine-state project began analyzing the data in terms of gender, they were both astonished and chagrined to discover that many of the gender effects observable in the centralized workplace carried into home-based work as well. On average, women homeworkers earned less; gravitated toward traditionally female occupations such as hairdressing, child care, clerical, and craft work; restructured their time more to meet family demands; and spent less time on income-producing work than did males. There are at least two ways of interpreting these findings. One is that women in certain family situations choose home-based work to combine income production with high family demands and so arrange their work to fit around their family by doing fewer hours of paid work. They may also choose occupations that have mainly female workers because these are the ones they know or are skilled in. In other words, rather than undertaking some research to discover what market niches they can fill, they base or combine their occupational choice on personal skills and interests and then go looking for a customer base.

It may also be that educational and experiential deficits in marketing, acquisition of outside capital, business structure, employee relations, cash flow management, and quantity production severely limit women's employment choices and income potential. Women earners may be particularly handicapped because the number of firms employing homeworkers is still small and because these jobs are often in communication, telemarketing and reservations services, craft or textile-related production, or semiskilled assembly work. Women business owners are particularly disadvantaged for they are working longer hours and earning less than women wage workers and less than a quarter of what men wage workers make. They are also spending 85% of their working time tied to the house—suggesting that, in addition to their home-based paid work, they are doing all or most of the housework as well. One study found that women who work at home spend the equivalent of three business days a week on grocery shopping, cooking, cleaning, washing dishes and clothes, doing family paperwork, and child care. The implications for women contemplating home-based work are clear: without successful negotiations with family members over sharing child care and domestic work, this "second shift" may take its toll through overwork, exhaustion, and resentment at "doing it all."

Most women home-based workers were able to carve out a separate space for their paid work, but women in adult-only and full-nest families shared that space with other family activities, sometimes while simultaneously performing their paid work. Other studies of homeworkers have noted that having a separate work space devoted solely to the needs of the work to be performed, secured with a sturdy (and soundproofed) door, and located away from family activities minimizes conflicts among home-based work, household production, and leisure. Some of the tools appropriate for the work (e.g., sewing scissors or garden herbicides) would be hazardous in the hands of small children. Some work spaces may need to be remodeled to make them appropriate for clients, customers, specialized equipment, or employees. The point is that home-based work takes space, sometimes all the household table space, basement storage area, spare bedroom closets, and the living room floor. Territorial problems arise when family members not involved in the business need to reclaim some of the space for family activities. Potential homeworkers will need to plan for the spatial needs of the business so as to minimize intrusions on home and family life and to avoid pushing family members into living with uncomfortable situations.

Owners versus Earners

On average, home business owners worked fewer hours and earned less than their earner counterparts. Although the nine-state sample was predominantly male, women chose home business ownership at a rate almost equal to that of men. Men's businesses were more likely to have been established longer and to employ paid helpers. Income from the home-based business is affected by gender, type of occupation, hours worked, having an outside job, and the number of and amount of care needed by dependent family members. Having children under 6 present depresses women's income by nearly $4,000 annually. Women business owners' annual incomes are so low ($7,691) that one is tempted to say, "Why do they do it?" Obviously, the flexibility to care for family members and the opportunity to work at their own pace are prime advantages. In addition, the experience of owning and managing a business can increase self-confidence and make one aware of hidden talents and abilities that could be translated into other, more financially remunerative work at another time.

Women earners face many of the same challenges women business owners do. They list the disadvantages as the inability to separate family life and work, working too much, and not being able to get away from work. Other challenges for off-site workers of either gender involve adequate and fair compensation for the hours worked, the amount and timing of work, opportunities for salary increases and advancement, and missing out on special assignments because of being "out of sight and out of mind." Off-site employees are not always eligible for fringe benefits such as paid sick leave and vacations, workers' compensation, or health, life, and disability insurance coverage. Home-based earners may also incur extra expenses in adding or remodeling work space, buying equipment, paying for extra property insurance, and transporting materials.

Most home-based earners are concentrated in white-collar jobs: marketing and sales, clerical and administrative support, and management. About 10% of male earners are in the mechanical and transportation trades, for example, long-distance truckers hauling for a larger company. Women earners are clustered in clerical and administrative support positions; only a minority of women are in higher-paying managerial positions. When sorting through their employment choices, prospective home-based workers may want to consider what the income potential of their home-based work is and whether they or another household member will need to have another job.

Inside the Homeworking Family

Management of household labor when income-generating activities are not spatially separated from household production and leisure activities can be a problem. Domestic work consists of essential, regular chores that must be performed by someone, either a household member or hired help. Families can reduce the pressure of home-based work either by changing standards or by accepting less work when important family activities conflict with times of high pressure in the home-based work. This study shows that home-based workers are more likely to adjust their personal time than to hire outside help. Only a quarter of the homeworking families in the nine-state sample use hired help, although during peak times nearly half have family and friends help out with either the paid work or domestic work.

Generally, it has been thought that because of flexibility of scheduling and the closeness of the work space, working at home would eliminate the need for child care for some home-based working women, since women tend to contribute most of the caregiving time within families. This study shows that while home-based work can alleviate the need for child care in some cases, home-based workers need and use child care services. Anecdotal evidence shows that children's needs and presence often determine the homeworker's time and ability to work. They report rarely or never having large blocks of time, free of distractions, to concentrate on the work. Some homeworkers plan their work activities for when children are in school and when they are asleep. Although this schedule may work in the short run, making rubber stamps or repairing lawn mowers at 2:00 A.M. night after night can increase a homeworker's sense of isolation and overwork burnout.

Even without children, household responsibilities have a way of perpetually interrupting paid work—houses and gardens demand attention, as do spouses. Family conflict is not an inevitable result of working at home, but homeworkers need to be aware that bringing income production into one's residence will affect everyone who lives there, even if only one family member is directly involved in the work. Cooperation, understanding, and assistance will be needed from all, and so will frank and honest negotiation. Familiar assumptions people make about who does what may no longer apply.

Finally, what does it mean for family life to have more time together and more opportunities to share physical space within the home? A centralized workplace separates the home and work for the worker, but homeworkers are responsible for maintaining that separation themselves. Many homeworkers in the nine-state sample maintain a separate work space to create a sense of distance between home and work. Other strategies to create boundaries between work activities and family activities could include restricting access to the work space, relocating social activities outside the home, and setting a strict schedule of work activities (e.g., setting times when people could call).

The Community Connection

One of the most significant findings from the nine-state study is the amount of income these businesses and wage workers are earning and the substantial contributions they are making to their local, state, and national economies. It is estimated that, in 1988 dollars, the total net income from home-based work amounted to 108.4 *billion* dollars. In some respects this is hidden income— "hidden" in the sense that home-based workers themselves are often invisible to each other and, sometimes, to their communities.

Some years ago, community developers investigating the impacts of an elderly population on rural communities discovered that retirement cash transfers constituted a substantial basic industry representing net money flow into the local economy and that these transfer payments were potential economic development instruments for local communities. It was suggested, not altogether facetiously, that chambers of commerce should quit "smokestack chasing" and begin recruiting the silver-haired economic base to improve their job and income situations.

It appears that planners have overlooked or underestimated the income stream generated by home-based workers. The home-based are consumers of goods and services, and as the nine-state study shows, they are more inclined to make their purchases in their local market whenever the desired goods and services are available. Yet home-based workers demand very little from their local communities in more miles of new roads, sewer and water lines, additional housing and schools, or expanded police and fire protection, as new industries sometimes do. Also, they contribute to the tax base of the community, for they are rarely given the same tax subsidies as the International Harvesters, Chryslers, or United Airlines.

Because three-quarters of the home-based sample are self-employed business owners, communities are missing a golden opportunity by ignoring or obstructing the formation of these desirable businesses. They create jobs, increase sales for existing businesses, and are responsible for innovation and technological gains that fuel state and national economies. Home-based workers, as a collective force, could have the political clout of another American Association of Retired Persons (AARP). But persons engaged in home-based work will need to support and be supported by organizations and networks that advance the home-based agenda to increase the awareness of their economic impact and reduce institutional barriers.

Continuation of Home-Based Work

Business failure data, as generated by the U.S. Small Business Administration (SBA), always make the odds of winning the lottery sound plausible. About one-third of all new establishments survive to their 5th birthday, but only one in five is still operating by the 10th year. These low survival rates often discourage small-business development, especially in rural areas. Yet retention rates for the nine-state sample are extremely high—75% of the sample was still actively engaged in home-based work 3 years after the original survey. Surprisingly, the amount of income generated by the work was not influential in predicting whether the worker would be performing the same work in the future, although not generating enough income is often given as a reason for exiting. What was significant, in addition to the age and education of the worker, was the number of years engaged in the work. In other words, the more years you had been in business, the more years you were likely to stay in business—a daunting statistic to someone just starting out. What is interesting is the subjective attitudes about home-based work that are influential in business continuation. Positive feelings about the work and expectations about changing one's attitude about the work are both predictors of business duration.

The retention rates displayed by these home-based workers are extremely encouraging. But home-based work is not for every individual or family. It requires a great deal of self-motivation, availability and access to capital, and discipline. Working at home can create feelings of isolation and tension over the division of labor and business responsibilities, family demands that undermine business activities, and too much or too little family togetherness. Prospective home-based workers need to be as aware of the pitfalls as of the successes before determining whether this employment choice is right for them.

SUGGESTIONS FOR THE FUTURE

Home-based work is a phenomenon of America's contemporary work force. Most observers predict that it will continue to grow in numbers and strength in the future. Some people have always worked at home: for example, salespeople, contractors, artists and writers, ministers, some professionals such as architects and accountants—and farming is the original home-based business. Being one's own boss has always been part of the American dream. The social and economic changes currently taking place in the United States are creating a large pool of dislocated workers and disaffected urban dwellers willing to take their experience and energy into ventures of their own—some of them at home, where the financial risk of start-up is lessened. Home-based work also offers employment opportunities to those who cannot hold traditional jobs because of physical disabilities, family responsibilities, or distance from traditional centers of employment. Shifts in lifestyle preferences are fueling the movement to home-based work. Workers want out of the commute to the central city, high costs, air and water pollution, overcrowded and understaffed schools, congestion, crime, and violence.

The trend toward home-based work has been a quiet revolution. Clearly, the popular press and media have failed to recognize fully the disparate nature of home-based work and its workers. Little, if any, attention has been paid to the part communities play in providing both incentives for and barriers against home-based work.

This book is dedicated to the hope that researchers, educators, practitioners, policy makers, and people in general will pay more and different attention to the world of home-based employment. The realities of this vital and economically important segment of the work force are not fully comprehended by public or private perspectives, including those of the home-based workers themselves.

Five Research Suggestions for the Future

As a direct result of the nine-state study, the literature is growing in the specific area of home-based work and the workers who perform it. By most judgments, the home-based work force is one of the fastest growing in the country. Building on the results of the nine-state study, future research is needed to *study a larger group of home-based workers*, to learn more about their characteristics and problems. Further studies are needed to explore the motivations behind the home-based work choice although the major advantages of such work are known. For example, what is the level of participation by minorities, low-income groups, and the disabled in the arena of home-based work? Researchers need to ask questions about job satisfaction, the ways in which this work meshes with family life, the human capital gains made through this employment, and the costs and benefits of alternative employment, if available.

How many more home-based businesses would there be if restrictions such as zoning, excessive regulation, exorbitant licensing fees, and unaffordable health insurance were alleviated? Based on the estimated contributions from the nine-state study, further research is needed to document in detail the economic impact of home-based businesses on their communities. With a larger sample of businesses, including both home-based ones and those on Main Street, the contributions by types of business could be further studied, as well as the differences between enterprises that are home-based and those that are not.

The nine-state data are limited relative to how much other income-generating activity takes place in homeworking families that detracts from home-based work income and time. To what extent do they use telecommuting or contract work out to other home-based businesses or to businesses that are not home-based? More research is needed concerning this more intricate look at overall work activities.

Additional information is needed to compare profiles of both home-based workers and workers who are not home-based for similarities in age, education, seasonality of work, and occupational choice; such comparisons would reveal whether certain occupations lend themselves more readily to home-based work. Data from the nine-state study did not permit a detailed examination of hourly wage rates and other returns to the home-based work effort for various groups of home-based workers such as owners and earners or for various occupation types. Future research needs to explore such aspects.

Based on the nine-state study and its finding concerning the sources of health insurance coverage, it would be useful to investigate the level or amount of health insurance coverage. It is not known if home-based workers suffer inadequate coverage more than other workers in the centralized workplace do.

The follow-up data in the nine-state study are the first of their kind to reveal factors related to home-based work over time. A *longitudinal study of a larger group of home-based workers* would pinpoint when it may be best to begin, change, or terminate home-based work considering various family or life course perspectives. Some of these would include transitions such as marriage, divorce, death, births or adoptions, and changes in dependency of family members. Longitudinal advantages and disadvantages of home-based work relating to family and self could be discovered.

It is important to make a proper estimate of the income stream generated by home-based work in its meaning for the household and to follow the income flow over time so that returns from such work choices can be properly evaluated. Even though the follow-up data are the first of their kind, low numbers prevent in-depth examination of workers who expanded or moved their businesses to Main Street or industrial parks. How many businesses start as home-based businesses? A larger sample of home-based businesses followed over time would make it possible to explore the dynamics of work and business, such as worker satisfaction, that are important for retention. Further investigation into starting, stopping, or changing work as it is structured by gender and gender issues, geographic location, perceived occupational opportunities, human capital characteristics, and market conditions such as the availability of other employment would enrich our present understanding.

Based on the findings of the nine-state study, further study is needed to *glean more detail about the work and the family*, particularly children and other dependents in the homeworking family. Are they better off than children of parents who work in a centralized workplace? Worse off? Nobody knows, and much further research is needed.

What part does home-based work play in creating stereotypical gender, family, and economic roles? More research is needed to understand the best combinations of family functioning types with different occupations. Although management behavior for the home-based work coincides with established conceptualizations, management behavior relative to the family needs further study to develop a more realistic representation of this aspect of family life.

Little is known about the size, arrangement, or amenities needed for the home office. Computers, modems, faxes, and cellular communication allow work to take place anywhere. Future studies outside the scope of this project are needed to understand more fully how work in the future will be carried out.

Based on the findings of the nine-state study, we *need more detail about the home business, especially about female owners and their home businesses* in general. Why do women business owners continue to work at such low pay? Why do rural owners feel less positive about their quality of life?

The findings about work space from the nine-state study show the need for more information about intensity of use of the chosen work space or spaces and how the work is spaced through the workday, possibly in different work sites. Much further research is needed to study interactions between work activities and home activities relative to intensity of effort, overlapping, dovetailing and sequencing, duration of work segments, and other details about the nature of the work or its tasks. More research is needed to study the specifics of work and family interactions and to investigate specific management practices such as planning and other managerial practices that may be innovated by the home-based work. How are disparate demands handled throughout the workday or over longer periods of time?

More research is needed to reveal a possibly different division of labor within the family relative to the unpaid household work. Do the amount of work and the responsibility for doing it change among family members and over time? To uncover the sequencing of work and family activities would necessitate the *collection of time-use data through open-ended time diaries to examine the true complexities and detailed nature of home-based work, family work, and leisure activities.*

Educational and Practitioner Suggestions for the Future

Educators and practitioners are a group of professionals that includes traditional classroom educators, cooperative extension faculty, community development specialists, and advisers or consultants of all types, but in particular family therapists, business consultants, and legal and financial advisers. The challenges to them in the future include some of the following.

First, traditional educators could *broaden their curricula to expose learners to a wide range of employment alternatives, including self-employment and home-based businesses.* Because management is the factor most closely linked with business success or failure, providing high-quality management education at a low cost to strengthen the managerial capacities of existing and potential home-based enterprises may be one of the most effective things educators can do. Experience, training, and development will help potential entrepreneurs identify and engage in profitable business opportunities. Implementation and follow-up assistance will help them succeed. For example, educators and business consultants can help start-up operations in obtaining financing and assist home-based entrepreneurs in evaluating capital investment decisions and marketing strategies based on their position in the formation and growth of their venture.

Second, educators providing high-quality education at public, secondary, and technical schools will improve the quality of the home-based work force, which will attract and create higher-paying jobs for home-based workers. Third, local universities and technical schools can sponsor week-long "hands-on" workshops, provide after-hours or weekend degree programs, enhance long-distance learning via satellite downlinks, and institute other innovative methods to provide vocational, professional, and technical education to keep homeworkers aware of the latest developments in their field.

Therapists and consultants can expand their practices to include assistance to home-based working clients. For example, consultants could start a business and industry visitation program in which community leaders visit home-based businesses on a regular basis to uncover limitations to growth. It may be possible to reduce these limitations through some form of local public or collective private action.

Practitioners can also provide advertising and marketing assistance, especially for businesses whose products or services could be sold in nonlocal markets. Data from the nine-state study show that businesses that did not limit their trade to the local area are more profitable.

Business consultants, accountants, legal advisers, and bankers can also identify and make available appropriate business and management training and technical assistance from small business development centers (SBDCs),[1] innovation centers, community development corporations, cooperative extension educators, industrial cooperatives, business incubators, community-based organizations such as the SBA's SCORE/ACE organization, small-business investment companies, and community and technical colleges.

Educators and practitioners can help individuals, families, and communities *recognize that home-based workers play a critical and insufficiently recognized role in the process of economic growth and development*. Their collective contributions to the family economy are discussed in detail in Chapter 6. In addition, small businesses are net job creators, profit producers, and key innovators. Approximately 50% of new jobs created in our various economies can be traced to small establishments. Small businesses are more profitable than firms of all other sizes except those with over $1 billion in assets. Small firms and independent investors are the main source of innovation—they innovate more efficiently and at a lower cost than larger firms. Local economic development in turn affects household compositions, geographic tenure patterns, social and physical environments, and quality of life.

Finally, therapists well versed in the complex interface between work and family can *assist in developing effective strategies for identifying and addressing issues in homeworking families* such as work overload, the parent-child subsystem, family power, communication styles, divisions of labor and territorial space, financial equity, and boundary overlap.

Policy Suggestions for the Future

On the whole, the home-based ventures in the nine-state study demanded very little from their local communities. An encouraging environment, however, would nurture and promote the development of home-based work. This condition exists in local communities where there are real development opportunities, available funds, rewards for risk taking, role models, and an absence of barriers. Public policy makers cannot by themselves create economic activity in a community. But there are policies and programs that can facilitate it, by removing those things that currently inhibit growth and development and by reinforcing and encouraging grass-roots investment.

First, taxes, zoning, signage requirements, and permit regulations and practices can be audited to ascertain their positive or negative impact on the home business community; then *suggestions can be proposed to change zoning laws and to streamline license and permit procedures that prove particularly onerous to home-based businesses and wage workers.*

Second, *financial support is often a critical missing piece in economic development.* Home-based businesses face significant problems in securing capital for both long-term investments in equipment and short-term inventory financing. Local policy makers can be of assistance in influencing credit unions, banks, and other lenders to extend their loan criteria to include deserving home-based businesses that would otherwise not be able to expand their operations. In this same vein, civic and community leaders can work with states and associations or councils of governments to establish a revolving loan fund as seed and venture capital or to meet a variety of fixed-asset and working-capital needs for existing home-based business ventures.

Community leaders can encourage and perhaps sponsor a business "incubator without walls" for one-step management and technical assistance at reasonable or subsidized rates. Rural policy makers interested in the growth of home-based work need to provide local and regional services that compete in quality and price with those of urban communities. This can improve efficiency in home-based work and open access to nonlocal markets. Communications is a good example. Cities, villages, and towns with outdated telephone systems present a major barrier in an increasingly computer-dependent society.

Finally, continuation and expansion at the state and national level of support for basic research in home-based work is *critical to document its impact on local economies, to point out critical areas at the interface of individual, family, and neighborhood, and to provide accurate information to homeworking families and their professional advisers.*

Suggestions for People in the Future

Continued growth in home-based work will be aided by advances in technology, which are developing more sophisticated tools that make it easier for the home-based to compete and be successful. At times, however, it seems as though home-based workers are the Rodney Dangerfields of employment choice—they must still battle for respect. There are initiatives that will need action in the next few years, at either the personal or the collective level, before home-based enterprises will be treated professionally.

One is to *reduce the number of marginal home business activities* through education, books, videos, and mentor programs. Too many home-based workers don't take themselves or their ventures seriously. For example, one man was running his upholstery business out of his garage—working a graveyard shift at a manufacturing plant, sleeping in the mornings, and "daylighting" at his business in the afternoons. He had no separate line for a business phone and no answering machine, and calls were being answered by any one of eight uninterested kids. He never returned any customer calls because he never got any messages. The onetime outlay for an answering machine and the monthly cost of a separate phone line would have paid for themselves within weeks. Similar examples can be found of homeworkers who have no business cards, no business license or resale number, no separate bank account, and no clear understanding of where their niche is or can be. These people need to be challenged to get professional or be pushed out by an increasing number of highly serious and well-trained entrepreneurs.

There is a need to *reverse the federal, state, and local opposition* that has kept home-based businesses small and vulnerable. They have been denied credit-card vendor status and access to wholesale suppliers, hampered by restrictive zoning laws and on-again/off-again tax deductions, and victimized by con artists who take advantage of their inexperience. Work-at-home schemes to stuff envelopes, raise worms, and sell on multilevel pyramids as well as telemarketing "boiler" rooms stigmatize and defeat legitimate home businesses.

Because growth in home-based work has been such a quiet revolution, many who are actually working out of their homes in the same or neighboring communities do not know about each other. As the nine-state study shows, the most popular form of advertising is word-of-mouth. Although testimonials are very powerful, they are no substitute for other marketing and promotional activities. Respect and success can be enhanced by *promoting and publicizing home-based business activities* in the press and in city/county council and other public meetings, by giving timely awards of merit for contributions to local economic development, and by encouraging chambers of commerce and other civic groups to expand their membership and focus to include home-based businesses.

In a similar manner, civic leaders and consumers can *encourage purchases from local home-based businesses*, promoting the theme "buy at home" as a bit of wordplay with a double meaning. This creates a win-win situation for everybody as increasing numbers of these businesses expand to create more local employment and income.

Finally, individuals can *increase the professionalism of home-based work* by joining local chapters of organizations such as the American Home Business

Association, the National Association for the Self Employed, the Home Executives National Networking Association, the National Alliance of Home-based Businesswomen, the National Association for Cottage Industry, and others. In addition to the political clout obtained from sheer numbers, homeworkers can inform, inspire, encourage, and support each other through newsletters and computer networks. The Home Office Network On-Line manages an electronic directory of member products and services, technical support panels, advice columns, and advertising opportunities.

The deliberation, ingenuity, flexibility, and resourcefulness with which home-based workers shape their environments will continue to sustain work, social, and private lives for themselves and their families. By investigating, sharing, and supporting the dimensions of these environments with past, current, potential, and hopeful home-based workers, researchers, educators, practitioners, and policy makers can also make a difference. These coordinated efforts assure home-based workers that they have willing associates in their quest toward lucrative and satisfying work environments as well as meaningful and integrated lives.

NOTE

1. Small business development centers (SBDCs) are a university- and college-based system now found in virtually every state in the country. Each center is headquartered on a university or college campus and is designed to serve as a focal point for the coordination of federal, state, local, and private resources to aid small businesses within a single area, at no cost to the small business or entrepreneur. It provides counseling and training for owners and operators of small firms in developing feasibility studies, business plans, financing, cash flow management, marketing, production, organization, engineering, and technical problem solutions.

Appendix A

Research Methods
Including Sample Design and
Questionnaire Development

Mary Winter and Kathryn Stafford

INTRODUCTION

This nine-state research study, "At-Home Income Generation: Impact on Management, Productivity, and Stability in Rural/Urban Families," examined households in which there was home-based work. This project, its data set, and its analyses are unique for three reasons. First, households in rural counties were oversampled so that there were numbers great enough to examine in detail the nature of home-based work in rural communities. Questions were asked so that the relationship between the household engaged in home-based work and its community could be explored to some extent. Second, the phenomenon of home-based work is essentially a rare event from a statistical standpoint. Although this form of employment is growing and is seen as a strategy for families to cope with a changing economic climate, few have studied its impact on the family. Third, data from this project permit researchers to examine the household's management and decision-making practices, the household's economic stability, and the county characteristics from U.S. census data.

The purpose of Appendix A is to describe the research methods used in the project and to provide basic information about the sample. The first section specifies the research design, including issues in sample selection. Then the development of the interview schedule is discussed. Interviewing procedures are outlined in the next section, followed by a discussion of data preparation. Chapters 3, 4, 5, 6, and 7 provide an overview of the socioeconomic and demographic characteristics of the overall sample and many and varied subanalyses, including a reinterview of 81.2% of the

The content of this appendix was developed in part by reprinting with permission from Human Sciences Press selected sections of an article previously published as the following: Stafford, K., Winter, M., Duncan, K. A., & Genalo, M. A. (1992). Studying at-home income generation: Issues and methods. *Journal of Family and Economic Issues*, *13*, 139–158.

original sample 3 years later, in 1992. When appropriate, the decisions that were necessary are highlighted and discussed.

RESEARCH DESIGN

The research objectives were to be accomplished through analyses of data gathered from households in which one or more individuals earned income by working at home. Face-to-face interviews were deemed prohibitively expensive, particularly if there was to be centralized data collection. Furthermore, both the depth and breadth of data required precluded a mailed questionnaire (Dillman, 1978). A short telephone interview, no more than 30 minutes, seemed to offer the highest quality while minimizing the cost.

Because of the desire to examine income-generating activities in both urban and rural areas, a stratified sampling plan would be needed, to ensure representation of the less populous rural areas. Data would be gathered from two strata in each state participating in the project, a rural stratum and an urban stratum.

As with most studies, decisions about the research design, the sample, and the techniques to be employed in data collection were not made independently. The interrelationships of such decisions in the present study were quite complex because they helped to define not only the project itself, but also the members of the research team. This section details the decisions made to select the sample of households for the study and to select the individual to be interviewed within each household.

Sampling Issues

Decisions made about sampling methods for the project affected a variety of outcomes, including the states that would be included in the study. The states that participated had a researcher who could devote at least 20% of his or her time to the project for 5 years and funds to support centralized, uniform data collection according to the protocol developed. Except for the salaries of the researchers and graduate assistants, the cost of the data collection represented the bulk of the costs of the study. Providing a reliable estimate of the cost of data collection was, therefore, essential to the formation of the research team itself, and it could only be accomplished after decisions had been made about the sampling and data collection methods.

A further complication was that funding from some states was contingent upon the ability to make inferences about at-home income generation in a particular state and/or the rural counties in that state. To meet those needs while also permitting generalizability beyond individual states, a stratified random sample was devised. For each state, the goal was 100 interviews, 40 from the urban stratum and 60 from the rural stratum. Counties containing at least one city with a population of 25,000 or more were designated as urban and the remaining counties as rural.

Sampling Home-Based Workers

As noted by Pratt (1987), the way in which home-based work has been defined has influenced estimates of the number of workers engaged in it. Estimates of the percentage of the population engaged in home-based work have ranged from 8% to 23% of the work force, depending on the definition used. Even if the least restrictive definition were used (i.e., that 23% of the work force is home-based), only one worker in four could be expected to be a home-based worker; the most restrictive definition would yield 1 home-based worker out of every 10 workers. Assuming the average number of workers per household is somewhere between one and two, three households would need to be contacted to locate one home-based worker; under the more restrictive definition, there would be one home-based worker in every eight households.

Home-based workers, then, are a rare population (Kalton & Anderson, 1986), one that is difficult to locate and study. One source of data about home-based workers is the decennial census. Researchers who have used the census to examine home-based workers (Kraut, 1988; Kraut & Grambsch, 1987) have defined home-based workers as those who responded "work at home" to the question about means of transportation to work. Analysis based on census data has been limited to characteristics of the worker, household, and the work.

Researchers who have examined the work-family interface with attitudinal data have employed a variety of methods to locate such individuals. Beach (1987), for example, used snowball techniques to locate her sample of 15 families in which one member was working at home. Ahrentzen (1990) used a number of lists and personal references to locate the 104 homeworkers in her sample. In their study of clerical workers, Gerson and Kraut (1988) used the yellow pages listings to identify local firms offering clerical services. Those firms were asked for a list of employees who worked at home. Christensen (1988a) included a questionnaire in one issue of *Family Circle* magazine; 14,000 women working at home responded. To locate their sample of individuals making and selling crafts, Littrell, Stout, and Reilly (1991) sampled from lists maintained by craft organizations, craft retailers, and cooperative extension.

If the conclusions of the present study were to be readily generalizable, nonprobability techniques were inappropriate. Scientific examination of the phenomenon required that a random sample of households be screened to yield the households of interest. The decision to use probability techniques to obtain the sample, along with the decision to administer the interview schedule only to households in which at least one member was a home-based worker, dictated a two-stage process for data collection. First, a short screening procedure would be used to identify eligible households from a sample of the population. Second, a 30-minute interview schedule would be administered to a respondent from each eligible household at a later date.

Sampling

The Statistical Laboratory of the Statistics Department at Iowa State University was selected as the subcontractor for data collection, coding, and data entry. The sample was purchased from Survey Sampling, a Connecticut firm that uses telephone directories supplemented with school registration lists, magazine subscription lists, voter registration lists, auto registration lists, and driver's license information to select random samples of specified populations. The firm provides names, addresses, and telephone numbers of the sample. The alternative for generating a random sample for a telephone interview, random digit dialing, was estimated to be considerably more expensive because of the time and money lost in dialing nonhousehold and nonworking numbers. In addition, using a listed sample, even though it might be somewhat outdated, would offer the advantage of having the name of the householder. Being able to call the householder by name increases the response rate.

The disadvantage of using a sample generated from telephone listings was that the sampling frame would be limited to those having a telephone with a listed number. Households in which someone worked at home should be less likely to have an unlisted number than other households, however, because the household telephone would also be the business phone.

Survey Sampling advertised their lists as expected to yield households at a rate of 85%. Previous estimates of the prevalence of households containing one or more home-based workers could not be used to estimate the number of initial phone calls needed to yield the desired sample size because the estimates differed widely according to the definition of home-based work upon which the estimate was based. Consequently, a pilot study was conducted to estimate the prevalence of working numbers on the list and the prevalence of eligible households in each stratum.

For the pilot study, 70 households in each stratum of each state except Hawaii were called. At the time of the pilot study, Hawaii had not joined the project. When that state joined the project, averages of the other states were used to calculate the number of phone contacts needed for Hawaii. To allow for attrition, it was assumed that a loss of 5% would be experienced at the screening stage and a loss of 15% at the interviewing stage. Table A.1 shows the prevalence of residences and eligible households in the pilot study, upon which the sample size estimates were based.

After the pilot study, a decision was made to exclude the five counties making up New York City; Philadelphia County, Pennsylvania; and three counties in the Detroit metropolitan area. The mean yield of residential numbers from the numbers provided was 84.75%, the rate promised by Survey Sampling. The percentage of telephone numbers yielding residences ranged from 76% in urban New York to 91% in rural Utah. In the pilot survey, the percentage of eligible households varied widely across strata, from 3.8% in urban New York to 17.9% in rural Vermont (Table A.1).

Based on the results of the pilot survey, a stratified random sample of 18,956 phone numbers was drawn. Each number was called during the winter of 1988–1989. Professional telephone interviewers administered a 3-to-5-minute interview schedule designed to elicit the information needed to ascertain if someone in the household was a home-based worker and, if so, a description of the work, the number of hours worked during the year, and the length of time the worker had been engaged in the at-home income-generating activity. Information was collected about a maximum of four different types of home-based work for each household. The majority of households had only one worker engaged in one home-based activity.

Table A.2 provides information on the proportion of residences, the proportion of eligible households, and the attrition rates encountered in the screening and interviewing stages of the project. At the screening stage, the list of telephone numbers yielded residences 88% of the time, and the range in yield rate among strata was narrower than in the pilot study. The list yielded residences at rates ranging from 86% to 91%. The proportion of households found to be eligible, based on responses to the screen, ranged

Table A.1
Results of the Pilot Survey, *N* = 1,120

Stratum	Proportion of numbers yielding residences	Proportion of residences eligible
Iowa urban	.800	.075
Iowa rural	.900	.095
Michigan urban	.857	.052
Michigan rural	.800	.056
Missouri urban	.900	.083
Missouri rural	.900	.115
New York urban	.757	.038
New York rural	.871	.107
Ohio urban	.857	.069
Ohio rural	.900	.081
Pennsylvania urban	.829	.073
Pennsylvania rural	.814	.053
Utah urban	.800	.111
Utah rural	.914	.095
Vermont urban	.829	.052
Vermont rural	.829	.179

Note: Hawaii did not participate in the pilot survey.

from 5.6% in urban Ohio to 12.8% in rural Vermont. Again, the range was narrower in the actual survey than in the pilot study.

Because of the two-stage process needed to locate the sample, an overall response rate could not be calculated. Instead, there were two attrition rates, one that applied at the screening stage and a second at the interviewing stage. The attrition rate at the screening stage, ranging from a low of 2.6% in rural Utah to a high of 9.5% in urban New York, represents the percentage of households who were found to be eligible for the 30-minute interview but who refused to provide the information necessary for the second contact. Attrition at the interview stage occurred because the respondent from eligible households could not be contacted or refused to answer the survey. Attrition at the interview stage ranged from 4.8% for rural New York to 43.2% in urban Hawaii.

THE DEVELOPMENT OF THE INTERVIEW SCHEDULE

The project objectives and the conceptual framework (Owen, Carsky, & Dolan, 1992) defined the parameters for the items to be included in the interview schedule, which were as follows:

1. Socioeconomic and demographic information about the household and its members: age, sex, and relationship to the respondent for each member of

Table A.2
Response to the Telephone Interview, *N* = 18,956

Stratum	Proportion of numbers yielding residences	Proportion of residences eligible	Attrition rate	
			Screen	Interview
Hawaii urban	.861	.058	.081	.432
Hawaii rural	.883	.076	.064	.222
Iowa urban	.860	.073	.043	.184
Iowa rural	.896	.082	.035	.100
Michigan urban	.877	.058	.048	.132
Michigan rural	.904	.069	.034	.137
Missouri urban	.877	.057	.094	.148
Missouri rural	.903	.062	.047	.175
New York urban	.888	.068	.095	.292
New York rural	.886	.069	.059	.048
Ohio urban	.864	.056	.062	.216
Ohio rural	.877	.082	.044	.159
Pennsylvania urban	.898	.055	.085	.250
Pennsylvania rural	.915	.066	.044	.126
Utah urban	.857	.073	.054	.303
Utah rural	.897	.108	.026	.092
Vermont urban	.856	.119	.060	.278
Vermont rural	.885	.128	.032	.137

the household, and marital status, education, and employment status for each individual over the age of 18

2. Information about the nature of the work: Self-employment versus wage work, occupation, advantages and disadvantages of the work, monetary and psychological rewards, number of other people involved, marketing techniques, use of other businesses; services and products, employment hours and experience, and seasonality of work

3. Information bout the nature of the work environment: location of employment activities in the home, where employment activities occur away from home, use of a special vehicle, and intrusiveness of employment on family life

4. Data on family functioning: management of household tasks, management of employment, and the interface between the worker, the family and the work

An initial draft of the interview schedule was assembled, and pretest interviews were conducted. The schedule was revised and refined based on the pretests.

INTERVIEWING PROCEDURES

The Individual to Be Interviewed

There were at least three alternatives in the selection of the individual to be interviewed. For the best information about the home-based work, an obvious choice would have been the person who was the home-based worker. A second approach would have been to interview any adult in the household who knew the details of both the work and the household. A third approach would have been to interview the individual who could be expected to know the details of family life and yet would be relatively conversant with the activities of the home-based worker. The latter approach was adopted. Interviews were conducted with the household manager, defined as "the person who actually manages the household, that is, the one who takes care of most of the meal preparation, laundry, cleaning, scheduling family activities, and oversees child care." The researchers believed the manager would be the household member best able to report accurately about issues in the work-family interface. The household manager was identified by the individual who responded to the screening questions.

The Worker and the Work

For the purposes of this project, home-based work was defined as working for pay at home or from the home at least 6 hours per week throughout the year or, in the case of seasonal work, for a minimum of 312 hours annually. Individuals were included in the sample if they had been engaged in the activity for at least 12 months prior to the interview and had no other office from which the work was conducted. For this research, "ordinary" farmers who raised crops or livestock and marketed their farm products by selling to processors were not included in the study. Farmers who performed "value-added" activities, such as selling farm products at a roadside market or processing sap into maple syrup, did qualify for inclusion in the sample, as did farmers who had other enterprises on the property.

The research objectives encompassed not only an understanding of the work and the worker, but an examination of the interface between work activities and family activities, both taking place in the same or contiguous space. An activity that did not require at least 6 hours a week or 312 hours a year would have had minimal impact on the family. By the same token, an activity that had been performed for less than a year would not have been in place long enough for the interface between the work activities and the family activities to have become routinized.

In the majority of households, only one individual generated income working at home. If more than one worker in the household were engaged in home-based work, or if one individual did more than one activity that qualified as home-based work, a decision was made about the work and/or worker that would be the focus of the interview schedule. The primary worker was designated as the household member who spent the greatest number of hours in home-based work. An exception to this rule was the case where the household manager met the minimum criteria but did not spend the highest number of total hours in home-based employment. In that case, the manager was considered the home-based worker. The primary home-based employment was the job in which the home-based worker spent the most time. When the home-based worker had more than one home-based job, questions about the job referred to the one that was most time-consuming.

Data Collection Procedures

After the initial screening, a letter was sent to the household manager of households in which there was a home-based worker eligible for the sample. The letter, signed by the state's member of the research team, described the project and requested the individual's cooperation. A trained interviewer from Iowa State University administered the interview schedule to the designated respondent during the winter and early spring of 1989. The first telephone contact was attempted between 5:00 and 9:00 P.M., local time of the respondent. Subsequent attempts were made during the daytime, later in the evening, and on a weekend. At least eight attempts were made to interview the respondent, four in the evening, two on weekends, and two during the day. As many as 12 attempts were made to reach some individuals.

Table A.3 details the results of telephone contacts with eligible households. The total number of questionnaires completed was 1 less than the target of 900, and the distribution between the urban and rural strata was 373 urban compared with the target 360, and 526 rural compared with the target 540. In some strata, the prevalence of households with a home-based worker in the actual survey differed widely from that in the pilot study. In others, the attrition rates differed widely from the assumed rates. As expected, the attrition rate was higher at the interview stage than at the screen stage. The attrition rate at the screen stage, 5.42%, was very close to the assumed rate of 5%. At the interview stage, the attrition rate of 19.05% was higher than the assumed 15%.

DATA PREPARATION

Data preparation was completed at the Statistical Laboratory at Iowa State University. Preliminary frequency analyses were used as a means of locating obvious errors in coding or data entry. Each state participating in the project received a data tape that included screening data and interview data for all participating states. Prior to delivery of the data, values for missing data were estimated and a weight for each stratum was calculated and included in the data set.

The Estimation of Missing Data

Because of the quality of the interviewing, there were very few cases with missing data. For all items except income, there were fewer than .1% of cases with missing information. To minimize their effects in the subsequent analyses (Kalton, 1983; Rubin, 1987), those cases with missing information were recoded to the appropriate, sample-based measure of central tendency.

Table A.3
Disposition of Eligible Households Contacted, $N = 1,107$

Stratum	Eligible contacts	Completed forms	Refusals	No answer	Language problem	Ill or dead
Hawaii urban	44	25	10	5	4	0
Hawaii rural	63	49	6	7	1	0
Iowa urban	49	40	7	2	0	0
Iowa rural	60	54	5	1	0	0
Michigan urban	53	46	6	1	0	0
Michigan rural	95	82	12	1	0	0
Missouri urban	61	50	8	3	0	0
Missouri rural	57	47	6	3	0	1
New York urban	89	63	22	4	0	0
New York rural	42	40	0	0	0	2
Ohio urban	37	29	5	2	0	1
Ohio rural	69	58	6	4	0	1
Pennsylvania urban	36	27	6	3	0	0
Pennsylvania rural	95	83	10	2	0	0
Utah urban	33	23	10	0	0	0
Utah rural	76	69	4	3	0	0
Vermont urban	97	70	20	6	0	1
Vermont rural	51	44	6	1	0	0

Four questions dealt with income: workers who were self-employed were asked gross and net income from the business in 1988; wage workers were asked net income from the work; all respondents were asked household income from all sources in 1988. Twenty-eight percent of the households with a self-employed individual who worked at home did not provide data on both gross and net business income; 15% of the wage workers did not provide net income from the work; and 22% of the total sample did not provide household income. Net income from self-employment or from wage work was estimated first, with regression equations that included hours worked, sex, and education of the home-based worker, and eight dummy variables representing occupation. Net income was then included in the equation to estimate gross business income. Income from the home-based work (i.e., either net business income or net income from wage work) was included in the equation to estimate total household income, along with household size, number of earners, a measure of rurality, and homeownership. The adjusted R^2s for the four reduced models ranged from .25 for net income from a business to .53 for net income from wage work.

Weighting

Households in the sample from each stratum represented different numbers of households in the population. Given the research design, rural areas and states with low populations were overrepresented in the sample. All research results are based on weighted data. Each observation was weighted so that it represents the same proportion of 899 as its proportion of all households in the 18 strata. To accomplish this, sample observations were weighted up to the total number of households in the stratum and then divided by the average number of households in all the strata. In this way observations from populous strata were weighted more heavily than observations from less populous strata. The weights can be found in Table A.4, along with the proportion of the sample from each stratum before and after the weighting procedure.

For the purpose of constructing the weights, the numbers of households in each stratum in 1985, as estimated by the U.S. Bureau of the Census (1989, 1990c), were used. Implicit in the weights was an additional adjustment for nonresponse. Two assumptions were made in using the weights. It was assumed that the lists compiled by Survey Sampling were reasonably representative of all households in the surveyed

Table A.4
Stratum Weights and Effect on Stratum Proportion in Sample

Stratum	Whole weight	Fractional weight	Unweighted proportion	Weighted proportion
Hawaii urban	668.5	0.542	0.028	0.015
Hawaii rural	64.4	0.052	0.055	0.003
Iowa urban	1022.1	0.829	0.044	0.037
Iowa rural	782.8	0.635	0.060	0.038
Michigan urban	1507.7	1.222	0.051	0.063
Michigan rural	560.9	0.455	0.091	0.041
Missouri urban	1353.6	1.097	0.056	0.061
Missouri rural	928.6	0.753	0.052	0.039
New York urban	2948.1	2.390	0.070	0.167
New York rural	1564.6	1.268	0.044	0.056
Ohio urban	5674.1	4.600	0.032	0.148
Ohio rural	1451.0	1.176	0.065	0.076
Pennsylvania urban	5115.4	4.147	0.030	0.125
Pennsylvania rural	958.5	1.176	0.065	0.076
Utah urban	1243.2	1.008	0.026	0.026
Utah rural	176.5	0.143	0.077	0.011
Vermont urban	65.9	0.053	0.078	0.004
Vermont rural	443.6	0.360	0.049	0.018

areas and that eligible households who declined to participate did not differ from those that were interviewed.

As noted, data were gathered from two strata in each state, a rural stratum, defined as counties in which the largest city contained fewer than 25,000 residents, and an urban stratum, defined as counties in which the largest city had a population of 25,000 or more. Almost three-fifths (59%) of the sample households lived in the rural strata; the weighting procedure reduced the projected percentage to 35.5%.

PREVALENCE OF HOME-BASED WORK

As noted previously, the estimated prevalence of home-based work varies widely with the definition used. With the procedures used in this study the effect of the definition on the estimated prevalence within the sample could be ascertained. Table A.5 reports findings on the prevalence of home-based work calculated in two different ways. Column 1 reports

Table A.5
Estimated Prevalence of Home-Based Work

Stratum	Proportion of households with any home-based work	Proportion of households with sample home-based work	Number of households with any home-based work	Number of households with sample home-based work
Hawaii urban	.104	.058	30,008	16,713
Hawaii rural	.106	.076	4,411	3,158
Iowa urban	.132	.073	73,425	40,885
Iowa rural	.118	.082	61,291	42,269
Michigan urban	.091	.058	108,608	69,352
Michigan rural	.098	.069	64,872	45,992
Missouri urban	.073	.057	86,543	6,781
Missouri rural	.100	.062	70,440	43,642
New York urban	.100	.068	275,463	185,729
New York rural	.102	.069	92,385	62,583
Ohio urban	.086	.056	253,495	164,549
Ohio rural	.124	.082	126,850	84,160
Pennsylvania urban	.067	.055	168,807	138,115
Pennsylvania rural	.100	.066	120,589	79,555
Utah urban	.146	.073	57,185	28,593
Utah rural	.165	.108	18,590	12,179
Vermont urban	.158	.106	6,844	4,610
Vermont rural	.170	.073	26,024	19,518
All strata	.096	.064	1,645,831	1,109,284

the proportion of all households in the strata that responded positively to the screen question of whether a member of the household worked at or from the home. In column 2 is the proportion of all households that met the study's criteria for inclusion in the sample. Columns 3 and 4 indicate the estimated numbers of households engaged in home-based work that each estimate of the prevalence rate would yield.

Almost 9.6% of all households in the nine states had at least one member engaged in an activity that generated income at home. Only 6.4% of the households had a home-based worker who met the study criteria (i.e., at least 312 hours annually and participation for at least a year in an activity that was not production agriculture). In other words, 536, 547 more households in these nine states reported a member engaged in home-based work under the most liberal definition than under the study's definition. Responses to the screen yielded an estimated 1,645,831 households engaged in home-based work in these nine states. The restricted definition used in this study yielded an estimated 1,109,284 households engaged in home-based work.

N A to end

Appendix B

Annotated Bibliography
from the Nine-State Study

REFEREED JOURNAL ARTICLES

Furry, M. M., & Lino, M. (1992). An overview of home-based work: Results from a regional research project. *Family Economics Review*, *5*(3), 2–8. ABSTRACT: This study uses data from a regional research project to provide an overview of the nature of home-based work, characteristics of home-based workers, and home-based workers' assessment of their work. Most home-based workers (75%) owned their own business, and 47% worked 40 or more hours per week. Home-based workers were a heterogeneous group in regard to occupation, sex, age, education, and presence of children. Most (83%) home-based workers were satisfied with their employment. Most planned to continue working at home. Results of this study should give policy makers a better understanding of this growing segment of the labor force.

Gritzmacher, J. E. (1993). Satisfaction with home-based employment. *Journal of Family and Economic Issues*, *14*, 145–161. ABSTRACT: Using data from the nine-state regional research project on at-home income generation, the relationships of three satisfaction variables to demographic and work situation variables of 899 household managers in households with home-based employment are investigated. The satisfaction variables include quality of life, family income, and control over everyday life. The majority of households are satisfied with income. One variable, the wage earner's control over the amount of work done in a day, is related to the three satisfaction variables.

Heck, R. K. Z. (1991). Employment location choices: Factors associated with generating income at home. *Lifestyles: Family and Economic Issues*, *12*, 217–233. ABSTRACT: The purpose of this research analysis is to investigate the factors that are associated with the likelihood of a worker choosing home-based employment. Using a sample of 6,744 employed men and women from the 1984 Panel Study of Income Dynamics, a logit estimation procedure is employed. Factors that decrease the likelihood of being a home-based worker include minority status, higher levels of total family labor income, a high school education or less, and longer working hours. Older workers, workers without children, workers with young children under age 6, the self-employed, and farmers are all more likely to be involved in home-based employment.

Heck, R. K. Z. (1992). The effects of children on the major dimensions of home-based employment. *Journal of Family and Economic Issues, 13*, 315–346. ABSTRACT: Using ordinary least squares regression procedure and data from the NE-167 sample of home-based employment households, the effects of children on seven major home-based work dimensions, respectively, are estimated along with remaining work dimensions and a series of control variables. The findings show that having a child equal to or under 18 years of age reduces home-based work hours by 407 hours per year, which equates to 1 workday per week. The separate effect of a child under 6 years of age reduces work hours by an additional 296 hours per year or about three-quarters of a workday per week. Being a male home-based worker offsets these children effects considerably compared with being a female home-based worker. Children in general are negatively related to large-scale businesses that hire employees or services. Younger children negatively affect the likelihood of being a home-based business owner and being involved in seasonal home-based employment.

Heck, R. K. Z., Saltford, N. C., Rowe, B. R., & Owen, A. J. (1992). The utilization of child care by households engaged in home-based employment. *Journal of Family and Economic Issues, 13*, 213–237. ABSTRACT: A logit procedure is used to examine the factors associated with the likelihood of using child care services among a sample of households with both a home-based worker and a child designated as needing care. Being a single parent, having high family income, and the presence of a 2-year-old child are positively associated with the likelihood of using child care. Being an older worker, having a child who is 1 year old or less or children who are 11 to 12 years old, and having a less professional occupation decrease the likelihood of using child care. Self-employment decreases the likelihood of usage; owning a business that hires employees or services increases the likelihood of usage. The major conclusion is that home-based work may be a coping strategy for some child care needs, but home-based working households often need and use child care.

Heck, R. K. Z., & Walker, R. (1993). Family-owned home businesses, their employees and unpaid helpers. *Family Business Review, 6*, 397–415. ABSTRACT: Family-owned home-based businesses traditionally utilize a work force of paid workers, contracting workers, and unpaid helpers. Each type of worker may be categorized as family, related, or unrelated. The research reported here shows that not all worker types increase business outputs. Family workers, family helpers, and unrelated workers contribute in positive ways to business outputs. In contrast, unpaid related helpers decrease net income, and contracting related workers increase the work hours of the business owner.

Heck, R. K. Z., Winter, M., & Stafford, K. (1992). Managing work and family in home-based employment. *Journal of Family and Economic Issues, 13*, 187–212. ABSTRACT: Two 10-item scales, one describing the management of the home-based work and the other describing the management of the family work, were administered to a sample of household managers who are also home-based workers. Scale items are designed to assess dimensions of input, planning, implementing, and output. *T*-tests are used to compare the means of the individual items and the scale means. Confirmatory factor analysis is used to assess whether the factoring of the scale items supports the theoretical framework. Scores are higher for the management of the home-based work than for the management of family work. Although both scales are highly reliable, the items in the home-based work scale factor clearly into the dimensions of standard setting and controlling. One interpretation may be that, given a choice, the home-based worker/manager may consciously choose to organize the paid work instead of the family work.

Loker, S., & Scannell, E. (1992a). Characteristics and practices of home-based workers. *Journal of Family and Economic Issues, 13*, 173–186. ABSTRACT: Using data collected by a nine-state regional research project, cluster analysis generates nine clusters of home-based workers from 853 usable cases. The clusters are named for their distinguishing characteristics as follows: Employed Outside the Home; Low Intrusion; Female Wage Workers; See Clients at Home; Lack of Health Insurance; Female Business Owners; Isolated; Two-earner Households; and Male One-earner Households. Ninety percent of home-based workers are covered by health insurance; 44% are covered through another job. Female home-based workers comprise 41% of the total sample and earn net home-based work incomes below the sample mean. The clusters with the highest net income are predominantly male and in marketing and sales, mechanical and transportation, and contracting occupational categories. Recommendations for prospective home-based workers are made.

Loker, S., & Scannell, E. (1992b). The unique nature of textile and craft home-based workers: A comparison. *Journal of Family and Economic Issues, 13*, 263–277. ABSTRACT: Using data collected by a nine-state regional research project, textile and craft home-based workers are compared with the rest of the home-based workers in the sample on several selected variables: home-based work and worker characteristics, income, adaptive behaviors to hectic work times, and advantages and disadvantages of home-based work. Significantly more females than males are engaged in textile and craft home-based work. The findings are related to gender; compared with other workers, textile and craft workers spend fewer hours on home-based work, have lower gross business incomes but greater gross family incomes, are more likely to have a spouse employed outside the home, and are more likely to use personal time than to hire help during hectic work times. Additional research should investigate gender effects and their relationship to the choice and context of home-based work as well as their impact on the household.

Loker, S., Scannell, E., Furry, M. M., & Heck, R. K. Z. (1990). Building home businesses in rural communities. *Journal of Extension, 28*(Summer), 18–20. NO ABSTRACT AVAILABLE.

Masuo, D. M., Walker, R., & Furry, M. M. (1992). Home-based workers: Worker and work characteristics. *Journal of Family and Economic Issues, 13,* 245–262. ABSTRACT: The purpose of the study reported here is to describe the worker and work characteristics of 899 home-based business owners and wage earners, using a definition that excludes farmers, hobbyists, and persons taking work home from a job located elsewhere. Contrary to predictions by futurists of an influx of white-collar workers from the office to home, the home-based workers in this research are more likely to be marketing and sales persons, contractors, or mechanical and transportation workers. Full- or part-time employment status, home tenure, seasonality of work, and occupation are significantly associated with ownership status. Findings show significant group differences on age, education, years in the community, household size, and net annual home-based income. Business owners, on average, are older, have less education, come from larger households, have lived in their communities more years, and have lower net annual home-based incomes than their wage earner counterparts.

Owen, A. J., Carsky, M. L., & Dolan, E. M. (1992). Home-based employment: Historical and current considerations. *Journal of Family and Economic Issues, 13,* 121–138. (Reprinted in *Family Business Review,* 1993, 6, 437–451.) ABSTRACT: The purposes of this article are threefold. First, there is a brief review of current and historical research on home-based business with special emphasis on female home-based employment and the impact of such employment on family life. Second, a conceptual model for family work activities is advanced. Finally, concepts related to home-based employment that could be used to frame and describe the empirical study are specified.

Owen, A. J., Rowe, B. R., & Gritzmacher, J. E. (1992). Building family functioning scales into the study of at-home income generation. *Journal of Family and Economic Issues, 13,* 299–313. ABSTRACT: This article describes testing of scales designed to measure the ways family members interact in a personal subsystem. The scales are intended to complement data about the managerial subsystem of a family and are to be used in conjunction with a regional research project focused on home-based work. The article includes conceptual underpinnings, construction of measures, and results of factor analysis of the measure administered. Suggestions for use of a family functioning scale in the context of a household that has a member working at home are explored in the final section.

Owen, A. J., & Winter, M. (1991). Research note: The impact of home-based business on family life. *Family Business Review, 4,* 425–431. ABSTRACT: Because family firms often unknowingly take on the roles, dynamics, and values of the family unit in which they began, it is useful to study businesses that began in, or are being run from, the home environment. This article examines a subset of cases drawn from a data base on home-based employment in nine states. The study sought to ascertain the extent to which the functioning of the family and that of the business are intertwined. Results from this subsample indicate that there are measurable family and business variables that can help researchers and practitioners understand the interactive effects of family and business life.

Rowe, B. R. (1993). Introduction: Home-based family businesses [foreword to topical issue on home-based family business and note for special section]. *Family Business Review*, 6, 351–354, 381–382. NO ABSTRACT AVAILABLE.

Rowe, B. R., & Bentley, M. T. (1992). The impact of the family on home-based work. *Journal of Family and Economic Issues*, 13, 279–297. ABSTRACT: This article reports on a study of 899 families with at least one member engaged in home-based work. Six work characteristics are examined in relation to family structure and gender of the home-based worker: business ownership, occupation of the home-based work, amount of income generated, location of the work space, number of hours worked, and availability of help with the work. Women in single-parent and full-nest families are found to do the most restructuring of work time and space, and women home-based workers generate less income from the work than do men. Male home-based workers experience less conflict between family and work scheduling, are more likely to have an exclusive work space, and tend to have help with the home-based work.

Rowe, B. R., Haynes, G. W., & Bentley, M. T. (1993). Economic outcomes in family-owned home businesses. *Family Business Review*, 6, 383–396. AB-STRACT: This study explored the financial success of 620 family-owned home businesses. Characteristics of the home business owner, of the business, and of the owner's managerial practices both within and outside the business arena were systemically evaluated. Personal and family characteristics of the owner-operator were more powerful variables in explaining the amount of income generated by the business than were dimensions of the business, although both categories played significant roles.

Rowe, B. R., Stafford, K., & Owen, A. J. (1992). Who's working at home: The types of families engaged in home-based work. *Journal of Family and Economic Issues*, 13, 159–172. ABSTRACT: As increasing numbers of families attempt to balance their need for paid wages with household and child care responsibilities, and corporations struggle with employee flexibility and global competitiveness, there has been a renewed interest in the home as a workplace. However, there is little literature on the kinds of families who engage in home-based work, where they live, the types of work they do, or how profitable home-based work can be. This descriptive analysis focuses on the family dimensions of home-based work. It is organized by the characteristics of the household, worker characteristics, characteristics of the work, and the effect of home-based work on family income.

Stafford, K., Winter, M., Duncan, K. A., & Genalo, M. A. (1992). Studying at-home income generation: Issues and methods. *Journal of Family and Economic Issues*, 13, 139–158. ABSTRACT: Methods used to locate and study 899 home-based workers and their households in nine states are described in detail, with emphasis on the rationale behind the decisions about the definition of home-based work, sampling, the development of the interview schedule, data collection procedures, and data preparation. More than 9.6% of all households in the nine states include someone who is engaged in home-based work; 6.4%

of the households have a member who has been engaged in the activity for more than 1 year and who spends at least 312 hours annually in the activity. The respondents have a mean age of 42.5 years and have completed a mean of 13.8 years of education. More than half have lived in communities of 2,500 or over for more than 10 years. More than 40% of the sample consist of individuals who are married and have children living in the home. The average household income in 1988 was just over $42,000.

Winter, M., & Fitzgerald, M. (1993). Continuing the family-owned home-based business: Evidence from a panel study. *Family Business Review, 6*, 417–426. ABSTRACT: A panel study of households in which someone is engaged in a home-based family business is analyzed to assess factors associated with the probability that the business will be operating 3 years later and reasons for quitting the business. Factors associated with the continuation of the business include age and education of the business owner, the number of years in business, positive feelings about the work, and expectations about changing attitudes toward the business. Neither income nor attitudes about income from the home-based work were significant predictors of the owner having the same business 3 years later.

Winter, M., Puspitawati, H., Heck, R. K. Z., & Stafford, K. (1993). Time management strategies used by households with home-based work. *Journal of Family and Economic Issues, 14*, 69–92. ABSTRACT: A sample of 899 households in which at least one member is engaged in home-based work is used to analyze two time-management strategies used to respond to the demands of home-based work. Analyses reveal that, first, personal time is reallocated more than additional help is obtained for either the home-based work or household production and, second, that different strategies are used depending on whether the household manager is also the home-based worker. Respondents holding both roles report reallocating personal time more often than respondents who are not home-based workers; the reverse holds for obtaining additional help. The results suggest that households generating higher incomes in which home-based work is a full-time occupation are more likely to use time-management strategies than those in which incomes are lower and the home-based work is part-time.

BOOKS AND BOOK CHAPTERS

Rowe, B. R., Owen, A. J., & Heck, R. K. Z. (Eds.). (in preparation). *Home-based businesses and their families*. [Negotiations initiated with Lexington Books for edited monograph structured as a practical manual based on research findings from NE-167].

Winter, M. (1993). Home-based work and work in the informal sector: It's the same the whole world over. In R. Von Schweitzer (Ed.), *Cross Cultural Approaches to Home Management* (pp. 74–98). Boulder, CO: Westview.

Winter, M., Heck, R. K. Z., & Rowe, B. (Eds). (in preparation). *Employment in the home: Research on home-based workers and their families*. [Negotiations initiated with Plenum Press, for reprinting of the collective works in two thematic issues in the *Journal of Family and Economic Issues* and a special issue of the *Family Business Review*].

DOCTORAL DISSERTATIONS AND MASTER'S THESES

Duncan, K. A. (1993). *Women's reservation wage for home-based work and its implications for their labor supply.* Unpublished doctoral dissertation, Ohio State University, Columbus.

Puspitawati, H. (1992). *Time-management strategies used in households in which income is generated at home.* Unpublished master's thesis, Iowa State University, Ames. ABSTRACT: The purpose of this study was to examine the relationship between socioeconomic and demographic characteristics of the household and the selection of management strategies to cope with the demands of home-based work. Two strategies, personal time reallocation and obtaining additional help, were examined in a sample of 899 households in which at least one member generates income working at or from the home. Findings indicate that respondents use personal time reallocation more than they obtain additional help. Total household income, pressure from the home-based work, age, and whether the respondent was the home-based worker are significant predictors of the use of both strategies.

Williams-Miles, K. (1992). *A comparison of nonfamily single-parent and full-nest families engaged in home-based employment.* Unpublished master's thesis, Utah State University, Logan.

NONREFEREED JOURNAL ARTICLES, EXTENSION PUBLICATIONS, AND CONFERENCE PROCEEDINGS AND PRESENTATIONS

Fan, X. (1993). Implicit income generated by home-based employment and its impact on household and social welfare. In T. A. Mauldin (Ed.), *Proceedings of 39th Annual Conference of the American Council on Consumer Interests* (pp. 371–372). Columbia, MO: American Council on Consumer Interests.

Furry, M. M. (1993). Home employment in rural and urban households. In E. P. Davis & J. G. Gilbreth (Eds.), *Diversity Among Economically Vulnerable Households*, Proceedings of a 1993 preconference workshop sponsored by the Family Economics–Home Management Section of the American Home Economics Association (pp. 77–81). Alexandria, VA: American Home Economics Association.

Furry, M. M., & Masuo, D. M. (1991). A comparison of self employed and wage workers: A rural/urban study of home-based work in nine states. In J. W. Bauer (Ed.), *Family Economic Well-Being in the Next Century: Challenges, Changes, Continuity*, Proceedings of a workshop sponsored by the Family Economics–Home Management Section of the American Home Economics Association (pp. 73–75). Alexandria, VA: American Home Economics Association.

Furry, M. M., & Radhakrishna, R. B. (1992). *Home-based workers in Pennsylvania* (unnumbered Extension Bulletin). University Park, PA: Pennsylvania State

University, College of Agricultural Sciences, Department of Agricultural and Extension Education.

Heck, R. K. Z. (1988). A profile of home-based workers. *Human Ecology Forum, 16*(4), 15–18.

Heck, R. K. Z. (1993). Children in rural households engaged in home-based employment. In E. P. Davis & J. G. Gilbreth (Eds.), *Diversity Among Economically Vulnerable Households*, Proceedings of 1993 preconference workshop sponsored by the Family Economics–Home Management Section of the American Home Economics Association (pp. 90–94). Alexandria, VA: American Home Economics Association.

Heck, R. K. Z., & Owen, A. J. (1993, November). Today's homeworking households: A summary of what we do and do not know and the implications of both. *Women working: Working differences*. Third Purdue University Women's Studies Symposium sponsored by Women's Studies Program, West Lafayette, IN.

Heck, R. K. Z., Rowe, B. R., Owen, A. J., & Saltford, N. C. (1991). Child care and home-based employment. In V. Haldeman (Ed.), *Proceedings of 37th Annual Conference of the American Council on Consumer Interests* (pp. 81–82). Columbia, MO: American Council on Consumer Interests.

Heck, R. K. Z., & Stafford, K. (1991). Earning income at home. *Human Ecology Forum, 19*(4), 21–23.

Heck, R. K. Z., Stafford, K., & Winter, M. (1991a). Family management practices. In J. W. Bauer (Ed.), *Family Economic Well-Being in the Next Century: Challenges, Changes, Continuity*, Proceedings of a workshop sponsored by the Family Economics–Home Management Section of the American Home Economics Association (pp. 75–77). Alexandria, VA: American Home Economics Association.

Heck, R. K. Z., Stafford, K., & Winter, M. (1991b). Home-based work and management practices. In V. Haldeman (Ed.), *Proceedings of 37th Annual Conference of the American Council on Consumer Interests* (pp. 79–80). Columbia, MO: American Council on Consumer Interests.

Heck, R. K. Z., & Walker, R. (1987). The incidence, characteristics, and types of home-based employment. In V. Hampton (Ed.), *Proceedings of 33rd Annual Conference of the American Council on Consumer Interests* (p. 341). Columbia, MO: American Council on Consumer Interests.

Heck, R. K. Z., Winter, M., Stafford, K., & Hennon, C. B. (1993). Home-based business and family outcomes. In T. A. Mauldin (Ed.), *Proceedings of 39th Annual Conference of the American Council on Consumer Interests* (pp. 352–356). Columbia, MO: American Council on Consumer Interests.

Loker, S., & Scannell, E. (1991). *Textiles and craft employment moves back home*. Paper presented at International Textile and Apparel Association Annual Conference, San Francisco, CA.

Masuo, D. M. (1993a). Health insurance coverage of home-based workers: A nine-state rural-urban study. In E. P. Davis & J. G. Gilbreth (Eds.), *Diversity Among Economically Vulnerable Households*, Proceedings of 1993 preconference workshop sponsored by the Family Economics–Home Management Section of the American Home Economics Association (p. 99). Alexandria, VA: American Home Economics Association.

Masuo, D. M. (1993b). [Review of *Homework: Historical and contemporary perspectives of paid labor at home*, by E. Boris and C. R. Daniels. Urbana: University of Illinois Press, 1989]. *Family Business Review, 6*, 453–455.

Masuo, D. M., & Kutara, P. B. (1991). *Home-based employment in Hawaii: Who, what, and where?* (Research Extension Series 131). Honolulu, HI: University of Hawaii, College of Tropical Agriculture and Human Resources.

Owen, A. J., & Gritzmacher, J. E. (1993). Family functioning when the family runs a business. In T. A. Mauldin (Ed.), *Proceedings of 39th Annual Conference of the American Council on Consumer Interests* (pp. 357–361). Columbia, MO: American Council on Consumer Interests.

Owen, A. J., Rowe, B. R., & Gritzmacher, J. E. (1991). Home-based work and family functioning. In V. Haldeman (Ed.), *Proceedings of 37th Annual Conference of the American Council on Consumer Interests* (p. 83). Columbia, MO: American Council on Consumer Interests.

Owen, A. J., & Walker, R. (1993, November). The economic outcomes of home-based work: The gender factor. *Women working: Working differences.* Third Purdue University Women's Studies Symposium sponsored by Women's Studies Program, West Lafayette, IN.

Rowe, B. R., & Arbuthnot, J. J. (1993). The economic contribution of home-based work to rural families. In E. P. Davis & J. G. Gilbreth (Eds.), *Diversity Among Economically Vulnerable Households*, Proceedings of 1993 preconference workshop sponsored by the Family Economics–Home Management Section of the American Home Economics Association (pp. 95–98). Alexandria, VA: American Home Economics Association.

Rowe, B. R., Heck, R. K. Z., Bentley, M. T., & Haynes, G. W. (1993). Family-owned home businesses and their economic outcomes. In T. A. Mauldin (Ed.), *Proceedings of 39th Annual Conference of the American Council on Consumer Interests* (pp. 362–365). Columbia, MO: American Council on Consumer Interests.

Rowe, B. R., & Masuo, D. M. (1993, November). The changing work environment: A focus on women and home-based work. *Women working: Working differences.* Third Purdue University Women's Studies Symposium sponsored by Women's Studies Program, West Lafayette, IN.

Rowe, B. R., & Williams, K. (1991). Who's working at home?: The types of families engaged in home-based work. In J. W. Bauer (Ed.), *Family Economic Well-Being in the Next Century: Challenges, Changes, Continuity*, Proceedings of a workshop sponsored by the Family Economics–Home Management Section of the American Home Economics Association (pp. 77–79). Alexandria, VA: American Home Economics Association.

Scannell, E. (1991). Home-based work affects household management. *Vermont Science, 15*(1), 3.

Scannell, E., & Loker, S. (1991). A typology of home-based workers. In J. W. Bauer (Ed.), *Family Economic Well-Being in the Next Century: Challenges, Changes, Continuity*, Proceedings of a workshop sponsored by the Family Economics–

Home Management Section of the American Home Economics Association (pp. 71–73). Alexandria, VA: American Home Economics Association.

Stafford, K. (1991). Households and workers engaged in home-based employment. In V. Haldeman (Ed.), *Proceedings of 37th Annual Conference of the American Council on Consumer Interests* (p. 77). Columbia, MO: American Council on Consumer Interests.

Stafford, K., Heck, R. K. Z., & Winter, M. (1993, November). Gender differences in family and business management behavior. *Women working: Working differences*. Third Purdue University Women's Studies Symposium sponsored by Women's Studies Program, West Lafayette, IN.

Stafford, K., & Olson, P. D. (1993). Health insurance coverage of home-based workers. In T. A. Mauldin (Ed.), *Proceedings of 39th Annual Conference of the American Council on Consumer Interests* (pp. 375–376). Columbia, MO: American Council on Consumer Interests.

Stafford, K., Owen, A. J., Winter, M., & Heck, R. K. Z. (1992). *Family resource management and family functioning: Critical pieces of a puzzle* (Family Resource Management Working Paper No. 92–02). Columbus, OH: Ohio State University, Department of Family Resource Management.

Walker, R., Furry, M. M., & Masuo, D. M. (1991). Working at home: Who is and at what? In V. Haldeman (Ed.), *Proceedings of 37th Annual Conference of the American Council on Consumer Interests* (p. 78). Columbia, MO: American Council on Consumer Interests.

Walker, R., Furry, M. M., & Masuo, D. M. (1993). Gender and family owned home businesses. In T. A. Mauldin (Ed.), *Proceedings of 39th Annual Conference of the American Council on Consumer Interests* (pp. 366–370). Columbia, MO: American Council on Consumer Interests.

Walker, R., & Heck, R. K. Z. (1992, August). *The utilization of paid and unpaid workers in home-based businesses*. Presentation at 1992 World Congress on the Family, Columbus, OH.

Walker, R., & Li, I. (1993). Gender, occupation, and earnings of home-based business owners. In E. P. Davis & J. G. Gilbreth (Eds.), *Diversity Among Economically Vulnerable Households*, Proceedings of a 1993 preconference workshop sponsored by the Family Economics–Home Management Section of the American Home Economics Association (pp. 82–89). Alexandria, VA: American Home Economics Association.

Winter, M. (1992, August). *The informal sector and home-based work: It's the same the whole world over.* Paper presented at the Family Resource Management Post-Conference Workshop, Rauischholzhausen (Marburg), Germany.

References

Aburdene, P., & Naisbitt, J. (1992). *Megatrends for women*. New York: Villard Books.

Ahrentzen, S. B. (1990). Managing conflict by managing boundaries: How professional homeworkers cope with multiple roles at home. *Environment and Behavior, 22*, 723–752.

Aldrich, H., & Weiss, J. (1981). Differentiation within the United States capitalist class: Workforce size and income differences. *American Sociological Review, 46*, 279–290.

Ambry, M. (1988). At home in the office. *American Demographics, 10*(12), 31–33, 61.

American Telephone and Telegraph. (1982). *The structure of the work-at-home market: Job/volunteer/school*. Unpublished manuscript.

Amos, O. M., Jr. (1987). Influence of urban areas on regional development. *Review of Regional Studies, 17*(3), 37–46.

Anderson, K. (1988). A history of women's work in the United States. In A. Stromberg & S. Harkess (Eds.), *Women working: Theories and facts in perspective* (2nd ed., pp. 25–41). Mountain View, CA: Mayfield.

Aram, J. D., & Coomes, J. S. (1985). Public policy and the small business sector. *Policy Studies Journal, 13*, 692–700.

Arden, L. (1988). *The work-at-home sourcebook: How to find "at-home" work that's right for you*. Boulder, CO: Live Oak Publications.

Aronson, R. L. (1991). *Self-employment: A labor market perspective*. Ithaca, NY: ILR Press.

Asinof, L. (1993, January 13). How Supreme Court's home-office ruling affects you. *Wall Street Journal*, pp. C1, C13.

Axel, H. (1985). *Corporations and families: Changing practices and perspectives*. New York: Conference Board.

Bacon, D. (1989, October). Look who's working at home. *Nation's Business*, pp. 20–31.

Balkin, S. (1989). *Self-employment for low-income people*. New York: Praeger.

Barkley, D. L., & Hinschberger, S. (1992). Implications of restructuring: Implications for the decentralization of manufacturing to nonmetropolitan areas. *Economic Development Quarterly, 6*, 64–79.

Bartik, T. J. (1991). *Who benefits from state and local economic development policies?* Kalamazoo, MI: W. E. Upjohn Institute for Employment Research.

Bates, T. (1989). Small business viability in the urban ghetto. *Journal of Regional Science, 29,* 625–643.

Bates, T. (1991). Financial capital structure and small business viability. In R. Yazdipour (Ed.), *Advances in small business finance* (pp. 63–78). Norwell, MA: Kluwer Academic Publishers.

Baysinger, B. D., & Mobley, W. H. (1983). Employee turnover: Individual and organizational analysis. In K. M. Rowland & G. R. Ferris (Eds.), *Research in personnel and human resources management* (Vol. 1, pp. 269–319). Greenwich, CT: JAI Press.

Beach, B. A. (1985). *Working at home: Family life/work life.* Unpublished doctoral dissertation, University of Connecticut, Storrs, CT.

Beach, B. A. (1987). Time use in rural home-working families. *Family Relations, 36,* 412–416.

Beach, B. A. (1988). Families in the home workplace. *Illinois Teacher of Home Economics, 32,* 23–26.

Beach, B. A. (1989). *Integrating work and family life: The home-working family.* Albany, NY: State University of New York Press.

Becker, E. H. (1984). Self-employed workers: An update to 1983. *Monthly Labor Review, 107*(7), 14–18.

Berger, P. S. (1984). Home management research: State of the art, 1909–1984. *Home Economics Research Journal, 12,* 252–264.

Bergmann, B. R. (1986). *The economic emergence of women.* New York: Basic Books.

Berk, S. F. (1985). *The gender factory: The apportionment of work in American households.* New York: Plenum Press.

Berney, R. E., & Owens, E. (1985). A theoretical framework for small business policy. *Policy Studies Journal, 13,* 681–691.

Bernstein, P. (1988). The ultimate in flexitime: From Sweden, by way of Volvo. *Personnel, 65*(6), 70–74.

Berry, L. L. (1979). The time-buying consumer. *Journal of Retailing, 55*(4), 58–69.

Bers, J. S. (1993). Telecommuting may cut real estate costs, but at what price? *Facilities Design and Management, 12*(10), 44–47.

Bianchi, S., & Spain, D. (1986). *American women in transition.* New York: Russell Sage Foundation.

Birch, D. L. (1987). *Job creation in America: How our smallest companies put the most people to work.* New York: Free Press.

Blau, D. M. (1987). A time-series analysis of self-employment in the United States. *Journal of Political Economy, 95,* 445–467.

Blau, F. D. (1978). Data on women workers, past, present, and future. In J. Freeman (Ed.), *Women working: Theories and facts in perspective* (2nd ed., pp. 25–41). Mountain View, CA: Mayfield.

Blau, F. D., & Ferber, M. A. (1986). *The economics of women, men, and work.* Englewood Cliffs, NJ: Prentice-Hall.

Bokemeier, J. L., & Garkovich, L. E. (1991). Meeting rural family needs. In C. B. Flora & J. A. Christenson (Eds.), *Rural policies for the 1990s* (pp. 114–127). Boulder, CO: Westview.

Boris, E. (1985). Regulating industrial homework: The triumph of "sacred motherhood." *Journal of American History, 71,* 745–763.

Boris, E. (1987). Homework and women's rights: The case of the Vermont knitters, 1980–1985. *Signs, 13,* 98–120.

Bower, B. (1988, October 1). From here to maternity. *Science News,* pp. 220–222.

Brock, W. A., & Evans, D. S. (1986). *The economics of small businesses—Their role and regulation in the U.S. economy.* New York: Holmes and Meier.

Brown, C., Hamilton, J., & Medoff, J. (1990). *Employers large and small.* Cambridge, MA: Harvard University Press.

Brown, J. N., & Light, A. (1992). Interpreting panel data on job tenure. *Journal of Labor Economics, 10,* 219–257.

Bruno, A. V., & Tyebjee, T. T. (1982). The environment for entrepreneurship. In C. A. Kent, D. L. Sexton, & K. H. Vesper (Eds.), *Encyclopedia of entrepreneurship* (pp. 288–307). Englewood Cliffs, NJ: Prentice-Hall.

Bubolz, M. M., Eicher, J. B., & Sontag, M. S. (1979). The human ecosystem: A model. *Journal of Home Economics, 71*(1), 28–31.

Burdette, P. A. (1990). Black and white female small business owners in central Ohio: A comparison of selected personal and business characteristics. (Doctoral dissertation, Ohio State University, 1990). *Dissertation Abstracts International, 51,* 3345A.

Buss, T. F., & Popovich, M. (1988). Rural enterprise development: An Iowa case study. In B. A. Kirchhoff, W. A. Long, W. E. McMullan, K. H. Vesper, & W. E. Wetzel, Jr. (Eds.), *Frontiers of entrepreneurship research, 1988* (pp. 75–76). Wellesley, MA: Babson College.

Butler, J. C. (1988). Local zoning ordinances governing the home. In K. E. Christensen (Ed.), *The new era of home-based work: Directions and policies.* Boulder, CO: Westview.

Campbell, A., Converse, P., & Rodgers, W. (1976). *The quality of American life: Perceptions, evaluations, and satisfactions.* New York: Russell Sage Foundation.

Carsky, M. L., Dolan, E. M., & McCabe, E. M. (1988). A typology to measure the impact of homebased work on quality of family life. In V. L. Hampton (Ed.), *Proceedings of the 34th Annual Conference of the American Council on Consumer Interests* (pp. 256–263). Columbia, MO: American Council on Consumer Interests.

Casson, M. (1991). *The entrepreneur: An economic theory.* Hampshire, England: Gregg Revivals.

Castro, J. (1993, March 29). Disposable workers. *Time,* pp. 43–47.

Cattan, P. (1991). Child-care problems: An obstacle to work. *Monthly Labor Review, 114*(10), 3–9.

Christensen, K. E. (1985). Women and home-based work. *Social Policy, 15*(3), 54–57.

Christensen, K. E. (1987). A hard day's work in the electronic cottage. *Across the Board, 24*(4), 17–23.

Christensen, K. E. (1988a). Introduction: White-collar home-based work—The changing U.S. economy and family. In K. E. Christensen (Ed.), *The new era of home-based work: Directions and policies* (pp. 1–11). Boulder, CO: Westview.

Christensen, K. E. (1988b). *Women and home-based work: The unspoken contract.* New York: Henry Holt.

Christensen, K. E. (1989). Home-based clerical work: No simple truth, no single reality. In E. Boris & C. R. Daniels (Eds.), *Homework: Historical and contemporary perspectives on paid labor at home* (pp. 183–197). Urbana: University of Illinois Press.

Clark, C. (1986). *The American family home, 1800–1960.* Chapel Hill: University of North Carolina Press.

Coates, V. T. (1988). Office automation technology and home-based work. In K. E. Christensen (Ed.), *The new era of home-based work: Directions and policies* (pp. 114–125). Boulder, CO: Westview.

Commissioner of Internal Revenue v. Soliman, 121 LEd 2d 634 (1993).

Constand, R. L., Osteryoung, J. S., & Nast, D. A. (1991). Assets-based financing and the determinants of capital structure in the small firm. In R. Yazdipour (Ed.), *Advances in small business finance* (pp. 29–46). Norwell, MA: Kluwer Academic Publishers.

Constantine, L. (1986). *Family paradigms: The practice of theory in family therapy.* New York: Guilford.

Cook, A. H. (1989). Public policies to help dual-earner families meet the demands of the work world. *Industrial and Labor Relations Review, 42,* 201–215.

Cooney, T. M., & Uhlenberg, P. (1991). Changes in work-family connections among highly educated men and women. *Journal of Family Issues, 12,* 69–90.

Coontz, S. (1992). *The way we never were: American families and the nostalgia trap.* New York: Basic Books.

Cooper, A. C., Dunkelberg, W. C., & Woo, C. Y. (1988). Survival and failure: A longitudinal study. In B. A. Kirchhoff, W. A. Long, W. E. McMullan, K. H. Vesper, & W. E. Wetzel, Jr. (Eds.), *Frontiers of entrepreneurship research, 1988* (pp. 225–228). Wellesley, MA: Babson College.

Cowan, R. (1987). Women's work, housework, and history: The historical roots of inequality in work-force participation. In N. Gerstel & H. Gross (Eds.), *Families and work* (pp. 164–177). Philadelphia: Temple University Press.

Cromie, S. (1987). Motivations of aspiring male and female entrepreneurs. *Journal of Occupational Behaviour, 8,* 251–261.

Crouter, A. C. (1984). Spillover from family to work: The neglected side of the work-family interface. *Human Relations, 37,* 425–442.

Crouter, A. C. (1994). The changing American workplace: Implications for individuals and families. *Family Relations, 43,* 117–124.

Dangler, J. (1986). Industrial homework in the modern world-economy. *Contemporary Crises, 10,* 257–279.

Deacon, R. E., & Firebaugh, F. M. (1975). *Home management context and concepts.* Boston: Houghton Mifflin.

Deacon, R. E., & Firebaugh, F. M. (1981). *Family resource management: Principles and applications.* Boston: Allyn and Bacon.

Deacon, R. E., & Firebaugh, F. M. (1988). *Family resource management: Principles and applications* (2nd ed.). Boston: Allyn and Bacon.

Deming, W. G. (1994). Work at home: Data from the CPS. *Monthly Labor Review, 117*(2), 14–20.

Devens, R. M. (1992). The employee turnover and job openings survey. *Monthly Labor Review, 115*(3), 29–32.

Devine, T. J. (1994). Characteristics of self-employed women in the United States. *Monthly Labor Review, 117*(3), 20–34.

Dickinson, K. (1975). Child care. In G. J. Duncan & J. N. Morgan (Eds.), *Five thousand American families—Patterns of economic progress* (Vol. 3, pp. 221–233). Ann Arbor: University of Michigan, Institute for Social Research.

Diebold Automated Office Program. (1981). *Office work in the home: Scenarios and prospects for the 1980's.* New York: Diebold Group.

Dillman, D. A. (1978). *Mail and telephone surveys.* New York: Wiley.

Donnelley, R. G. (1964). The family business. *Harvard Business Review, 42*(4), 93105.

Duncan, G. J., & Hill, C. R. (1975). Modal choice in child care arrangements. In G. J. Duncan & J. N. Morgan (Eds.), *Five thousand American families—Patterns of economic progress* (Vol. 3, pp. 235–258). Ann Arbor: University of Michigan, Institute for Social Research.

Dunne, T., Roberts, M., & Samuelson, L. (1987). *Plant failure and employment growth in the U.S. manufacturing sector*. Unpublished manuscript. Pennsylvania State University, Department of Economics, University Park.

Edwards, F. R. (1965). The banking competition controversy. *National Banking Review, 3,* 1–34.

Edwards, K. P. (1970). A theoretical approach to goal-oriented family behavior. *Journal of Home Economics, 62,* 652–655.

Edwards, P., & Edwards, S. (1991). *Making it on your own*. New York: Tarcher/Putnam.

Edwards, P., & Edwards, S. (1994a). Government wages war on the SOHO [small office/home office] movement. *Points West* (Special Report, 94-05-02-A). Denver, CO: Center for the New West.

Edwards, P., & Edwards, S. (1994b). *Working from home*. New York: Tarcher/Putnam.

Eigsti, M. (1984, March). *Family and peer assessment as a basis for identifying normative managerial behavior*. Paper presented at the annual meeting of NCR-116, Committee on Family Resource Management, Minneapolis, MN.

Elliehausen, G. E., & Wolken, J. D. (1990). *Banking markets and the use of financial services by small and medium sized businesses*. Washington, DC: Board of Governors of the Federal Reserve System.

Employee Benefit Research Institute. (1988, December). *Dependent care: Meeting the needs of a dynamic work force* (EBRI Issue Brief No. 85). Washington, DC: Author.

Employee Benefit Research Institute. (1993, June). *The changing environment of work and family* (EBRI Issue Brief No. 138). Washington, DC: Author.

Employee Benefit Research Institute. (1994, May). *Characteristics of the part-time work force: Analysis of the March 1993 Current Population Survey* (Special Report and Issue Brief No. 149). Washington, DC: Author.

Epstein, B. (1982). Industrialization and femininity: A case study of nineteenth-century New England. In R. Kahn-Hut, A. K. Daniels, & R. Colvard (Eds.), *Women and work: Problems and perspectives* (pp. 88–100). New York: Oxford University Press.

Ericksen, J. A., Yancey, W. L., & Ericksen, E. P. (1979). The division of family roles. *Journal of Marriage and the Family, 41,* 301–313.

Eriksson, G. (1991). Human capital investments and labor mobility. *Journal of Labor Economics, 9,* 236–254.

Evans, D. S., & Leighton, L. S. (1989). Some empirical aspects of entrepreneurship. *American Economic Review, 79,* 519–535.

Fan, X. J. (1993). Implicit income generated by home-based employment and its impact on household and social welfare. In T. A. Mauldin (Ed.), *Proceedings of the 39th Annual Conference of the American Council on Consumer Interests* (pp. 371–372). Columbia, MO: American Council on Consumer Interests.

Farkas, G. (1976). Education, wage rates and the division of labor between husband and wife. *Journal of Marriage and the Family, 38,* 473–483.

Ferber, M. A., & O'Farrell, B. (Eds.). (1991). *Work and family: Policies for a changing work force*. Washington, DC: National Academy Press.

Fitzsimmons, C., Larery, D. A., & Metzen, E. J. (1971). *Major financial decisions and crises in the family life span* (North Central Regional Research Publication No. 208). West Lafayette, IN: Purdue University, Agricultural Experiment Station.

Flora, C. B., & Christenson, J. A. (1991). Critical times for rural America: The challenge for rural policy in the 1990s. In C. B. Flora & J. A. Christenson (Eds.), *Rural policies for the 1990s* (pp. 1–7). Boulder, CO: Westview.

Flora, J. L., & Johnson, T. G. (1991). Small businesses. In C. B. Flora & J. A. Christenson (Eds.), *Rural policies for the 1990s* (pp. 47–59). Boulder, CO: Westview.

Foley, J. D. (1992, February). *Sources of health insurance and characteristics of the uninsured: Analysis of the March 1991 Current Population Survey* (EBRI Issue Brief No. 123). Washington, DC: Employee Benefit Research Institute.

Fox, W., & Murray, M. (1991). Local public policies and interregional business development. *Southern Economic Journal, 57*, 413–427.

Fredland, J. E., & Little, R. D. (1981). Self-employed workers: Returns to education and training. *Economics of Education Review, 1*, 315–337.

Friedman, D. E. (1986). Child care for employees' kids. *Harvard Business Review, 64*(2), 28–34.

Friedman, D. E. (1987). Work vs. family: War of the worlds. *Personnel Administrator, 32*(8), 36–38.

Fuchs, V. R. (1971). Differences in hourly earnings between men and women. *Monthly Labor Review, 94*(5), 9–15.

Fuchs, V. R. (1982). Self-employment and labor force participation of older males. *Journal of Human Resources, 17*, 339–357.

Fuguitt, G. V., Brown, D. L., & Beale, C. L. (1989). *Rural and small town America.* New York: Russell Sage Foundation.

Fullerton, H. N. (1991). Labor force projections: The baby boom moves on. *Monthly Labor Review, 114*(11), 31–44.

Furry, M. M. (1993). Home employment in rural and urban households. In W. P. Davis & J. G. Gilbreth (Eds.), *Diversity Among Economically Vulnerable Households*, Proceedings of 1993 preconference workshop sponsored by the Family Economics–Home Management Section of the American Home Economics Association (pp. 77–81). Alexandria, VA: American Home Economics Association.

Galinsky, E., & Stein, P. J. (1990). The impact of human resource policies on employees: Balancing work/family life. *Journal of Family Issues, 11*, 368–383.

Garrison, M. E., & Winter, M. (1986). The managerial behavior of families with preschool children. *Journal of Consumer Studies and Home Economics, 10*, 247–260.

Gaston, R. J. (1989). The scale of informal capital markets. *Small Business Economics, 1*, 223–230.

Gerson, J. M., & Kraut, R. E. (1988). Clerical work at home or in the office: The difference it makes. In K. E. Christensen (Ed.), *The new era of home-based work: Directions and policies* (pp. 49–64). Boulder, CO: Westview.

Giele, J. Z. (1984). Changing sex roles and family structure. In P. Voydanoff (Ed.), *Work and family: Changing roles of men and women* (pp. 191–208). Palo Alto, CA: Mayfield.

Googins, B. (1991). *Work/family conflicts: Private lives—public responses.* New York: Auburn House.

Gordon, H. A., & Kammeyer, K. C. W. (1980). The gainful employment of women with small children. *Journal of Marriage and the Family, 42*, 327–336.

Gramm, W. L. (1975). Household utility maximization and the working wife. *American Economic Review, 65*, 90–100.

Gramm, W. S. (1987). Labor, work and leisure: Human well-being and the optimal allocation of time. *Journal of Economic Issues, 21*, 167–188.

Grayson, P. (1983). Male and female operated nonfarm proprietorships, tax year 1980. *Statistics of Income Bulletin, 2*(4), 35–39.

Greenhouse, L. (1993, January 13). Home-office tax breaks are curbed. *New York Times*, pp. C1, C2.

Gringeri, C. E. (1990, May). *The nuts and bolts of subsidized development: Industrial home-workers in the heartland.* Paper presented at the 3rd Annual Meeting of the National Rural Studies Committee, Cedar Falls, IA.

Gronau, R. (1977). Leisure, home production and work—The theory of the allocation of time revisited. *Journal of Political Economy, 85*, 1099–1123.

Gross, I. H., Crandall, E. W., & Knoll, M. M. (1973). *Management for modern families* (3rd ed.). New York: Appleton-Century-Crofts.

Gross, I. H., Crandall, E. W., & Knoll, M. M. (1980). *Management for modern families* (4th ed.). Englewood Cliffs, NJ: Prentice-Hall.

Gumpert, D. (1984). Work in the home: Trends and implications. *Entrepreneur, 12*(3), 54–56.

Gutman, H. (1976). *Work, culture and society in industrializing America: Essays in American working-class and social history.* New York: Knopf.

Haber, S. E., Lamas, E. J., & Lichtenstein, J. H. (1987). On their own: The self-employed and others in private business. *Monthly Labor Review, 110*(5), 17–23.

Hagan, O., Rivchun, C., & Sexton, D. (Eds.). (1989). *Women-owned businesses.* New York: Praeger.

Hall, C. P., & Kuder, J. M. (1990). Health benefits and small business: What now and what next? *Benefits Quarterly, 6*(4), 14–47.

Hansen, N. M. (Ed.). (1972). *Growth centers in regional economic development.* New York: Free Press.

Hansen, N. M. (1988). Regional consequences of structural changes in the national and international division of labor. *International Regional Science Review, 11*, 121–136.

Hareven, T. (1987). The dynamics of kin in an industrial community. In N. Gerstel and H. Gross (Eds.), *Families and work* (pp. 55–83). Philadelphia: Temple University Press.

Hareven, T. (1991). The history of the family and the complexity of social change. *American Historical Review, 96*, 95–124.

Hayghe, H. (1990). Family members in the work force. *Monthly Labor Review, 113*(3), 14–19.

Heck, R. K. Z. (1983). A preliminary test of a family management research model. *Journal of Consumer Studies and Home Economics, 7*, 117–135.

Heck, R. K. Z. (1988). A profile of homebased workers. *Human Ecology Forum, 16*(4), 15–18.

Heck, R. K. Z. (1991). Employment location choices: Factors associated with the likelihood of home-based employment. *Lifestyles: Family and Economic Issues, 12*, 217–233.

Heck, R. K. Z. (1992). The effects of children on the major dimensions of home-based employment. *Journal of Family and Economic Issues, 13*, 315–346.

Heck, R. K. Z., & Douthitt, R. A. (1982). Research modelling implications of conceptual frameworks in family management. *Journal of Consumer Studies and Home Economics, 6*, 265–276.

Heck, R. K. Z., Saltford, N. C., Rowe, B. R., & Owen, A. J. (1992). The utilization of child care by households engaged in home-based employment. *Journal of Family and Economic Issues, 13*, 213–237.

Heck, R. K. Z., Winter, M., & Stafford, K. (1992). Managing work and family in home-based employment. *Journal of Family and Economic Issues, 13*, 187–212.

Henry, M., Drabenstott, M., & Gibson, L. (1987). Rural growth slows down. *Rural Development Perspectives, 3*(3), 25–30.

Hershon, S. (1975). *The problems of management succession in family businesses.* Unpublished doctoral dissertation, Harvard University, Cambridge, MA.

Hill, C. R., & Stafford, F. P. (1985). Lifetime fertility, child care and labor supply. In F. T. Juster & F. P. Stafford (Eds.), *Time, goods, and well-being* (pp. 471–492). Ann Arbor: University of Michigan, Institute for Social Research, Survey Research Center.

Hill, M. S. (1985). Patterns of time use. In F. T. Juster & F. P. Stafford (Eds.), *Time, goods, and well-being* (pp. 133–176). Ann Arbor: University of Michigan, Institute for Social Research, Survey Research Center.

Hill, M. S., & Juster, F. T. (1985). Constraints and complementarities in time use. In F. T. Juster & F. P. Stafford (Eds.), *Time, goods, and well-being* (pp. 439–470). Ann Arbor: University of Michigan, Institute for Social Research, Survey Research Center.

Hisrich, R. D., & Brush, C. G. (1986). *The woman entrepreneur: Starting, financing and managing a successful new business.* Lexington, MA: D.C. Heath.

Hochschild, A. (1989). *The second shift.* New York: Viking.

Hofferth, S. L., Brayfield, A., Deich, S., Holcomb, P., & Glantz, F. (1991a). *National child care survey, 1990: Low income supplement.* Washington, DC: Urban Institute.

Hofferth, S. L., Brayfield, A., Deich, S., & Holcomb, P. (1991b). *National child care survey, 1990: A National Association for the Education of Young Children (NAEYC) study.* Washington, DC: Urban Institute.

Hollander, B. S., & Elman, N. S. (1988). Family-owned businesses: An emerging field of inquiry. *Family Business Review, 1,* 145–164.

Hoover, C. (1986). *The entrepreneurial activities of farm-based women.* Unpublished master's thesis, Ohio State University, Columbus.

Horvath, F. W. (1986). Work at home: New findings from the current population survey. *Monthly Labor Review, 109*(11), 31–35.

Hukill, C. (1990). Homework. *Monthly Labor Review, 113*(5), 53–54.

Huth, S. A. (1989). Corporations provide variety of child care options. *Employee Benefit Plan Review, 44*(3), 48–50.

Igbaria, M., & Siegel, S. R. (1992). The reasons for turnover of information systems personnel. *Information and Management, 23,* 321–330.

Illich, I. (1981). *Shadow work.* Boston: Marion Boyers.

Jovanovic, B. (1982). Selection and the evolution of industry. *Econometrica, 50,* 649–670.

Juster, F. T. (1985a). A note on recent changes in time use. In F. T. Juster & F. P. Stafford (Eds.), *Time, goods, and well-being* (pp. 313–332). Ann Arbor: University of Michigan, Institute for Social Research, Survey Research Center.

Juster, F. T. (1985b). Investments of time by men and women. In F. T. Juster & F. P. Stafford (Eds.), *Time, goods, and well-being* (pp. 177–204). Ann Arbor: University of Michigan, Institute for Social Research, Survey Research Center.

Juster, F. T., & Stafford, F. P. (Eds.). (1985). *Time, goods, and well-being.* Ann Arbor: University of Michigan, Institute for Social Research, Survey Research Center.

Kahn, A. J., & Kamerman, S. B. (1987). *Child care: Facing the hard choices.* Dover, MA: Auburn.

Kahn-Hut, R., Daniels, A., & Colvard, R. (1982). Women and the division of labor: Limiting assumptions. In R. Kahn-Hut, A. Daniels, & R. Colvard (Eds.), *Women and work* (pp. 17–23). New York: Oxford University Press.

Kalleberg, A. L., & Berg, I. (1987). *Work and industry: Structures, markets, and processes.* New York: Plenum Press.

Kalleberg, A. L., & Leicht, K. T. (1991). Gender and organization performance: Determinants of small business survival and success. *Academy of Management Journal, 34*(1), 136–161.

Kalton, G. (1983). *Compensating for missing survey data.* Ann Arbor: University of Michigan, Survey Research Center.

Kalton, G., & Anderson, D. W. (1986). Sampling rare populations. *Journal of the Royal Statistical Society, 149,* 65–82.

Kamerman, S. B. (1983). *Meeting family needs: The corporate response.* New York: Pergamon Press.

Kanter, R. (1977). *Work and family in the United States: A critical review and agenda for research and policy.* New York: Russell Sage Foundation.

Kantor, D., & Lehr, W. (1975). *Inside the family: Toward a theory of family process*. New York: Harper Colophon.

Katona, G. (1975). *Psychological economics*. New York: Elsevier.

Kent, C. A. (1982). Entrepreneurship in economic development. In C. A. Kent, D. L. Sexton, & K. H. Vesper (Eds.), *Encyclopedia of entrepreneurship* (pp. 237–256). Englewood Cliffs, NJ: Prentice-Hall.

Keough, J., & Forbes, C. (1991). Family business: Enduring generations of change. *Industrial Distribution, 80*(13), 27–36.

Kessler-Harris, A. (1982). *Out to work: A history of wage-earning women in the United States*. New York: Oxford University Press.

Key, R. J. (1990). Complementarity and substitutability in family members' time allocated to household production activities. *Lifestyles: Family and Economic Issues, 11*, 225–256.

Kim, J., & Mueller, C. W. (1981). *Factor analysis: Statistical methods and practical issues* (Series 1, No. 07-014). Beverly Hills, CA: Sage.

Kleiman, C. (1988, August 29). Cottage industries battle to stay in-house. *Chicago Tribune*, Section 4, p. 5.

Kmenta, J. (1986). *Elements of econometrics*. New York: Macmillan.

Knoll, M. M. (1963). Toward a conceptual framework in home management. *Journal of Home Economics, 55*, 335–339.

Kolb, R. W. (1987). *Financial management*. Glenview, IL: Scott Foresman.

Kraut, R. E. (1988). Homework: What is it and who does it? In K. E. Christensen (Ed.), *The new era of home-based work: Directions and policies* (pp. 30–48). Boulder, CO: Westview.

Kraut, R. E., & Grambsch, P. (1987). Home-based white collar employment: Lessons from the 1980 census. *Social Forces, 66*, 410–426.

Krinsky, I., & Roteberg, W. (1991). The valuation of initial public offerings: The small firm case. In R. Yazdipour (Ed.), *Advances in small business finance* (pp. 1–8). Norwell, MA: Kluwer Academic Publishers.

Kroll, D. (1984). Telecommuting: A revealing peek inside some of industry's first electronic cottages. *Management Review, 73*(11), 18–23.

Lacy, W. B., Shepard, J. M., & Houghland, J. G. (1979, August). *The relationship between work and nonwork satisfaction*. Paper presented at the annual meeting of the American Sociological Association, Boston, MA.

Lambert, S. (1990). Processes linking work and family: A critical review and research agenda. *Human Relations, 43*, 239–257.

Lansberg, I. (1988). The succession conspiracy. *Family Business Review, 1*, 119–143.

Lasch, C. (1977). *Haven in a heartless world: The family besieged*. New York: Basic Books.

Lehrer, E. (1983). Determinants of child care mode choice: An economic perspective. *Social Science Research, 12*, 69–80.

Leibowitz, A., Waite, L. J., & Witsberger, C. (1988). Child care for preschoolers: Differences by child's age. *Demography, 25*, 205–220.

Levitan, S. A., & Gallo, F. (1990). Work and family: The impact of legislation. *Monthly Labor Review, 113*(3), 34–40.

Lieberson, S., & O'Connor, J. F. (1972). Leadership and organizational performance: A study of large corporations. *American Sociological Review, 37*, 117–130.

Lin, X., Buss, T. F., & Popovich, M. (1990). Entrepreneurship is alive and well in rural America: A four-state study. *Economic Development Quarterly, 4*, 254–259.

Littrell, M. A., Stout, J. A., & Reilly, R. (1991). In-home businesses: Profiles of successful and struggling craft producers. *Home Economics Research Journal, 20*, 27–39.

Loker, S. (1985). Home knitters design nontraditional lives. *Vermont Science, 9*(2), 3.

Lopata, H. Z. (1993). The interweave of public and private: Women's challenge to American society. *Journal of Marriage and the Family, 55*, 176–190.

Loscocco, K. A., & Robinson, J. (1991). Barriers to women's small business success in the United States. *Gender and Society, 5*, 511–532.

Loscocco, K. A., Robinson, J., Hall, R. H., & Allen, J. K. (1991). Gender and small business success: An inquiry into women's relative disadvantage. *Social Forces, 70*, 65–85.

Lozano, B. (1989). *The invisible work force: Transforming American business with outside and home-based workers.* New York: Free Press.

Maguire, S. R. (1993). Employer and occupational tenure: 1991 update. *Monthly Labor Review, 116*(6), 45–56.

Maloch, F., & Deacon, R. E. (1966). Proposed framework for home management. *Journal of Home Economics, 58*, 31–35.

Mamorsky, J. D. (Ed.). (1987). *Employee benefits handbook.* Boston, MA: Warren, Gorham & Lamont.

Markey, J. P., & Parks, W. (1989). Occupational change: Pursuing a different kind of work. *Monthly Labor Review, 112*(9), 3–12.

Marsh, L. C. (1981). Hours worked by husbands and wives. *Journal of Family Issues, 2*, 164–179.

Marshall, C. M. (1991). Family influences on work. In S. J. Bahr (Ed.), *Family research: A sixty-year review, 1930–1990* (Vol. 2, pp. 115–166). New York: Lexington Books.

Masuo, D. M., Walker, R., & Furry, M. M. (1992). Home-based workers: Worker and work characteristics. *Journal of Family and Economic Issues, 13*, 245–262.

Mayo, J. W., & Flynn, J. E. (1989). First entry and exit: Causality tests and economic-base linkages. *Journal of Regional Science, 29*, 645–662.

Mazur, J. (1987, September 1). Industrial homework and sweatshops. *Vital Speeches of the Day, 53*, 701–702.

McGee, L. F. (1988). Setting up work at home. *Personnel Administrator, 33*(12), 58–62.

McLaughlin, M. (1981). *Physical and social support systems used by women engaged in home-based work.* Unpublished master's thesis, Cornell University, Ithaca, NY.

McLaughlin, S. D., Melber, B. D., Billy, J. O., Zimmerle, D. M., Winges, L. D., & Johnson, T. R. (1988). *The changing lives of American women.* Chapel Hill: University of North Carolina Press.

Meirs, M. (1988). Parental leave and the bottom line. *Personnel Journal, 67*(9), 108–133.

Miller, B. (1992, October). *The distribution of family oriented benefits* (EBRI Issue Brief No. 130). Washington, DC: Employee Benefit Research Institute.

Miller, J. P. (1985). Rethinking small businesses as the best way to create rural jobs. *Rural Development Perspectives, 1*(2), 9–12.

Miller, J. P. (1989). The product cycle and high technology industry in nonmetropolitan areas, 1976–1980. *Review of Regional Studies, 19*(1), 1–12.

Miller, J. P. (1990). *Survival and growth of independent firms and corporate affiliates in metro and nonmetro America* (Rural Development Research Report No. 74). Rockville, MD: Economic Research Service.

Miller, J. P. (1991). New rural businesses show good survival and growth rates. *Rural Development Perspectives, 7*(3), 25–29.

Mintz, S., & Kellogg, S. (1988). *Domestic revolutions: A social history of American family life.* New York: Free Press.

Moen, P. (1992). *Women's two roles: A contemporary dilemma.* New York: Auburn House.

Mokry, B. W. (1988). *Entrepreneurship and public policy: Can government stimulate business startups?* New York: Quorum Books.

Moore, R. L. (1983). Employer discrimination: Evidence from self-employed workers. *Review of Economics and Statistics, 65*, 496–501.

Morgan, J. N., Sirageldin, I., & Baerwaldt, N. (1966). *Productive Americans: A study of how individuals contribute to economic progress.* Ann Arbor: University of Michigan, Institute for Social Research.

Murphy, N. B. (1983). Loan rates, operating costs and size of loan: The evidence from cross-section data. In P. M. Horvitz & R. R. Petit (Eds.), *Small business finance: Problems in financing of small business* (pp. 51–62). Greenwich, CT: JAI Press.

Near, J., Rice, R., & Hunt, R. (1980). The relationship between work and nonwork domains: A review of empirical research. *Academy of Management Review, 5*, 415–429.

Nelson, G. (1991). Locus of control for successful female small business proprietors. *Mid-Atlantic Journal of Business, 27*, 213–224.

Newton, D. L. (1979). *Managerial behavior, goal achievement, satisfaction with managerial behavior, and life satisfaction.* Unpublished master's thesis, Iowa State University, Ames.

Nickell, P., Rice, A., & Tucker, S. (1976). *Management in family living.* New York: Wiley.

Nickols, S. Y., & Fox, K. D. (1983). Buying time and saving time: Strategies for managing household production. *Journal of Consumer Research, 10*, 197–208.

Nollen, S. D. (1982). *New work schedules in practice: Managing time in a changing society.* New York: Van Nostrand Reinhold.

Oakley, A. (1974). *The sociology of housework.* New York: Pantheon Books.

O'Connell, M. (1990). *Who's minding the kids? Child care arrangements: Winter 1986–1987* (CPR Series P-70, No. 20). Washington, DC: Department of Commerce, Bureau of the Census.

Olson, G. I., & Beard, D. M. (1985). Assessing managerial behavior. In S. Y. Nickols (Ed.), *Thinking globally, acting locally* (pp. 138–148). Washington, DC: American Home Economics Association.

Olson, M. H. (1983). *Overview of work-at-home trends in the United States* (CRIS Working Paper No. 57). New York: New York University, Center for Research on Information Systems.

O'Malley, S. (1994). The rural rebound. *American Demographics, 16*(5), 24–29.

Orpen, C. (1978). Work and nonwork satisfaction: A causal-correlational analysis. *Journal of Applied Psychology, 63*, 530–532.

Owen, A. J., Carsky, M. L., & Dolan, E. M. (1992). Home-based employment: Historical and current considerations. *Journal of Family and Economic Issues, 13*, 121–138.

Owen, A. J., Rowe, B., & Gritzmacher, J. (1992). Building family functioning scales into the study of at-home income generation. *Journal of Family and Economic Issues, 13*, 299–313.

Owen, J. (1986). *Working lives: The American work force since 1920.* Lexington, MA: Lexington Books.

Owen, W. (1984). *Some pros and cons of having a business in your home* (CDFS-9-84). Columbus: Ohio State University, Cooperative Extension Service.

Paolucci, B., Hall, O. A., & Axinn, N. (1977). *Family decision-making: An ecosystem approach.* New York: Wiley.

Pleck, J. H. (1977). The work-family role system. *Social Problems, 24*, 417–427.

Pleck, J. H., Staines, G. L., & Lang, L. (1980). Conflicts between work and family life. *Monthly Labor Review, 103*(3), 29–32.

Pratt, J. H. (1984). Home teleworking: A study of its pioneers. *Technological Forecasting and Social Change, 25*, 1–14.

Pratt, J. H. (1987). Methodological problems in surveying the home-based workforce. *Technological Forecasting and Social Change, 31*, 49–60.

Pratt, J. H. (1993). *Myths and realities of working at home: Characteristics of homebased business owners and telecommuters* (U.S. Small Business Administration, Office of Advocacy Contract SBA-6647-OA-91). Washington, DC: U.S. Government Printing Office.

Pratt, J. H., & Davis, J. (1986). *Measurement and evaluation of the population of family-owned businesses and home-based businesses* (Final Report, SBA-9202-AER-85). Washington, DC: Small Business Administration.

Quinn, J. F. (1980). Labor force participation patterns of older self-employed workers. *Social Security Bulletin, 43*(4), 17–28.

Rauch, J. (1981). Anatomy of a regulator proposal—The battle over industrial homework. *National Journal, 13*(23), 1013–1016.

Rhyne, E. H. (1988). *Small business, banks, and SBA loan guarantees: Subsidizing the weak or bridging a credit gap.* Westport, CT: Greenwood Press.

Ries, P., & Stone, A. (1992). *The American woman, 1992–93: A status report.* New York: Norton.

Robinson, J. P. (1977). *How Americans use time: A social-psychological analysis of everyday behavior.* New York: Praeger.

Robinson, J. P. (1985). Changes in time use: An historical overview. In F. T. Juster & F. P. Stafford (Eds.), *Time, goods, and well-being* (pp. 289–312). Ann Arbor: University of Michigan, Institute for Social Research, Survey Research Center.

Rose, S. (1987). Gender segregation in the transition to the factory: The English hosiery industry, 1850–1910. *Feminist Studies, 13*, 163–184.

Rosenblatt, P. C. (1987). *Family tension and the home-based business* (HE-FS-3095). St. Paul: University of Minnesota, Minnesota Extension Service.

Rosenblatt, P. C., de Mik, L., Anderson, R. M., & Johnson, P. A. (1985). *The family in business: Understanding and dealing with the challenges entrepreneurial families face.* San Francisco: Jossey-Bass.

Rosow, J. M., & Zager, R. (1983). Punch out the time clocks. *Harvard Business Review, 61*(2), 12–30.

Rowe, B. R., & Arbuthnot, J. J. (1993). The economic contribution of home-based work to rural families. In E. P. Davis & J. G. Gilbreth (Eds.), *Diversity Among Economically Vulnerable Households,* Proceedings of 1993 preconference workshop sponsored by the Family Economics–Home Management Section of the American Home Economics Association (pp. 95–98). Alexandria, VA: American Home Economics Association.

Rowe, B. R., & Bentley, M. T. (1992). The impact of the family on home-based work. *Journal of Family and Economic Issues, 13*, 279–297.

Rubin, D. B. (1987). *Multiple imputation for nonresponse in surveys.* New York: Wiley.

Saltford, N. C., & Heck, R. K. Z. (1990, February). *An overview of employee benefits supportive of families* (EBRI Special Report). Washington, DC: Employee Benefit Research Institute.

Sanik, M. M. (1981). Division of household work: A decade comparison: 1967–1977. *Home Economics Research Journal, 10*, 175–180.

Satir, V. (1972). *People making.* Palo Alto, CA: Science and Behavior Books.

Schor, J. B. (1991). *The overworked American: The unexpected decline of leisure.* New York: Basic Books.

Scott, J., & Tilly, L. (1980). Women's work and the family in nineteenth-century Europe. In A. Amsden (Ed.), *The economics of women and work* (pp. 91–139). New York: St. Martin's Press.

Scott, J. T. (1977). *Price and nonprice competition in banking markets: A study of the theoretical and empirical justification for regulating attempts to promote competition in banking markets* (Research Report No. 62). Boston: Federal Reserve Bank of Boston.

Sehgal, E. (1984). Occupation mobility and job tenure in 1983. *Monthly Labor Review, 107*(10), 18–23.

Shank, S. (1988). Women and the labor market: The link grows stronger. *Monthly Labor Review, 111*(3), 3–8.

Sharpe, D. L. B. (1988). *Time devoted by women to selected household tasks, 1975–1981: Implications for assessing change in standards.* Unpublished doctoral dissertation, Iowa State University, Ames.

Silver, H. (1989). The demand for homework: Evidence from the U.S. census. In E. Boris & C. R. Daniels (Eds.), *Homework: Historical and contemporary perspectives on paid labor at home* (pp. 103–129). Urbana: University of Illinois Press.

Sloane, L. (1993, February 6). When a home also shelters a business. *New York Times,* p. 26.

Smith, R. E. (1979). The movement of women into the labor force. In R. E. Smith (Ed.), *The subtle revolution* (pp. 1–29). Washington, DC: Urban Institute.

Solomon, S. (1986). *Small Business USA.* New York: Crown.

Stackel, L. (1987). The flexible work place. *Employment Relations Today, 14*(2), 189–197.

Staff. (1984, November 12). Tip of the ski cap: Labor department's decision on home labor. *Wall Street Journal,* p. 24.

Staff. (1986, November). Taking brakes off working at home. *Nation's Business,* p. 14.

Staff. (1993, February 22). Family friendliness. *U.S. News and World Report,* pp. 59–66.

Stafford, F. P. (1980). Women's use of time converging with men's. *Monthly Labor Review, 103*(12), 57–62.

Stafford, F. P., & Duncan, G. J. (1985). The use of time and technology by households in the United States. In F. T. Juster & F. P. Stafford (Eds.), *Time, goods, and well-being* (pp. 245–288). Ann Arbor: University of Michigan, Institute for Social Research, Survey Research Center.

Stafford, K., Longstreth, M., Gritzmacher, J., & Smith, J. (1986). Use of family care services by women who earn income at home, versus away from home. In G. L. Pyles (Ed.), *Consumer Services for the Family: Who, What, When, Where, Why,* Proceedings of the Southeastern Family Economics and Home Management Conference (pp. 133–141). Kent, OH: Kent State University.

Stafford, K., Winter, M., Duncan, K. A., & Genalo, M. A. (1992). Studying at-home income generation: Issues and methods. *Journal of Family and Economic Issues, 13,* 139–158.

Staines, G. L., & Pleck, J. H. (1983). *The impact of work schedules on the family.* Ann Arbor: University of Michigan, Institute for Social Research, Survey Research Center.

Staines, G. L., & Pleck, J. H. (1986). Work schedule flexibility and family life. *Journal of Occupational Behaviour, 7,* 147–153.

Starrels, M. E. (1992). The evolution of workplace family policy research. *Journal of Family Issues, 13,* 259–278.

Steers, R. M., & Mowday, R. T. (1981). Employee turnover and post-decision accommodation process. In L. L. Cummings and B. M. Staw (Eds.), *Research in organizational behavior* (Vol. 3, pp. 235–281). Greenwich, CT: JAI Press.

Steinmetz, G., & Wright, E. O. (1989). The fall and rise of the petty bourgeoisie: Changing patterns of self-employment in the postwar United States. *American Journal of Sociology, 94,* 973–1018.

Steinnes, D. N. (1984). Business climate, tax incentives, and regional economic development. *Growth and Change, 15,* 38–47.

Stevens, S. (1994). *Independent contractor vs. employee: Exploring the categories* (NCR 546). Columbia: University of Missouri at Columbia, University Extension.

Stiglitz, J. E., & Weiss, A. (1981). Credit rationing in markets with imperfect information. *American Economic Review, 71*, 393–410.

Stoll, H. R. (1981). *Small firm's access to public equity financing*. Washington, DC: Interagency Task Force of Small Business Finance.

Stoll, H. R., & Whaley, R. E. (1981). *Transaction costs and the small firm effect* (Working Paper No. 81–116). Nashville, TN: Vanderbilt University, Owne Graduate School of Management.

Strober, M. H., & Weinberg, C. B. (1980). Strategies used by working and nonworking wives to reduce time pressures. *Journal of Consumer Research, 6*, 338–348.

Sullivan, S. (1992). Is there a time for everything? Attitudes related to women's sequencing of career and family. *Career Development Quarterly, 40*, 234–243.

Sweet, J. A., & Bumpass, L. L. (1987). *American families and households*. New York: Russell Sage Foundation.

Swoboda, F. (1990, October 28). Congress passes $22 billion child-care package. *Washington Post*, p. A19.

Tepper, T. P., & Tepper, N. D. (1980). *The new entrepreneurs: Women working from home*. New York: Universe Books.

Thornton, A., & Freedman, D. (1983). The changing American family. *Population Bulletin, 38*(4), 3–44.

Tilly, L. A., & Scott, J. W. (1987). *Women, work and family*. New York: Methuen.

Toffler, A. (1980). *The third wave*. New York: William Morrow.

Topel, R. (1991). Specific capital, mobility, and wages: Wages rise with job seniority. *Journal of Political Economy, 99*, 145–176.

U.S. Bureau of the Census. (1975). *Historical statistics of the United States, colonial times to 1970* (Bicentennial ed., Pt. 1). Washington, DC: U.S. Government Printing Office.

U.S. Bureau of the Census. (1981). *Statistical abstract of the United States* (101st ed.). Washington, DC: U.S. Government Printing Office.

U.S. Bureau of the Census. (1987). *Who's minding the kids? Child care arrangements: Winter, 1984–85* (CPR Series P-70, No. 9). Washington, DC: U.S. Government Printing Office.

U.S. Bureau of the Census. (1989). *Household and family characteristics: March 1988* (CPR Series P-20, No. 437). Washington, DC: U.S. Government Printing Office.

U.S. Bureau of the Census. (1990a). *County statistics file 4* (COSTAT 4) [Machine-readable data file]. Washington, DC: U.S. Bureau of the Census (Producer and distributor).

U.S. Bureau of the Census. (1990b). *Money income and poverty status in the United States, 1989* (CPR Series P-60, No. 168). Washington, DC: U.S. Government Printing Office.

U.S. Bureau of the Census. (1990c). *Residents of farms and rural areas: 1989* (Current Population Reports, Series P-20, No. 446). Washington, DC: U.S. Government Printing Office.

U.S. Bureau of the Census. (1991a). *Census of population and housing, 1990: Summary tape file 3, United States* [Machine-readable data file]. Washington, DC: U.S. Bureau of the Census (Producer and distributor).

U.S. Bureau of the Census. (1991b). *Household and family characteristics: March 1991* (CPR Series P-20, No. 458). Washington, DC: U.S. Government Printing Office.

U.S. Bureau of the Census. (1991c). *Money income of households, families, and persons in the United States: 1988 and 1989* (CPR Series P-60, No. 172). Washington, DC: U.S. Government Printing Office.

U.S. Bureau of the Census. (1991d). *Statistical abstract of the United States* (111th ed.). Washington, DC: U.S. Government Printing Office.

U.S. Bureau of the Census. (1992a). *Marital status and living arrangements: March 1991* (CPR Series P-20, No. 461). Washington, DC: U.S. Government Printing Office.

U.S. Bureau of the Census. (1992b). *Who's minding the kids? Child care arrangements: Fall, 1988* (CPR Special Series P-70, No. 30). Washington, DC: U.S. Government Printing Office.

U.S. Bureau of the Census. (1993). *Statistical abstract of the United States* (113th ed.). Washington, DC: U.S. Government Printing Office.

U.S. Bureau of Labor Statistics. (1989a). *Employee benefits in medium and large firms, 1988* (Bulletin No. 2336). Washington, DC: U.S. Government Printing Office.

U.S. Bureau of Labor Statistics. (1989b). *Employment and wages, annual averages, 1988* (Bulletin No. 2341). Washington, DC: U.S. Government Printing Office.

U.S. Bureau of Labor Statistics. (1989c). *Employment in perspective: Women in the labor force* (Third Quarter, Report No. 75). Washington, DC: U.S. Government Printing Office.

U.S. Bureau of Labor Statistics. (1989d, April 4). *News*. Washington, DC: U.S. Government Printing Office.

U.S. Bureau of Labor Statistics. (1994). *Employment and earnings* (Bulletin No. 2307). Washington, DC: U.S. Government Printing Office.

U.S. Department of Commerce, Office of Federal Statistical Policy and Standards. (1980). *Standard occupational classification manual*. Washington, DC: U.S. Government Printing Office.

U.S. Department of Health and Human Services. (1990, October). *Child care arrangements: Health of our nation's children, United States, 1988* (Advance data from vital and health statistics, No. 187). Washington, DC: National Center for Health Statistics.

U.S. Department of Labor. (1988). *Child care: A workforce issue* (Report of the Secretary's Task Force). Washington, DC: U.S. Government Printing Office.

U.S. Department of Labor. (1990, June). *Facts on working women* (No. 90-1). Washington, DC: U.S. Government Printing Office.

U.S. Department of Labor. (1992). *Work and family provisions in major collective bargaining agreements* (BLMR Report No. 144). Washington, DC: U.S. Government Printing Office.

U.S. Small Business Administration. (1991). *The state of small business: A report to the president*. Washington, DC: U.S. Government Printing Office.

U.S. Small Business Administration. (1992). *The state of small business: A report to the president*. Washington, DC: U.S. Government Printing Office.

U.S. Small Business Administration. (1993). *The state of small business: A report to the president*. Washington, DC: U.S. Government Printing Office.

Voydanoff, P. (1987). *Work and family life*. Newbury Park, CA: Sage.

Walker, J. R. (1991). Public policy and the supply of child care services. In D. M. Blau (Ed.), *The economics of child care* (pp. 51–78). New York: Russell Sage Foundation.

Walker, K. E., & Woods, M. E. (1976). *Time use: A measure of household production of family goods and services*. Washington, DC: Center for the Family of the American Home Economics Association.

Walker, R., Bubolz, M., & Lee, M. (1991). Contributions of family resource management to quality of family life of mid-life women and men. In J. W. Bauer (Ed.), *Family Economic Well-Being in the Next Century: Challenges, Changes, Continuity*, Proceedings of the Family Economics–Home Management Section of the American Home Economics Association (pp. 129–143). Washington, DC: American Home Economics Association.

Walker, R., Lee, M., & Bubolz, M. (1989). The effects of family resources and demands on quality of life: A rural-urban comparison of women in the middle years. In H. L. Meadows & M. J. Sirgy (Eds.), *Quality-of-Life Studies in Marketing and Management:*

Proceedings of the Third Quality-of-Life Marketing Conference (pp. 397–411). Blacksburg, VA: Virginia Polytechnic Institute and State University.

Whatmore, S., Lowe, P., & Marsden, T. (Eds.). (1991). *Rural enterprise: Shifting perspectives on small-scale production.* London: David Fulton.

White House Conference on Families. (1980). *Listening to America's families: Action for the '80s* (Report to the President, Congress, and Families of the Nation). Washington, DC: U.S. Government Printing Office.

Williams, F. L., & Manning, S. L. (1972). Net worth change of selected families. *Home Economics Research Journal, 1,* 104–113.

Winter, M., & Fitzgerald, M. (1993). Continuing the family-owned home-based business: Evidence from a panel study. *Family Business Review, 6,* 417–426.

Winter, M., Puspitawati, H., Heck, R. K. Z., & Stafford, K. (1993). Time-management strategies used by households with home-based work. *Journal of Family and Economic Issues, 14,* 69–92.

Index

About the Contributors

PAUL and SARAH EDWARDS are the authors of the best seller *Working from Home* (1985) and four other books on the subject of self-employment. They founded and manage the "Working from Home Forum" on CompuServe Information Service, and have developed a course for nonentrepreneurs seeking self-employment entitled "Hire Yourself." They have produced and cohosted the radio show "Working from Home" and cohost the show "Working from Home with Paul and Sarah Edwards" for cable TV.

MARGARET FITZGERALD is an Instructor in the Department of Child Development and Family Science at North Dakota State University. She has published in *Family Business Review*. Her research interests include home-based employment and economic issues related to delayed childbearing.

MARILYN M. FURRY* is Associate Professor in the Agricultural and Extension Education Department at Pennsylvania State University. Her work experience includes counseling, teaching, research, and cooperative extension. She has published in *Journal of Family and Economic Issues*, *Family Economics Review*, *Journal of Home Economics*, *Journal of Extension*, and *Extension Review*, and has authored over 75 extension publications and mass media programs that help families with financial management, risk management, life

*The researcher listed was a member of the original Cooperative Regional Research Project (i.e., the nine-state study), entitled "At-Home Income Generation: Impact on Management, Productivity and Stability in Rural/Urban Families," NE-167, that was approved for a 6-year period from October 1, 1987, through September 30, 1993.

changes such as marriage, divorce, death, and retirement, and related economic and management topics.

JOAN E. GRITZMACHER* is Professor of Home Economics Education at Ohio State University. Her research and experience are in program evaluation, evaluation of teaching and learning, and entrepreneurship. She is an entrepreneur in the teaching of this content, which she has been doing for more than 10 years. She has published in *Home Economics Research Journal, Journal of Vocational Home Economics Education, Journal of Vocational Education Research, Journal of Home Economics*, and *Journal of Family and Economic Issues*. She has twice been a recipient of the university's Distinguished Teaching Award and was recognized as a 1991 American Home Economics Association Leader.

GEORGE W. HAYNES is an Assistant Professor in the Department of Health and Human Development at Montana State University. He has published in *Family Business Review* and *Advancing the Consumer Interest*. His research interests include small-business finance, economic linkages between the family and the business in Native American populations, and the economics of health promotion in rural areas.

RAMONA K. Z. HECK* is Associate Professor in the Department of Consumer Economics and Housing at Cornell University. She holds the designation of J. Thomas Clark Professor of Entrepreneurship and Personal Enterprise at Cornell University. Her current research interests include family-owned businesses, home-based employment, and working families and employers' benefits. She is editor of *Journal of Family and Economic Issues*, on the editorial boards of *Family Business Review* and *Journal of Consumer Affairs*, and a member of the overseas advising board for *Journal of Consumer Studies and Home Economics*. Her work has been published in *Family Business Review, Journal of Consumer Affairs, Lifestyles: Family and Economic Issues, Journal of Family and Economic Issues, Journal of Consumer Studies and Home Economics, Journal of Home Economics, The Service Industries Journal*, and *Science*.

CHARLES B. HENNON is Associate Director of the Family and Child Studies Center at Miami University, Oxford, OH. He is the former editor of *Journal of Family and Economic Issues* and serves on the editorial boards of several national and international journals. He is coeditor of two books and has published in *AIDS Education and Prevention, Family Relations, Families in Society, Journal of Divorce and Remarriage, International Journal of Human Development*, and several other journals and books. His scholarship interests include the family dynamics and self-defined success of family-owned and operated businesses, rural families, family life education, and family stress.

SUZANNE LOKER* is Director of the School of Family and Consumer Sciences at the University of Idaho (formerly in the Department of Merchandising, Consumer Studies and Design at the University of Vermont). She has published in *Journal of Family and Economic Issues, Home Economics Research Journal, Clothing and Textiles Research Journal, Journal of Home Economics, Journal of Extension, Journal of Retailing and Consumer Services*. Her research interests include home-based work, the work-family interface, the evolution of apparel manufacturing and retailing in Eastern Europe, and apparel catalog marketing.

DIANE M. MASUO* is Assistant Professor in the Department of Human Resources at the University of Hawaii at Manoa. Currently, she is president of the Western Region Home Management Family Economics Educators. She has published in *Journal of Family and Economic Issues*, and *Journal of Computer Based Instruction* and has authored publications and developed computer programs aimed at helping consumers with financial management and consumer buying. Her research interests include underemployment, home-based employment, and minority family-owned businesses.

ALMA J. OWEN* is Associate Professor in the Department of Consumer Sciences and Retailing at Purdue University (formerly in the Department of Agriculture, Natural Resources and Home Economics at Lincoln University Cooperative Extension). Her primary areas of research are rural families, household production, family time use and its meaning, and the interactive aspects of managerial, productive, and affective functions of families. She has published in *Family Business Review, Journal of Family and Economic Issues, Lifestyles: Family and Economic Issues, Journal of Consumer Studies and Home Economics, Home Economics Research Journal*, and *Journal of Extension* and is the author of numerous extension publications.

BARBARA R. ROWE* is Associate Professor in the Department of Consumer Sciences and Retailing at Purdue University (formerly in the Department of Human Environments at Utah State University). Her research interests include the economics of divorce, child support guidelines, work and family, and the economic well-being of women and children. She is coauthor of a series of extension publications designed to assist small- and home-business owners/-managers and has presented over 100 workshops on home business management. Her work is published in *Family Business Review, Journal of Contemporary Law, Journal of Divorce and Remarriage, Conciliation Courts*

Review, *Journal of Family and Economic Issues*, and the *Encyclopedia of Marriage and the Family*.

NANCY C. SALTFORD** is Professor in the College of Human Ecology at Cornell University. She is also a fellow at the Employee Benefit Research Institute, a public policy research organization in Washington, D.C., where she specializes in employer policies for working families. She served as associate dean in the College of Human Ecology at Cornell University from 1980 to 1988 and was deputy administrator, Home Economics and Human Nutrition, Extension Service, U.S. Department of Agriculture from 1989 to 1991. Her current teaching is in the areas of management and public policy.

ELIZABETH SCANNELL* is Extension Associate Professor in the Department of Community Development and Applied Economics at the University of Vermont. She is on the editorial board of *Financial Counseling and Planning*. Her work is published in *Journal of Family and Economic Issues*, *Financial Counseling and Planning*, *Journal of Extension*, *Journal of Consumer Studies and Home Economics*, and *Journal of Vocational Home Economics Education*, and she has written numerous extension publications on financial management. Her research interests include an international comparison of housing costs relative to income and the characteristics and occupations of home-based and family-owned businesses.

KATHRYN STAFFORD* is Associate Professor in the Department of Consumer and Textile Sciences at Ohio State University. Her current research work includes such topics as divorce settlements, at-home income generation, and management practices of households who are engaged in home-based employment. Her research has been published in *Home Economics Research Journal*, *Journal of Family and Economic Issues*, *Lifestyles: Family and Economic Issues*, *Journal of Consumer Studies and Home Economics*, *Journal of Small Business Management*, *Family Perspective*, and *Adolescence*.

ROSEMARY WALKER* is Professor in the Department of Family and Child Ecology at Michigan State University. Her current research interests include home-based employment, effects of management and economic variables on quality of life, and farm families in economic transition. She is on the editorial board of *Journal of Family and Economic Issues*. Her work has been published in *Family Business Review*, *Journal of Consumer Affairs*, *Journal of Family and Economic Issues*, *Journal of Consumer Studies and Home Economics*, *Journal of Home Economics*, and *American Behavioral Scientist*.

**Dr. Nancy C. Saltford was the first administrative adviser to the Technical Committee for the Cooperative Regional Research Project NE-167.

MARY WINTER* is Professor in the Department of Human Development and Family Studies at Iowa State University. Her current research work includes an analysis of family resource management in Mexico and two-way transfers in intergenerational living arrangements. She is also involved in the study of households who work at home for pay and their associated management practices and coping strategies. She is associate editor of *Journal of Family and Economic Issues*. Her research has been published in *Family Business Review*, *Home Economics Research Journal*, *Housing and Society*, *Journal of Family and Economic Issues*, *Lifestyles: Family and Economic Issues*, *Journal of Consumer Studies and Home Economics*, *Journal of Consumer Affairs*, *Journal of Marriage and the Family*, *Social Science and Medicine*, *Urban Anthropology*, and *City and Society*.

ISBN 0-86569-214-9

EAN

9 780865 692145

90000>

HARDCOVER BAR CODE